Rich Russians

Rich Russians

From Oligarchs to Bourgeoisie

ELISABETH SCHIMPFÖSSL

OXFORD
UNIVERSITY PRESS

OXFORD
UNIVERSITY PRESS

Oxford University Press is a department of the University of Oxford. It furthers
the University's objective of excellence in research, scholarship, and education
by publishing worldwide. Oxford is a registered trade mark of Oxford University
Press in the UK and certain other countries.

Published in the United States of America by Oxford University Press
198 Madison Avenue, New York, NY 10016, United States of America.

© Oxford University Press 2018

Library of Congress Cataloging-in-Publication Data
Names: Schimpfössl, Elisabeth, author.
Title: Rich Russians : from oligarchs to bourgeoisie / Elisabeth Schimpfössl.
Description: New York : Oxford University Press, [2018] |
Includes bibliographical references and index.
Identifiers: LCCN 2017049314 (print) | LCCN 2018000033 (ebook) |
ISBN 9780190677770 (Updf) | ISBN 9780190677787 (Epub) |
ISBN 9780190677763 (hardcover : alk. paper)
Subjects: LCSH: Elite (Social sciences)—Russia (Federation) |
Social classes—Russia (Federation)
Classification: LCC HN530.2.Z9 (ebook) |
LCC HN530.2.Z9 S45 2018 (print) | DDC 305.5/20947—dc23
LC record available at https://lccn.loc.gov/2017049314

9 8 7 6 5 4

Printed by Sheridan Books, Inc., United States of America

Contents

Preface and Acknowledgments

THE SUMMER SUNSHINE that year was ideal for a day out at the Henley Royal Regatta, Britain's most prestigious rowing competition. Well-dressed spectators who had not anticipated such a glorious day donned sunglasses with brightly colored frames handed out by people advertising *The Daily Telegraph*. It was hot too, and the Regatta officials fastidiously checked that the ladies had not broken the dress code by wearing dresses that did not cover their knees. In the jovial queue, people made final calls before their phones disappeared into their pockets for the rest of the day. Inside it was a quintessentially English event: impeccable riverside lawns and the Thames marked with straight rowing lanes. The races began. There was a Wimbledon-like atmosphere, but with industrial quantities of Pimm's and cucumber sandwiches rather than champagne and strawberries.

I was with four young British men: George, Dave, Matt, and Harry. They were Oxbridge graduates and now worked in the corporate world. All of them were sporting their respective college rowing-club ties and blazers. We were in Leander Club, one of the world's oldest rowing clubs, on a terrace overlooking the Thames. The water was quietly lapping against the river's banks, its sparkle fading as the sun slowly set behind the charming houses of Henley-on-Thames. When we realized that we had been drinking for nine hours, a change of scene was suggested. Dave, a tall, cocky Old Etonian of Scottish aristocratic descent (the prominence of which he tends to inflate), remembered that a financier friend of his owns Henley's only nightclub. The strip club in the basement was a must, he said, and he sent his friend a text.

While we were waiting for the friend to reply, the four young men started swapping table-dancing stories. Many of their tales involved being ravished by "high quality girls" in Russia. Matt, whose physique marks him out neither as a rower nor a cox, but who is confident and brash and can be charming when required, lived in Moscow more than a decade ago. He fondly recalled those halcyon days, when pretty girls would throw themselves at him, despite his receding hairline and expanding waistline. That was just before the oil boom of the 2000s. Later, pragmatic young Russian females switched their focus from modestly well-off Western expats to extravagantly rich Russian businessmen and bureaucrats. Now married and with a good job in a large pharmaceutical company, Matt still visits Moscow as often as he can arrange for his work to send him there.

Turning the discussion to rich Russians, Matt laughingly recounted a business meeting in New York, which took place in a suite at The Pierre hotel overlooking Central Park. The billionaire host, with his sleek, slim businessman looks, could have been mistaken for a visiting Englishman, were it not for his manners. "Bring me Dover sole!" he ordered briskly, Matt told us. The room service waiter apologized for not having any Dover sole and suggested alternatives. The billionaire raised his voice and repeated angrily: "Bring me fucking Dover sole and bring it now!" He then added a long list of side dishes and the poor waiter crawled off to comply with the guest's orders. As one of the top thousand richest men in the world, this pharmaceutical billionaire loves expensive cars, beautiful girls—and good food. "There are some things one never gets tired of," Matt remarked.

With a glass of pink champagne in one hand and rosé in the other, Dave recalled a rather peculiar Russo–Henley link. Through his work, he had met the man who bought Britain's most expensive house, the $180 million, 300-year-old grade II listed mansion Park Place Estate, just down the road from where we were still (just about) standing. The buyer, Andrey Borodin, is a Russian banker billionaire, who was granted political asylum in the United Kingdom in 2013 so that he could not be extradited to Russia on charges of corruption, charges which he has denied.[1] (He had lost his protection in Russia when his ally, the then mayor of Moscow, was elbowed out of office in 2010.) Safe in Henley, Borodin now tries to integrate himself into British high society in whatever ways he can, including taking up polo. At one charity auction he bought a dress for $156,000 for his young supermodel wife; at a Conservative Party fundraising event he blew $36,000 on a portrait of Margaret Thatcher.[2] Everybody in our corner of the terrace at Leander Club agreed that everything about the house and its owner sounded intriguing. In any event, "they're terribly nice people," Dave assured us.

George joined in the conversation. It turned out that even he, a polite, old-fashioned, and somewhat helpless bachelor with a very round face and rose complexion, does business with Russians. George has been advising a rich client who is even more intriguing than the Dover sole billionaire or the expensive house buyer. He has never actually met Sergey Polonsky, a real estate magnate who was extradited from Cambodia to Russia on charges of fraud and who, at that time, was awaiting trial in Matrosskaya Tishina, Moscow's most dreaded jail. Polonsky is eccentric even by Russian standards. He once ate a tie on screen in a television show after losing a bet. He was punched in the face on live television by the Russian co-owner of the *London Evening Standard*, Alexander Lebedev. He was arrested and jailed in Cambodia for allegedly detaining unlawfully several local seamen while on a drinking binge with some Russian mates. He named one of his sons and a dog after his company Mirax.[3] George thought he might be a little out of his depth in his dealings with Polonsky; he was not sure he could fulfill his brief of helping his client save at least some of his money from Russian bureaucrats. George had never been to Russia and found it all rather too much for him. Are they all like Polonsky, he wondered?

The public perception of rich Russians in the United Kingdom is not flattering, and it is little wonder that the Western media love sensationalizing the decadence of uncouth Russian *nouveaux riches*: sugar daddies who splash out $2 to $3 million in an evening at Mayfair clubs; paparazzi scoops about their young mistresses shopping for diamond-encrusted Bentleys, and sometimes even mysterious deaths. Nevertheless, in answer to George's question, they are not all like Polonsky. Harry, the fourth member of this group, from a solid middle-class background and the first in his family to make "proper" money, has considerable experience of working with Russians and has done business with Len Blavatnik, who was ranked number one in Britain's 2015 *Sunday Times Rich List.*

Born in 1957 in the Soviet Union, Blavatnik emigrated to the United States in 1978 and now lives in London, from where he controls an estimated fortune of $17 billion. Blavatnik got rich on Russian oil during the privatization in the 1990s. He later pulled all of his assets out of Russia and now engages in safer activities, including philanthropy. He has funded Oxford University's School of Government and a new wing of London's Tate Modern, both of which bear his name. Harry mused that if the funds had come from any number of other Russians, the university and the museum might one day have cause to regret this choice of benefactor.

However, our Leander Club group agreed that Blavatnik could not really be compared to the "normal" Russian rich. What exactly is a "normal" Russian rich, I asked, but nobody was listening. Blavatnik was in a different league entirely, they said, waving away my interjection.

Blavatnik's PR people had to work hard to present him as "different" and distance him from the negative "oligarch" label. They have done a good job; he is now accepted as perfectly "legit" in elite circles in both the United States and the United Kingdom,[4] and was even awarded a knighthood in the 2017 honors list. However, it surprised me that these four young men, with all their experience of working with Russians, could not see that there had been a more general shift from decadent money-splashing *nouveaux riches* to the knighted Blavatnik variety. For them, as for most other people, rich Russians were still on par with figures like F. Scott Fitzgerald's Jay Gatsby who, despite his claims to be a cultivated Oxonian with an affected "old sport" accent, ultimately failed to legitimize himself. The British public expects the same from wealthy Russians: However hard they try, they will never make it, and some do not even bother trying.

This book sets out to challenge those ideas. It is the first attempt to apply to the Russian upper class the insights of research into what it means to "make it" from sociological studies of upper classes outside of Russia. It argues that many members of the Russian upper class have indeed "made it," with their new money becoming what we think of as respectable money. They might not have achieved Blavatnik's extreme achievements and publicity, but the means to success are similar: more refined tastes, a bourgeois public image, and active engagement in philanthropy.

The book begins by providing the context for the rise of Russia's upper class and employing key ideas from studies of how upper classes form and reproduce themselves as social groups. It applies a historical perspective to support the claim that there has been a shift away from crude conspicuous consumption; rich Russians strive to consolidate their social positions and legitimize themselves and their offspring, just as the bourgeoisie in the West did. Early chapters address the elite's path to riches and the quest on the part of its members to seek distinction both in terms of their family history and their lifestyles. The middle section of the book explores their narratives of legitimacy, which demand the practice of philanthropy on the one hand, and yet the justification of both a pronounced social inequality and patriarchic norms on the other. With an eye to the future, the final chapters consider the further development of today's Russian bourgeoisie, paying particular attention to the transfer of their wealth to their children, and their increasingly tangled relations with the West.

THE RESEARCH FOR this book began back in 2005. When I first approached potential PhD supervisors in politics and sociology at the University of Vienna, they were skeptical. They did not believe a Russian upper class existed, and insisted that it would be at least another twenty years before a study of Russian social legitimacy, passed on across generations, could be carried out. They also doubted that rich Russians would agree to talk to me.

After this feedback, I did consider abandoning my project; all the same, I sent my father the draft of the proposal. This was shortly before he left for an expedition to the Himalayas to climb Annapurna III. I did not expect him to find the time during the hectic preparations to read my draft, but I was wrong. When I spoke to him by phone the night before his flight, I suggested he focus on getting the equipment together for his expedition, and that we could talk about my proposal on his return. However, he insisted on discussing it there and then. Unlike the university academics, he was excited about the subject. He looked at it from an historical perspective and saw the familiar story of raw robber barons beginning the journey to becoming gentlemen.

My father was not to return from his Himalayan expedition. The night before the final ascent, at 23,000 feet above sea level, he suffered high altitude sickness and died the next day. My last conversation with my father was about Russian history and my idea for a PhD.

Ignoring the professors' skepticism, I stuck to the topic. I conducted my research at the University of Manchester, and finished it off during a postdoctorate fellowship at University College London. Among the many people who helped me along the way, I am deeply grateful to Angela Chnapko, Yoram Gorlizki, Lynne Attwood, Vera Tolz, Stephen Hutchings, Pete Duncan, Tom Rollings, Mike Savage, Elke Krahmann, Mark Fowler, Jean-Pascal Daloz, Jukka Gronow, Alexander Gasparishvili, Alexander Chvorostov, Simon Pirani, Dieter Segert, Eva Kreisky, Friedhelm Kröll, Michael Hartmann, Yelena Kryukova, Leif Wenar, Eduard Steiner, Tudor Jenkins, Yekakterina Vizirova, Leonid Kogan, Natalia Koslova, Marina Tsenter, Alan Warde, Katharina Hecht, Boris Kagarlitsky, Nathan Brooker, Dorian Khoo, Heiko Khoo, David Mayer, Ilya Yablokov, Mark Hollingsworth, Peter Zusi, Jan Kubik, Verena Hable, Marjeta Jernej, Christina Klemenjak, Eugenia Romanova, Talyana Tobert, Natalia Yamshchikova, my interviewees, and hundreds of anonymous experts.

I would also like to acknowledge, most crucially, the support of the funding bodies that helped me through the years: The Leverhulme Trust awarded me a three-year Leverhulme Early Career Fellowship at the University College London, the Austrian Ministry of Science and Research supported my PhD at the University of Manchester, and the Austrian Research Association financed some of my fieldwork trips to Moscow.

Rich Russians

Introduction

THIS BOOK IS about the current generation of powerful and wealthy Russians who grew up at a time of unprecedented economic and social change. They bore witness to the collapse of the Soviet Union, the opening up of Russia to the West, and the introduction of the market economy, all of which helped to shape the way they see the world and how they see their position within it. *Rich Russians* dissects their stories and ideas through a series of key questions: What strategies do rich Russians employ in their desire to acquire bourgeois tastes and habits? How do they justify their wealth in a society as unequal as today's Russia? How do they cultivate a sense of legitimacy in their children, who are set to inherit great fortunes?

Among the eighty people I interviewed for this book was the entrepreneur and banker Boris Mints. In 2015, he ranked number 53 on the Russian *Forbes* list.[1] The interview was scheduled for a Friday in July 2015 in a Park Lane hotel in London's wealthy Mayfair district. I had to wait for him for a while because the Wimbledon women's doubles semifinal had gone on longer than expected. When he finally strutted into the hotel lobby, dressed in shamrock green trousers and a white T-shirt with a Hopper-esque print, his arrival was unmissable. In both stature and demeanor, he looked like Pavarotti gearing up to perform: round-faced, bearded, and barrel-chested.

Mints was born in 1958 into a family with a background in the intelligentsia. His father was a military engineer, his mother a librarian. Both parents were Jewish. After graduating with a degree in theoretical physics, Mints taught at university and conducted research. These were the dying days of the Soviet Union, and during this time the Centers for Scientific-Technical Creativity of the Youth (abbreviated in Russian as NTsTM), which commercialized technology, would prove to be hotbeds for the emergence of businessmen, and Mints ran one of them. Then, in the 1990s, during the market liberalization, he tried politics rather than going into business. He became the deputy mayor of Ivanovo, the country's nineteenth-century textile manufacturing capital, sometimes referred to as Russia's Manchester. In 1994 he moved to Moscow to join President Boris Yeltsin's team as Head of the Directorate of the Federal Agency for State Property Management. From 1996 to 2000 he headed the presidential department for municipal governments. Like many others of his generation, he was a liberal in the 1990s, working closely with the young reformers Anatoly Chubais, who was Russia's privatization chief at that time, and Yegor Gaidar, the architect of Russia's economic "shock therapy." Unlike many others of his generation, he remained a liberal under Putin.

Mints's ascent to the *Forbes* list came nearly a decade later. In the early 2000s, he cofounded one of the most prosperous commercial banks in Russia and set up an investment company, O1 Group, which owns and manages real estate and financial sector assets. After joining the ranks of Russia's billionaires in 2014, his wealth rose to $1.6 billion in 2015. In recent years, Mints has taken a back seat in business. "If you do things right, you attract strong managers and you can then do other stuff yourself," he explained to me. "In my position, you can't do any management anymore. I can't run the daily business. That's for the new generation." In his case this has fallen on his sons, whom he feels have inherited his entrepreneurial talent. Instead of business, Mints now does mainly philanthropy.

As in most Soviet intelligentsia families, Mints's parents regularly took him to museums as a child and encouraged him to learn a musical instrument. The whole family was musical, and his grandmother had a successful acting career. In keeping with the family tradition, Mints today supports the theater, classical music, and fine art. In particular he cherishes artworks by Russian impressionists, which he started collecting in 2001. At one time he kept the paintings in a special storage place, hidden away from public view. However, he considered this to be a great shame. Some of them were too big for the storage place, so he hung them in his office. But that too was wrong: "They should hang in the right place," he said. His solution was to build a museum for them on the site of a former Moscow chocolate and biscuit factory, Bolshevik. Rather than restore the building, Mints tore it down and commissioned top British architects to rebuild it in the same shape for $20 million.[2] The gallery is housed in a copy of the previous windowless warehouse that was used to store flour and sugar.

Like Mints, many of my interviewees have turned their back on crude conspicuous consumption and are now cultivating Russia's heritage in the arts. In doing so, it is not only their art that is on show (rather than jewels and cars), but their pioneering identities as billionaire art patrons, collectors, and philanthropists. As Mints said, "We are first-generation rich." This generation is fascinating in many respects, not least because its members are not held back by bourgeois traditions. *Rich Russians* charts where they have come from, how they are evolving in the present, and how they are planning to mold the next generation via a transfer of bourgeois status and respectability.

Studying Russia's Rich

After the breakup of the Soviet Union in 1991, when free market reforms were introduced, Russia's population experienced a sharp decline in their living standards, and there was an explosion of poverty: Within three years, the proportion of people living in poverty had tripled to more than a third of Russia's population.[3] Numerous writers, artists, scientists, and academics found themselves among the "new poor." Many emigrated, while back home, to add insult to injury, medieval epidemics—including bubonic plague—reappeared to strike the weak. The birth rate declined dramatically, and the death rate soared.[4] Male life expectancy, which in the Soviet Union of the early 1960s was higher than in the United States, fell to around fifty-seven years by the mid-1990s, lower than anywhere else on the globe apart from sub-Saharan Africa.[5] It was, in the most basic physical terms, a time of the survival of the fittest.

Meanwhile, a small number of people came to flourish and rose to the ranks of the *novye russkie*, the "new rich," accumulating great wealth faster than anybody else had ever done throughout history. These characters—many of them resembling the Soviet caricature of tasteless capitalists[6]—thrived in this dog-eat-dog world and celebrated a new hedonism. This soon attracted the interest of many writers and filmmakers,[7] as well as political scientists. The latter set about tracing the fate of former Soviet elites and the background of the emerging new elites. Their debates revolved around the extent to which the post-Soviet political and business elite consisted of people who had not previously belonged to the Soviet elite. Some scholars concluded that Russia's upper strata weathered the changes following 1991 particularly well in comparison to those in other countries in the Eastern bloc. According to these studies, many of those who held political positions at the very top lost them, but those just below them were very successful in making their way up.[8]

In the course of the 1990s, a tiny group of bankers and other tycoons appeared at the top of the new rich stratum. They came to be know as oligarchs, a term which originates from ancient Greek (*oligarkhia* meaning "government by the few," made up of *oligoi*, meaning "few, small, little," and *arkhein*, "to rule"), and suggests that they were the few who ruled.[9] The early Russian oligarchs seemed to have appeared from nowhere, plundered the country's resources, and then, directly or indirectly, got their hands on the driving wheel of government. The political scientist Jeffrey A. Winters suggests that when oligarchs enter politics, they do so not in order to run their country, but to defend their wealth.[10] That was very much the case when seven banker oligarchs orchestrated President Boris Yeltsin's re-election in 1996.

The oligarchs' capture of the state in the 1990s was short-lived. Those who continued to focus on politics in the early 2000s fell foul of Putin and were forced off the scene. Their rise and fall was chronicled most famously in two journalistic works, *Sale of the Century* (2000) by the former *Financial Times* Moscow correspondent and subsequent foreign minister of Canada, Chrystia Freeland, and David E. Hoffman's *The Oligarchs* (2001). All of the six big players of the 1990s who were scrutinized by Hoffman fell from grace, went into exile, lost their money, or died, with one exception, the politician and businessman Anatoly Chubais.[11] Mikhail Khodorkovsky, to whom Freeland paid special attention, rose to become the richest Russian, but was arrested in 2003 and eventually imprisoned.[12]

Meanwhile, Putin consolidated his power base by prioritizing the so-called *siloviki*. The term derives from *silovye struktury*, which literally means "force structure" but is better rendered into English as "power structures."[13] It refers to government personnel with a security or military background.[14] The consolidation of *siloviki* power meant that the road to riches for aspiring billionaires took new routes. For example, one could now become rich by entering the top management of state-aligned companies, but not only. Those who had enriched themselves by means of gas, coal, oil or oil refining, metals, and banking were joined by an influx of newcomers who had made their wealth in finance, information technology, real estate, trade, and retail.[15]

Putin's ascendancy coincided with a long oil boom. Strong economic growth reconstituted the profile of Russia's business actors, and a new glamour culture mushroomed among the newly rich in the 2000s. This, again, inspired numerous filmmakers, novelists, and journalists, as did the bleak ethical vacuum that came with it.[16] The journalist Mikhail Zygar called these years the "strangest period" in Russia's history, a decade of superlatives, with the rich gorging themselves on the high oil price feast and splashing out on the biggest yachts, the best parties, and the most enormous and sparkling mansions. They discovered the Côte d'Azur and the French Alps ski resort Courchevel, to which Moscow's high society would fly in their private jets, sometimes just for an evening.[17]

During the 2000s oil boom, Russian society moved from mass poverty to mass low-income.[18] At the same time, the wealth held by the very rich grew much faster than that held by the general population. Inequality rose throughout the decade, especially after the onset of the 2008 economic crisis.[19] Russia's wealth inequality over took that of other emerging powers such as Brazil, India, Indonesia, or South Africa. In 2013 Credit Suisse declared Russia the country with the highest level of wealth inequality in the world, apart from small Caribbean nations with resident billionaires.[20] In their 2014 report the Credit Suisse researchers contemplated inventing a separate category for Russia, as the country's wealth inequality had become so extreme that it had begun to skew the wealth report's statistics.[21]

This gap between Russia's rich and poor became even more acute after the 2014 economic crisis. The plunge in oil prices and the slump in the ruble–dollar exchange rate destroyed much of the gain made in the early 2000s in the living standards of ordinary Russians.[22] By contrast, rich Russians did not feel the consequences of the 2014 economic crisis that heavily. When the number of dollar billionaires declined from 117 in 2013 to 88 by 2015, this was to a large extent due to the 2014 ruble devaluation. By 2017 the ruble had recovered slightly, and the number of billionaires was back up to ninety-six.[23] In sum, within two decades Russia had gone from a country with relative equality—especially in comparison with the capitalist West—to a country of extreme inequality, which was, according to Freeland, far starker than it was under the tsars.[24]

While we know a fair deal about the businesses of most top billionaires,[25] academics have been slow to follow journalists, writers, and filmmakers in identifying the changing character of the Russian elite beyond their most salient political and business activities. There has been a notable gap in academic studies concerning the ways in which Russia's rich in 2017 differ from their former selves in the 1990s and what the vast wealth inequality in Russia means in terms of individual and collective strategies to gain legitimacy. With the exception of a few studies by Russian academics, there is a big gap in scholarly material relating to family, lifestyle, and identity of the new upper class.[26] In the few cases of Western academic researchers paying attention to any of these issues—for example, work has been done on the 2000s' glamour culture—they have usually analyzed media representations of their subjects rather than engaging with them directly.[27]

This gap has several historical reasons. First, in post-war social sciences there was an international trend to question the very concept of social class. Second, when the concept of class was finally revived, it was generally deemed not to be applicable to post–Soviet Russian society.[28] Third, when social science in the United States and Western Europe has addressed questions of power in Russia, this field has been dominated by Sovietologists and Kremlinologists, who have traditionally focused on political elites in and around the Kremlin.[29] The upper class in social and cultural terms has barely figured in academic research on Russia; neither has a discussion on wealth and inequality from the lived perspective of the superrich, nor their ideas and practices that shape the reproduction of the elite.

Sociological Studies on the Rich

In contrast to this apparent blind spot in Russian studies, the upper ranks and the lives they lead in other countries have been perennial topics for social scientists. One of the intellectual foundations of this enduring sociological interest in elites was laid by the economist and sociologist Thorstein Veblen, who studied the new rich of late nineteenth-century America.[30] Whereas previous privileged classes sought to demonstrate their status and wealth by not working, the upper classes in industrial society were characterized by a peculiar mix of industriousness and "leisureness." In relation to the latter, the new rich indulged in what Veblen termed "conspicuous consumption" and "conspicuous leisure," which the male elite often exercised vicariously through their women.

This idea of displaying wealth through women was further developed by Veblen's fellow sociologist and economist Werner Sombart in *Luxury and Capitalism*. Sombart considered social distinction to be exercised through qualitative luxury in the form of refined goods of superior quality, for example, food and dresses.[31] At around the same time, in the early twentieth century, the German philosopher and sociologist Georg Simmel, who was studying social interaction and individualization in modern society, developed a theory of fashion.[32] He argued that fashion serves as a means of both identifying with and dissociating oneself from others. New styles of consumption are often developed by those just below the top rungs of the social ladder. They then trickle down the status hierarchies, becoming devalued and vulgarized in the process.

Simmel's and Sombart's more famous contemporary, their friend and colleague Max Weber, developed his own concept of stratification.[33] Examining German society and its social structure, he identified class, status, and power as the main components of social stratification. He also introduced social prestige and popularity into the discussion; these, he claimed, potentially increase an individual's ability to raise their social position and have influence on society. Weber considered the private sphere—friendship circles, family, and social life—to be crucial for the perpetuation of social class across generations.

Many sociologists have taken up Weber's ideas as the basis for their research. One of the most famous was the American sociologist and social conflict theorist C. Wright Mills, whose sociological study *The Power Elite*, published in 1956, set the tone for much of the postwar scholarship on elites. Mills saw the US elite as a strongly interrelated group, whose members were highly dependent on each other. This group was drawn from a socially recognized upper class located in the economy, politics, and the military. Mills, like Weber before him, also paid attention to his subjects' social lives. He considered how frequently people interact, and how freely and unreservedly they marry each other, to be important indicators of the social class they belong to.[34] Despite the book's title, Mills dedicated around two-thirds of his analysis not to the power elite (the very top level of society), but to a broadly defined upper class or property class.

Mills's approach to an analysis of the upper class was replicated in many follow-up studies. His principal inheritor was G. William Domhoff, who used a wider definition of Mills's elite, moving away from a narrow focus on institutional leaders and including the managers of large enterprises and high-level employees in private institutions—that is, the 1 percent of Americans who possessed more than a third of the overall US wealth in the early 1990s. Other US scholars zoomed in on specific aspects of the subject: Susan Ostrander researched women in the upper class in the late 1970s and early 1980s (see chapter 6), while Francie Ostrower explored the reasons for the wealthy's engagement in philanthropy (see chapter 5), arguing that elites use culture to set themselves apart from others and to protect their status.

The postwar boom from 1947 through 1973—the Golden Age of capitalism, as Eric Hobsbawm termed it—saw a huge rise in living standards in the West.[35] Against this background, the study of elites and upper ranks became secondary for social scientists in Western Europe, who shifted their focus to a range of other themes, among them social movements, gender, and ethnicity. One of the few voices addressing elite culture during those years was that of the French sociologist Pierre Bourdieu. His research from the 1960s onward dealt with aspects of class reproduction that are noneconomic—for which, famously, he introduced the idea of different kinds of "capital:" economic, cultural, social, and symbolic capital (for example, education, cultural skills, social networks, and political influence). To Bourdieu, the fundamental benefit of being part of a privileged social class is to be able to distance oneself from economic necessity. The dominant classes possess what they see as superior culture and knowledge. They have the power to impose their own categories of taste and appreciation upon the lower classes. Upper-class children who are socialized in that dominant culture enjoy the advantage of internalizing the "right" skills and knowledge during their junior years.[36]

Bourdieu triggered a renewed interest in the upper ranks among sociologists in Europe and the United States, who developed his ideas further. Michèle Lamont explored how upper-middle-class French and Americans create symbolic distinctions between themselves and others, using culture as a resource by which to recognize one another.[37] Examining the top boarding school in the USA, St. Paul's, Shamus Khan showed how elite educational institutions help students justify their social positions in society by instilling in them the perception that they are talented and they achieve their success through merit and hard work, rather than appealing to social ties or to other powerful institutions such as grand family dynasties. In doing so, they obscure the systemic inequality which they help reproduce.[38] Based on her research among wealthy New York families, Rachel Sherman identified strategies used by parents to deal with privilege in the upbringing of their children and the ways in which they strive to raise morally "good" children, a process that serves both their own and their children's legitimization.[39] Michael Hartmann scrutinized German elites with regard to their business activities, demeanor, and educational paths, comparing them to elites across the globe and questioning the existence of a truly transnational elite.[40] Jean-Pascal Daloz compared the ways in which elites display themselves publicly in different cultures and epochs, using settings as different as Norway and Nigeria. In contrast to Bourdieu's conception of distinction, which focuses on the discreet and seemingly natural superiority of dominant classes, Daloz included ostentatious forms of distinction in his comparative analysis. This wider understanding of social distinction makes his analysis very useful for the Russian context.[41]

In the mid-2010s a new wave of interest in elites emerged. This was triggered by the fact that the 2008 financial crisis had not eased social inequality; on the contrary, the rich quickly recovered and increased their share of the economic pie. At this time the French economist Thomas Piketty published his seminal work *Capital in the Twenty-First Century*, which showed that the super-rich are, to a large extent, the engines of inequality, and that wealth differences are increasingly vast even amongst themselves.[42] This was echoed by the British sociologist Mike Savage, who has pointed to the huge economic inequality within the top 1 percent.

A number of Savage's ideas are pertinent to the analysis of Russia's rich.[43] First, Savage reminds us that the top 1 percent is more sharply divided internally than any other income group. This is particularly relevant in Russia because of its extreme inequality. Second, Savage argues that sociological analysis must go hand in hand with historical analysis, which is essential to an understanding of the unusual origins of Russia's bourgeoisie. Third, he points out that accumulation and inheritance are more crucial factors in forming social classes today than cross-sectional employment position. This is something which we can, again, observe in Russia where the children of the very rich do not derive their wealth from their own effort. Finally, following Bourdieu, Savage stresses that the various forms of capital stand in relation to each other: That is, one form of capital can be converted into another. Russia's rich have been actively using their economic capital to gain a foothold in other areas and attach great importance to adopting a new lifestyle that is independent of their business activities.[44]

Recent sociological studies on elites, conducted in the tradition of Weber, Veblen, and Bourdieu, have not included Russian case studies in their empirical base. The chaotic situation in which the Russian elite emerged in the 1990s did not fit into the theoretical models developed on the basis of Western experience in an earlier, twentieth-century context.

However, the stabilization that Russia's elite has enjoyed in the 2000s removed this mismatch, making an analysis that focuses on the cultural and social dimension of power and social class timely and topical.

Russian Bourgeoisie

The academic literature on elites is characterized by notions and concepts that reflect diverse theoretical backgrounds. Some studies focus on the economic assets of elites, looking at the rich (with a variety of prefixes, such as super-, uber-, hyper-, mega-). Others use concepts that relate to the elite, or elites in plural (sometimes specified as occupational or positional elites), the ruling class, or the upper class in an effort to explore the political, social, and cultural resources of those at the top of society. Bourdieu's *la classe dominante* can be placed in this category. There are additional terms that apply specifically to contemporary Russia, which include *nouveaux riches*, "new Russians," oligarchs, "Putin cronies," and the moneyed classes. These terms are all valid in accordance with the various research goals that academics have pursued. In this study, however, they do not quite fit the bill. My goal is, ultimately, to capture the social development of the upper ranks in Russian society in the conditions of political and economic stabilization that followed the chaos of the 1990s. This means identifying their transition from rival individuals and clans to a more coherent social class. Accordingly, I have settled for "bourgeoisie" as an overarching frame for my research. The logic behind this choice of term is that its familiarity adds explanatory power, facilitating analysis of the similarities and differences between the bourgeoisie in Russia and elsewhere, as well as making historical comparison easier.[45]

Karl Marx famously declared that the ruling ideas of each age are the ideas of its ruling class.[46] His argument, expounded in the 1840s, was that, although philosophical and legal discourse has a certain autonomy, over time it is reshaped in the context of new socioeconomic relations. However, Marx stopped short of undertaking a sociological analysis because he was interested in the bourgeoisie primarily in economic terms. An important sociological perspective was added more recently by Pierre Bourdieu; his description of what he called *la classe dominante* was similar to Marx's understanding of the ruling class, but he shifted the focus to the importance of cultural and social resources in forming a social class.[47]

I use the term "bourgeoisie" in a similar way to Bourdieu's use of *la classe dominante*.

The term "bourgeoisie" has etymologies and associations that are culturally specific and diverse. After the restoration of the monarchy in England in 1660 following the collapse of the Republic, the nascent bourgeoisie adopted aristocratic culture. In France the bourgeoisie took power by force and demonstratively counterposed itself to the aristocracy. (After 1815, the French bourgeoisie followed Britain in the sense that a new post-revolution aristocracy emerged, with bourgeois upstarts taking on aristocratic manners.)[48] From the mid-nineteenth century, the term bourgeoisie came to be associated with two contrasting traditions. On the one hand it has been linked to middle-class values. On the other, it has been associated with the ideas of Marx, who saw the bourgeoisie as a social class defined by its ownership of the means of production, and functioning as the ruling class in capitalist society. I define membership in the Russian bourgeoisie on the basis of capitalist ownership.

In Russia the bourgeoisie did not emerge as an economic class with strong political clout. It failed both in 1905 and, more monumentally, in 1917 to modernize social and political relations. This was due to the weakness of capitalist production at a time when the impoverished peasantry constituted the overwhelming majority of the Russian population. As Leon Trotsky explained in his *History of the Russian Revolution*, the Russian economic elite formed part of a coalition composed of the tsarist autocracy and landowners that opposed the transfer of land to the peasants.[49] In this context, the Russian Bolsheviks came to power in October 1917 not on a socialist program of planned industry, but on the slogan of land to the peasants. This was also what the French bourgeoisie had advanced during the French Revolution of 1789.[50]

The fact that there was no Russian bourgeoisie to speak of for most of the twentieth century goes a long way toward explaining why it does not function today as a ruling class on the model of its British or French equivalents. Russia's new oligarchs of the 1990s did not inherit their wealth from an existing bourgeois class. Their property ownership followed the privatization of Soviet industry, which was pushed by Russian reformers in the 1990s. The bulk of this new wealth emerged from asset-stripping what had been state property, while many state enterprise managers privatized what was under their control and thus became capitalists. Unlike in the West, they initially commanded political power as individual tycoons, not as representatives of a cohesive social group.

As a reaction to the chaos of the 1990s, Putin brought economic liberalization under his personal control and significantly reined in Russia's oligarchs. As a result, the bourgeoisie today holds little political power. Russia's richest have to be content to remain on the political sidelines, or else risk a ruinous run-in with Putin. All the same, they own significant parts of Russia's economy, which puts them very much in line with Marx's concept of the bourgeoisie. While they do not directly participate in politics as a class, Russia's media elite and Kremlin spin doctors heavily influence the dominant cultural and social discourse.[51]

In short, the new Russian bourgeoisie has not emulated either its French or English counterpart in its historical trajectory. However, from a sociological perspective that explores its values and its practices of legitimacy, it has acquired over time many of their features, some of which have been documented in the stories of literary and nonliterary figures. In *Downton Abbey* we see aristocrats marrying "dollar princesses" to save their estates; a similar phenomenon occurs in the novels of Honoré de Balzac, which have recently been used by the economist Thomas Piketty as social-historical sources. Although post-Soviet history is unique, it replicates processes we have seen in numerous other societies and on numerous occasions in the past: how new money becomes respectable money and how *parvenus* can become an accepted part of the social elite. Most of Russia's so-called robber barons are thus well on the way to transforming themselves into respectable gentlemen.

Becoming Bourgeois in Post–Soviet Russia?

In Russia, the land of ostentation, limousines, and fake baroque palaces— in short, of "glitz" and "bling"—how is such a rapid move toward more respectable conduct possible? In the opaque situation of post–Soviet Russia, where the new rich had no memory of a bourgeois tradition to fall back on, the Russian intelligentsia has served as a substitute. The Russian word "intelligentsia" is one of the few words that English has borrowed, in part thanks to the translation of such works as Ivan Turgenev's *Fathers and Children* (1862). In Soviet times the term was officially extended to people who were engaged in mental labor: professionals or white-collar workers who defied Marxist social classification, such as engineers, teachers, educationalists, cultural workers, medical doctors, scientists, researchers, writers, and artists, as well as state and party functionaries. Being able to trace their descent from the Soviet intelligentsia provides an ideal provenance and cultural legacy for today's bourgeois elite, effectively offering them an alternative to "aristocratic" ancestry and accelerating their journey to bourgeoisification.

Resuscitating their intelligentsia roots to gain respectability does not mean that rich Russians have become "better" people. Neither does the process of bourgeoisification imply that they are less inclined to take part in corrupt business practices. The same is true on a global scale. A Russian does not become less bourgeois when engaging in criminal practices, just as the English, French, or Italian do not become less bourgeois by engaging in illegal tax avoidance or any other more heinous crimes. What it means is that intelligentsia backgrounds provide historical reference points for the new rich to draw boundaries that set them apart from other groups in society.

With the economic meltdown that started in 2008 and was further stimulated by the onset of the 2014 ruble crisis, Russia's rich have become even more concerned about legitimizing their position. As is the case almost anywhere, in the long run upper-class Russians also wish to feel worthy of their positions in society, and that they deserve them because of who they are and their superior characters and qualities.[52] They want to be accepted by their peers and live in an environment of social cohesion.

How can this work in a country where there is widespread antipathy toward the rich, who are often considered to be thieves and crooks, and where more than half the population is convinced that it is impossible to make big money by honest means?[53] In modern societies there is generally an ambivalent attitude toward the rich: a combination of respect and obedience toward them on the one hand, and contempt and rebellion against them on the other. In Russia, these attitudes are more dramatic. (I have lost count of the number of Russian mothers I have met who, despite viewing the rich as hateful thieves, would be quite happy to marry off their daughters to one.)

Rich Russians have acquired a variety of cultural and social resources that help them consolidate not only their personal power, but also, ultimately, their power as a social class. They have set out to develop more distinguished, cultured, and refined tastes and manners, to rediscover their family histories, and to actively engage in philanthropy. Some principles of noblesse oblige have become obligatory for the upper ranks of Russian society.[54] They have now become more self-restrained and "European" in their public personae, which has helped them shed the *nouveaux riches* image of the 1990s. This enables them to set the tone for those who are lower down the pecking order. Most importantly, they have begun to work out a narrative for themselves, which justifies their elitist position in society by grounding their self-image in ideas about who they are and what they see as their superior qualities in relation to others.

The absence of the term "bourgeoisie" in Russian studies from the multiplicity of terms applied to the elite, as mentioned earlier, reflects the widespread assumption that Russia still does not have a bourgeoisie comparable to that in the West. The reasoning is that, while there is an extremely wealthy elite, it is not supported by that wider layer that constitutes the bourgeoisie. In addressing this issue, my research points to the diversity within the Russian bourgeoisie, but also unlocks shared features within a broader layer of Russia's rich that have so far not been considered or analyzed by researchers.

The Interviews

Using the term "bourgeoisie" as a frame for my research informed my approach to gathering empirical data. I interviewed and observed wealthy entrepreneurs, their spouses, and their adult children from the top richest 0.1 percent of the Russian population in Moscow, London, and New York between 2008 and 2017.[55] About a third of my eighty interviewees were "super-rich" (that is, according to *Forbes* magazine, someone with a net worth of more than $500 million)[56] or "hyper-rich" (that is, billionaires).[57] Most of the others are "ultra high net worth" individuals (those with investable assets of more than $50 million), with some "high net worth" individuals (those with investable assets of between $1 million and $50 million).[58] This means that almost all of those interviewed belong to the richest 0.1 percent of the Russian population which totals nearly 144 million people.[59] (The exceptions were a couple of post-2008 crisis dropouts, a political exile, and another downshifting migrant.) What they all have in common is that they share a certain lifestyle predicated on financial privilege, but not wholly contingent on it.

As for the content of the interviews, my approach was inspired by the work of the French sociologist Daniel Bertaux, who collected life histories in order to study social mobility in post–Soviet Russia.[60] I conducted biographical narrative interviews, which contained questions about people's lives, their family history, what they considered to be important in life, what they thought helped them become successful, what values and skills they wanted to pass on to their children, and what they wished for in the future. Further questions concerned philanthropy, education, and leisure time activities; how they related to the West; and how they related to questions concerning gender. Another tranche of questions referred to housing, lifestyle tastes, preferences in literature and culture, and preferences in the people they chose to have around them.[61]

There is a widespread perception that interviews can be biased because people try to present themselves in the best light, and this tendency is often exacerbated in print media appearances and autobiographies. Research interviews have a slightly different dynamic from media interviews as people believe that what they say will be safely stored away in libraries. Of course, giving an interview simply for the sake of scholarship does not necessarily stop people from distorting and varnishing their lives and deeds. However, we need to consider the extent to which this actually matters.

In the case of my interviews, I was not on a mission to find out the "truth" in terms of deeds and misdeeds, facts, and figures.[62] As the historian of Soviet society, Sheila Fitzpatrick, noted during a 2015 book launch in London, all data is biased in one way or another, and this is particularly the case with autobiographies; however, this does not mean that they do not contain highly interesting and revealing information. For the purpose of this book, "boasters" were especially welcome. Inflated narratives provide fertile grounds for analysis, as they demonstrate how people wish to be seen and how they relate to the world around them.

This leads to my second point: In sociological research self-presentation and self-perception are just as important as facts. The sociologists Michèle Lamont and Ann Swidler regard interviews as a tool to probe "where people live imaginatively—morally but also in terms of their sense of identity."[63] Autobiographies are one mode of story telling, but few of us ever engage in it. However, most of us tell numerous stories in our everyday lives, to others and to ourselves, about what has passed and what we hope will pass. When doing so, we make sense of ourselves and of others and, simultaneously, interpret our own stories and lives. In this way we continuously produce and reproduce our own identities, through the lens of our current perspective.[64] This process of interpreting our lives and producing identities is particularly intense in interview settings because it allows us to fully focus on ourselves. However, I also observed my interviewees when they were moving about in society and interacting with others in order to gain a sense of their everyday life practices.[65]

The interviewees ranged in age from twenty-one to over seventy. About two-thirds of them were entrepreneurs, and the rest were people with high status in art, media, or politics (though these also often had business projects running in the background).[66] Three-quarters of the sample were male. Of the female interviewees, half were businesswomen. About fifteen interviewees were grown-up children, whose ages ranged from twenty-one to thirty-two. If the interviewees gave me their permission, I recorded our conversation. They were conducted in Russian and lasted from half an hour to four hours.[67] I did not include in this book all of the eighty persons interviewed to avoid a surfeit of names and characters.

My sample of interviewees reflected two key characteristics of the Russian elite that have been identified in previous studies.[68] First, more than 90 percent of them have university degrees, with a large majority in science, engineering, economics, international relations, and law. The younger generation tends to choose business-related degrees, which are more often than not gained in the West. Thirty percent (all male) hold advanced degrees, roughly equivalent to a PhD, of which more than a third possess a higher doctoral degree (*doktor nauk*, which was taken from the German system). Second, they often have strong political ties with the Kremlin and other power structures. (This was often visible when I stepped into their offices: Some were terribly exhausted from a late-night dinner with Putin; others had photographs of themselves with the world's elite hanging on their walls.)

Pyotr, a businessman in the retail industry, embodies these and other characteristics, which are typical for upper-class Russians.[69] I met him in his bright office in a newly renovated red-brick loft building in the center of Moscow. With an estimated $50 million to $100 million to his name, Pyotr was considered "poor" amongst the rich; nevertheless, he was acutely aware that this amount of money puts him among the elite— the "service elite," as he called it. "What makes one belong to the elite?" Pyotr asked, repeating my question. "It is, yes, a) financial resources; but also b) lifestyle, and c) one's cultural-social position in society." Lines from the introduction of Pierre Bourdieu's *Distinction* came to my mind: "Taste classifies, and it classifies the classifier."[70] As if Pyotr were familiar with them, he said: "The high level I occupy implies not only access to luxury and comfort, but also the ability to correctly evaluate luxury and comfort."[71]

Pyotr occasionally teaches at a university: "Of course, if it is written somewhere that I'm a professor of a higher educational institution, actually one of the best in Russia, yes, that's a bonus, but not one that has value in its own right." What has more value, he said, is his culturally privileged background: He was born into the Moscow intelligentsia.[72] As if to honor this, he writes poetry and art reviews in his spare time, which are of sufficient quality to bestow on him esteem in Moscow's high society. If this makes Pyotr sound earnest, it should not. As he spoke, he looked at me through burning red eyes with puffy bags beneath them, perhaps the result of a long night out on the town. Indeed, he told me that he did not deny himself when it came the hedonistic side of life. He planned to take this principle to the grave, literally, having already come up with his epitaph: "The inscription will read something like: '*bylo zabavno*' ('game over—it was fun')."

The name Pyotr is a pseudonym. While I use the full names of some individuals, I gave interviewees who preferred to remain anonymous a fictitious first name. When I anonymized them, I also changed a number of their basic characteristics to make them unidentifiable. This occasionally required the inclusion of some fictional elements, though I chose them in such a way that they conveyed the basic flavor of the interviewee's personality and gave an indication of the setting in which the interview took place. I also anonymized some of my interviewees who did not actually asked to be anonymous. Some of the material the interviews produced could potentially have caused upset. In a few cases, I was not able to obfuscate the stories and anonymize the actors sufficiently. Here I eventually exercised self-censorship and left them out.

My interviewees' responses and my observations of them are complemented by information drawn from the media. About 80 percent of the interviewees are people who attract a certain level of publicity. The Internet accordingly provides abundant information on them, which includes everything from feature stories to interviews and professional biographies. Half of the remaining 20 percent are present on social media. Media reports provided me with plenty of information about the ways these rich people tried to build their public identities, as well as how the media perceives them.

In addition to the interviews with rich Russians, I conducted over a hundred "expert" interviews with people who know members of this group of upper-class Russians and have had intimate dealings with them; these include wealth managers, lawyers, consultants, former personal assistants, artists, architects, interior decorators, private jet operators, travel agents, psychotherapists, glossy magazine editors, journalists, teachers, drivers, and builders. Some of these "experts" paved the way to interviews with the rich they catered to. Others helped me by taking me along, or organizing access, to social functions and events.[73] Their diversity ensured that there was a wide range of types among the elite recruits. Their impressions, observations, and knowledge provided me with information both on rich people's lives, and the perception of the rich on the part of a group that was subordinate to them, and yet also profited from knowing them. With a few exceptions, these "experts" will not be mentioned individually.

Structure of the Book

The first part of the book highlights the practices through which upper-class Russians relate to themselves, their peers, and those beyond their group. The opening chapter starts by reviewing how Russia's new rich emerged during the years of post-Soviet social transformation. It shows how they used the social assets they had to hand, were quick to recognize which parts of their expertise and skill sets were of no value in the turmoil of those times, and realigned their resources accordingly. The chapter then considers their strategies for narrating their path to enrichment.

Chapter 2 explores what it means to become bourgeois, analyzing everything related to gaining distinction. It explains how upper-class Russians have learned not to show off their money but to embrace more cautious tastes, which are a mark of discerning, bourgeois distinction. Chapter 3 analyzes how this need for distinction has informed the ideological beliefs that endorse the legitimacy of members of the Russian bourgeoisie in their own eyes—for example, which of their qualities they think explain their success in business.

The second part of the book elaborates further on the theme of distinction, analyzing it in relation to family background, philanthropy, gender relations, and the younger generation. Chapter 4 considers how today's upper-class Russians trace their origins and status traits back to their family history, especially to parents and grandparents from the Soviet intelligentsia, and the ways in which they reinterpret crucial chapters in their country's history through the lens of their current elite status and identity. Chapter 5 explores the cultivation of philanthropy by upper-class Russians after the early 2000s to provide proof of their legitimacy, and how this propelled them into a narrative of obligation toward the less fortunate that is reminiscent of Russia's nineteenth-century tradition of elite aristocratic philanthropy. Chapter 6 looks at the relationship between upper-class men and women, unpacking the ways in which changing attitudes toward money-making and social status are affecting notions of masculinity and femininity in what is still a highly patriarchal elite. Chapter 7 discusses the task that rich Russians have yet to face in finding a convincing narrative to justify their children's legitimate entitlement to wealth that does not contradict their own story of being self-made.

The final chapter, chapter 8, looks at the paradox whereby the exposure of the Russian elite to Western life is taking place at the same time that political ties between Russia and the West are deteriorating. It suggests that rich Russians have overcome their old inferiority complex in dealings with Westerners after decades of Cold War isolation. On the contrary, they now display a growing sense of their own superiority, and, echoing nineteenth-century Slavophile views, are expressing disillusionment with the West.

Drawing on ideas outlined by Max Weber, I argue that the bourgeoisie profiled in this book wish to be convinced that they deserve their position because of who they are and their superior qualities. For now, the approval of their bourgeois peers is far more important than gaining social legitimacy vis-à-vis society at large. This is a task that lies ahead of the second generation. With the current move away from crude ostentation toward greater etiquette, a stronger family orientation, and some degree of modesty, philanthropy, and patriotism are essential if the upper class is to reproduce itself and keep its place in a post-Putin Russia.

1

A Short Story of Enrichment

AMONG THE INTERVIEWS I looked forward to conducting most was the one with Konstantin Ernst, the head of Russia's main TV station, Channel One. It was one of the most difficult to organize. When it was provisionally scheduled for a Sunday, I knew only at midday that it would actually take place, at 2 p.m. When I saw Ernst, a tall, imposing man, I realized that I had caught him on a good day.[1] He was taking a couple of hours out to relax. After about an hour, he walked me to a large screen to show me parts of *Viking*, the new blockbuster film he was producing about Vladimir the Great, Prince of Novgorod. He had a budget of more than $20 million, and the film later turned out to be very successful.

Despite his apparent good mood, he seemed a little restless. Sitting on a huge, dark, glossy wooden table in a conference room adjacent to his office, he pressed a button every five minutes or so. Usually his secretary brought him cigarettes in response, plus a device that allowed him to smoke without producing any fumes. Once in a while he had a different request: For example he wanted her to find a copy of *An Alien Girl* (*Chuzhaya*), a gangster movie he had produced, for me to take home. The movie depicts the brutality of 1990s Russia.

Ernst never showed the movie on his channel or promoted it in any way. When I got to my friends' house and watched it with their two sons, aged thirteen and fifteen, thinking it was safe for family viewing, I understood why. The violence is hardcore, even by Russian standards. The thirteen-year-old ran off to hide. My friends, however, appeared to love it. It was violent, certainly, but at the same time it had meaning.

After all, the 1990s *were* brutal. The dismantling of the planned economy unleashed violence and a surge in unemployment and impoverishment. Organized crime emerged from the shadows of the Soviet Union's prison network and grew stronger as the state weakened and it became obvious that a new, more impartial judiciary was not in the cards.[2] The death toll was particularly high among business people, but those in other professional fields also can remember violent incidents. Ernst's predecessor as head of what is now Channel One, Vladislav Listyev, was shot dead on the stairs of his apartment building in March 1995.[3] Ernst himself had bullets fly through his window, followed by death threats sent to his pager.

Such violence was instrumental to the rupture in Russian society as rival clans struggled to carve up assets in the 1990s. It also left the impression that Russia's early post-Soviet elite was a group of rough upstarts from simple social backgrounds. Scholars, however, soon suggested that the new post-Soviet elite was not actually that "low-born," nor entirely new. Many so-called newcomers to the upper echelons of society in the 1990s were in fact the descendants of privileged or highly educated families.[4]

In politics, perhaps the most famous example was Yegor Gaidar. The liberal reformer was born in 1956 into a family that was the nearest thing the Soviet Union had to royalty, as the *Financial Times* Moscow correspondent Chrystia Freeland described Gaidar's family background.[5] Both his grandfathers were well-known writers and his father a famous journalist, and Gaidar himself joined the Communist Party while he was in college. Gaidar first worked for the Institute of Economic Forecasting, which was attached to the Academy of Sciences, and then became head of the economic policy department of *Kommunist*, the Communist Party Central Committee's main theoretical journal. In November 1991 he joined Boris Yeltsin's team. As minister of economics and, in 1992, acting prime minister, he set about demolishing the Soviet economic system with the help of his fellow liberals (among them were Pyotr Aven in Moscow, and Anatoly Chubais and Alfred Kokh in Leningrad).[6]

From Oligarchs to Bourgeoisie

Russia has more wealth related to resources, privatization, and political connections than any of the other BRIC countries (Brazil, Russia, India, and China).[7] This statement does not convey the drama of the transfer of assets, which had been built up during the Soviet period, into private hands in the immediate post-Soviet period. In effect, the oligarchs inherited assets from the ousted Soviet government. While ordinary Russians—who saw their living standards plummet—mourned the loss of the security provided by the Soviet benefits system, at the top table business clans queued up to stake their claim to Soviet assets. Many of these entrepreneurs had already made significant sums following the tentative reforms that Gorbachev pushed during perestroika. The scandalous privatizations of the 1990s then turned a few individuals into powerful super-rich almost overnight.

During these years, the goal of these new business players was to grab as much as they could. They cultivated the necessary ties with the reformers and important government officials, and even took up key government posts out of political self-interest. Rather than engaging in productive economic activity, they specialized in deal-making, and in outsmarting their rivals.

The first wave of privatizations occurred in 1992, starting with the voucher privatization process, the brainchild of the reformer Anatoly Chubais, a Gaidar ally and chairman of the State Committee for the Management of State Property (GKI), the government body that would administer the privatizations.[8] Every citizen received a voucher with a face value of 10,000 rubles, which was worth about $25, and the right to participate in voucher auctions where properties were sold. The vouchers could be exchanged for shares in an enterprise. Voucher privatization was initially very popular as it promised participation for everybody in the newly emerging market economy. However, these promises were illusory: Ordinary people, for the most part, had no idea what to do with their vouchers or were so poor that they had to sell straightaway in order to meet basic needs.[9]

Some of those who had already accumulated wealth and set up their own banks during perestroika bought vouchers from those who did not know what to do with them. In other cases it was insiders, mostly Soviet-era factory managers, who ended up purchasing the vouchers for a pittance, often from their employees, and gaining control over large assets. The latter process was assisted by the fact that Chubais had made a deal with the incumbent factory directors in order to reduce their resistance and push through privatization: Workers and managers could buy 51 percent of the voting share in their company at a nominal price. As workers were often in desperate need of money in the crumbling economy, the bosses usually took over the assets. Admittedly, many of these enterprises were worthless ruins at that time. Some, however, were relatively well-functioning monopoly suppliers of goods with a guaranteed demand. Thus nomenklatura privatization—that is, the handover of property to the managers or bureaucrats in charge of them (something Chubais had officially meant to avoid by opening the sale of state property to the public via auctions)—became the norm.[10]

The 1992 voucher privatization was "nothing" compared to what was to come, the oligarch Pyotr Aven explained to me. He had observed things firsthand as Gaidar's minister of foreign economic relations in 1992.[11] In 1995 the government desperately needed money to pay pensions and state-sector salaries, which were months in arrears. To meet this deficit, the banker Vladimir Potanin (who in 2015 was at the top of Russia's *Forbes* list) suggested loans-for-shares auctions.[12] Under the terms of Potanin's program, private businesses would, through their banks, provide loans to major enterprises in exchange for shares in companies.[13] The idea was that the banks (which were owned by the most powerful oligarchs, among them Potanin) would get the ownership of forty-three state enterprises transferred to them, which would be held in trusts for five years. In return, they would provide loans to the government. During these five years, the government could in theory buy back these enterprises from the banks—though this was clearly not going to happen.[14]

The government, pushed by deputy prime minister Chubais, took up the plan. The first auctions proceeded in late 1995 in an atmosphere of confusion and scandal. The main players, Oneksimbank (owned by Potanin) and Menatep (owned by Khodorkovsky), had divided up in advance the assets they wanted.[15] The auctions were opaque, mostly held in secret, and run by banks owned by the oligarchs, who awarded the assets to favored insiders or, in the overwhelming majority of the cases, to themselves. Eventually, a dozen major Russian enterprises, which constituted some of the country's largest assets, were auctioned off at a bargain price to some of the biggest new oligarchs. For instance, Potanin, who was right at the center of the program, won Norilsk Nickel. Chubais later acknowledged that the loans-for-shares program was a trade-off. He needed the oligarchs' support to get Yeltsin reelected in the 1996 presidential elections.[16]

Yeltsin was indeed very much in need of their support. The first Chechen war, which had started in 1994, and the economic and social hardship the population endured had both taken their toll. In early 1996 Yeltsin's popularity plummeted to less than 5 percent. The voters' discontent and yearning for stability and social security played into the hands of the Communist Party, with its leader Gennady Zyuganov the clear favorite for the next presidency. The new elite was panicking. The oligarch Boris Berezovsky and Alfred Kokh, then deputy head of the Committee for State

Property Management, took the initiative to organize the leading oligarchs around them in order to save Yeltsin. The core group consisted, alongside Berezovsky, of the tycoons Vladimir Gusinsksy, Alexander Smolensky, Mikhail Khodorkovsky, Mikhail Fridman, Pyotr Aven, Vladimir Potanin, and Vladimir Vinogradov, all of them bankers. With the help of a massive propaganda campaign, they succeeded in turning things around by activating their media might, their talented staff, and their financial power. According to official figures, Yeltsin beat Zyuganov. As a result, the power of the oligarchs was reinforced.[17]

After Yeltsin's re-election relations among the oligarchs quickly turned sour. The following year, in 1997, the media oligarchs Vladimir Berezovsky and Vladimir Gusinsky hoped to cash in their investment in Yeltsin's campaign by gaining control of Svyazinvest, the holding company that was created to bring together telecom assets that were up for privatization. By then, Chubais, now head of the presidential administration, had changed his tune and insisted on doing everything "properly"—that is, according to all formal rules. Vladimir Potanin, whom Yeltsin had appointed as first deputy prime minister, outbid his rivals with the help of capital advanced by the US-based Hungarian financier George Soros.[18] The ousted oligarchs, who had backed Potanin's appointment to the cabinet as their representative in the Kremlin, felt betrayed and did not take this defeat lightly. Soon bitter feuds broke out in the media outlets owned by Berezovsky and Gusinsky and among the State Duma deputies they funded.[19]

On August 17, 1998, Russia defaulted on its international debts and the ruble was devalued. People who had ruble savings (that is, most poor and middle-class Russians) were ruined, as were those international investors and Russian banks that had gambled on the market for government short-term bonds (GKOs). These bonds were short-term state securities—treasury bills with maturity dates from six weeks to twelve months—which had been launched by the Ministry of Finance in May 1993. For most of the period 1994–1996, investors had been able to realize large positive returns by lending the state short-term money far above the inflation rate. Now, the GKOs turned into sharply devalued titles and many banks went under. Oligarchs whose wealth was mostly based on banking (for example, the oligarch bankers Smolensky and Vinogradov) were hit hard. In contrast, those who had assets in the extraction of natural resources enjoyed ample cash flow from exports, which were starting to experience a fantastic boom at that time due to rising prices on the world market.[20] This made Mikhail Khodorkovsky, who had acquired the oil company Yukos in the loans-for-shares auctions, Russia's richest man with, according to the 2004 *Forbes* rich list, a net-worth fortune of $15 billion.

After the shockwaves of the August 1998 default, the volatility and instability of the early 1990s ebbed. However, instead of the Western-type capitalism the reformers dreamed of, Russia established crony capitalism. According to some scholars, the mass privatizations of the 1990s were directly responsible for this development.[21] Due to the anarchic legal field in the 1990s, characterized by corporate raiding,[22] rich Russians chose to syphon money into safe havens abroad rather than reinvest. Although the Central Bank had clear rules that should have hindered capital flight, these were widely ignored or never enforced.[23] Capital flight totaled as much as $56 billion to $70 billion even in 1992–1993—a time when there was purportedly "no money around" in Russia. Chronic lack of reinvestment left Russia's economy underdeveloped and dependent on the extraction and exportation of natural resources.[24]

These years were the apogee of Boris Berezovsky's influence. The oligarch was almost running the Kremlin, in due course playing a major role in ensuring Putin's rise to power.[25] After his election as president in March 2000, however, Putin bolstered his position by publicly attacking some of the 1990s oligarchs, accusing them of having looted the country's wealth—an announcement that was well-received by the general electorate.[26] Putin utilized the backlash against the oligarchs to strip Boris Berezovsky of the TV station NTV and Vladimir Gusinsky of ORT. The fate of these two fallen oligarchs, who fled abroad in 2000, taught the rest to keep a low profile politically.

One exception was Mikhail Khodorkovsky, who did not back off from political machinations (such as buying the loyalty of Duma deputies).[27] Arguably still more important was that he was prepared to sell large stakes in Yukos to ExxonMobil and Chevron Texaco.[28] In 2003 he was arrested for tax evasion and sent to the labor camp Krasnokamensk near Chita in eastern Siberia, not far from the border with China and Mongolia (a place where, incidentally, many Decembrists were exiled after their uprising in 1825 against Tsar Nicholas I's absolute monarchy). Khodorkovsky was imprisoned there for the next ten years. He was released in 2013, as part of the Kremlin's amnesty campaign to improve Russia's image on the eve of the 2014 Winter Olympic Games.[29]

The Kremlin destroyed Yukos and forcibly brought some oil and gas assets back under state control. Its aim was to shift the balance of power, gain control over key taxpayers, and establish a national flagship company.

The latter was achieved by the expansion of the state-owned oil company Rosneft and by reasserting control over the state-owned gas company Gazprom. Western observers started fearing a renationalization of private industry. These fears proved to be unfounded. The state-owned portion of Russia's oil and gas sector remained small when compared to oil countries such as Saudi Arabia, Mexico, or Kuwait.[30] Although oil companies usually have strong ties to the Kremlin, most of them are in private hands, apart from Rosneft and Gazprom.[31]

Together with the oil sector, the state also retained control over defense industries, gas and electricity, and the railways, which led to the emergence of a new category of oligarchs with very close ties to the state. Some of them were *siloviki*, personnel with a security service or military background, such as Igor Sechin, who became head of Rosneft. Many of Putin's friends and protégés also became very wealthy, literally overnight.[32] In contrast to the insider trading of the 1990s, when the government traded favors on unfavorable terms, now the leadership could show largesse out of a position of strength, thanks to the oil boom.

In the course of renationalizing strategic sectors such as oil, President Putin and German Gref, minister of economics and trade from 2000 to 2007, reiterated during the attack on Yukos that the clock would not be turned back on the privatizations of the 1990s.[33] They were true to their word: Gref initiated privatizations and liberalizations on a scale and in areas that the market reformers of the 1990s could only have dreamed of. While Russianists usually regard the 1990s as the peak of neoliberal policies, from a comparative perspective the political scientists Hilary Appel and Mitchell Orenstein identify the Gref era as outstanding in neoliberal ambition.[34] For example, Gref introduced a flat tax of 13 percent in 2001, a symbolic hallmark of a hyperliberal economic policy. Gref's biggest coup was to break up the state-owned electricity monopoly United Energy System of Russia, which owned the grid and most of the power stations (and was headed by Chubais prior to its sell-off).[35] In addition, municipal services (the free provision of which had meant the difference between poverty and misery for millions of Russians) started to be privatized.

Russia's economy developed in great strides in the 2000s, though this had little to do with Gref's economic policies. The devaluation of the ruble in 1998 multiplied the effect of high export prices of oil and other natural resources when hard currency revenue was converted back into rubles.[36] New groups of players emerged from the shadows of the oligarchs of the 1990s.[37] In the first half of the 2000s the oil and manufacturing sectors secured their owners with a place on Russia's *Forbes* list. The devaluation of the ruble also boosted import substitution in sectors outside oil and gas. Economic growth pushed forward a process of diversification beyond the oil and gas sector and changed the composition of the elite. By the second half of the 2000s finance and technology (mainly telecoms) had expanded significantly. New billionaires also emerged in construction, retailing, and online marketing.[38]

Following the onset of the global financial recession after the sub-prime crisis in 2008–2009, Putin forced some oligarchs, such as Oleg Deripaska, to rescue loss-making enterprises and thereby protect jobs. Putin's actions once again highlighted how big money is still closely tied to the Kremlin. Yet if in the 1990s business leaders exploited the weakness of the government to pursue their own commercial ends, the subsequent consolidation in the vertical organization of power meant that the oligarchs now had to listen to Putin's demands. Those who did had the best chance to do well. Very much in contrast to what we usually hear about Putin's dislike of (selected) oligarchs, the Kremlin actively protected the interests of billionaires. According to the Credit Suisse *Global Wealth Report* of 2015, some 96 percent of the billionaires who were on the Russian *Forbes* list in 2005 were still on it in 2010. The corresponding average across the G7 countries was 76 percent; for the BRIC countries, it was 88 percent.[39]

Narratives of Enrichment

The 1990s have left a legacy of popular distrust in the reformers and the entrepreneurs who had made great gains. Against this background, the consensus among the elite is that talking about the 1990s is unnecessary, if not risky, as it could easily challenge their legitimacy. This study does not aim to analyze rich Russians as economic agents, and so unmask their path to wealth during the transition. Rather, it aims to explain how they respond to their privileged positions by developing appropriate narratives to justify their high status. From this perspective it is not a paradox that, although the privatization of wealth is essential to their origin as a social class, the stories they presented to me in my interviews largely glossed over this chapter in their lives.

Those who did mention the privatizations did so in order to distance themselves from the toxic legacy they have left. Thus Pyotr Aven, switching into English, told me that the loans-for-shares auctions of 1995 were "totally unfair" and continue to have repercussions today. "It will be many years till private property will be seen as legitimate in Russia," he said in 2017, when, he continued, 70 percent of the Russian population still has a negative view of these privatizations. (His own bank, Alfa-Bank, which he has run with Mikhail Fridman since 1994, was not allowed to take part in the 1995 auctions, something for which, in hindsight, he said he was very grateful.)

The Entrepreneurial Spirit of the Oligarchs

Russia's rich usually stress the dynamic nature of their entrepreneurial activity. For the oligarchs of the 1990s, whose murky activities behind closed doors lack legitimacy, the focus is on their bold initial rise to riches before the privatizations. As students they ventured into commerce well before the collapse of the Soviet Union. Their stories of adventurous risk-taking and initiative back then have been placed into context by Chrystia Freeland: She has described the social starting position of many of the later oligarchs as close enough to the levers of power to take advantage of the market transition, but far enough away to do new things outside of the existing system.[40]

An insider position was indeed essential to taking advantage of Gorbachev's reforms. The 1987 Law on State Enterprises gave these state enterprises the freedom to determine output levels according to consumer demand. A joint-venture law enacted in January 1988 permitted foreign investment in the Soviet Union for the first time since the 1920s, and abolished the monopoly on foreign trade previously held by the Ministry of Foreign Trade.[41] The May 1988 Law on Cooperatives allowed for small-scale private ownership in services, consumer goods, and manufacturing. As a result, restaurants, shops, and manufacturers sprang up. The *Komsomol*, the Young Communist League, which was controlled by the Communist Party of the Soviet Union, started running a virtual empire of small and large service and production entities.[42]

Mikhail Khodorkovsky was deputy head of his institute's *Komsomol* committee when he graduated from the D. Mendeleev Institute of Chemical Technology in 1986. This allowed him to set up a Youth Center for Technical and Scientific Creativity (NTsTM) and engage in financial and credit businesses. In this he enjoyed the patronage of senior Communist Party officials.[43] Khodorkovsky then set up Menatep Bank in 1988, again with the support of senior officials, who passed state credits to enterprises via his bank.[44] This move was made possible by substantial reforms in 1987–1988 that enabled state banks to be privatized by their managers and new banks to be set up. The ex-*Komsomolites* at Menatep soon discovered that it was highly profitable to carry out financial operations that state enterprises were banned from.[45]

Mikhail Khodorkovsky and Mikhail Fridman, born in 1963 and 1964 respectively, fell into an ideal age cohort: First, they were too young to have advanced high up the bureaucratic career ladder and hence far enough from the top of the Soviet hierarchy to be independent of it.[46] Second, unlike more senior officials, they did not remember the reversals that followed the economic reforms of the mid-1960s and, therefore, unburdened by prior experience, did not fear anything like this happening again. Instead, they pursued all of the opportunities that came their way.[47]

Another factor that made them relatively peripheral was that they were Jewish. Covert anti-Semitism was still pervasive in late Soviet times. Pyotr Aven, the billionaire president of Russia's biggest private bank, Alfa-Bank, remembered:

> Jews didn't have any choice. Their choice of career was limited. They couldn't go into the Foreign Service, they couldn't join the party apparatus, several academic disciplines were closed to them. My business partner, Mikhail Fridman, was not allowed to do a PhD.

The anti-Semitism of the time encouraged some of them to be active in the emerging private sector.[48]

Soviet Jews lived in an ambiguous state, being Jews according to their passports and in the social and public perception, but being Russians through and through in a cultural sense. Jewish identity was seen as a "negative nationality."[49] The official classification of Jewish nationality was a status that did not guarantee rights, but only restrictions. Thus although they were fully assimilated, discrimination and deeply rooted anti-Semitism both among the Soviet population and the state in fact reinforced Jewish identity, fostering loyalty within their communities and suspicion of outsiders. In Moscow and St. Petersburg, where there were (and still are) large numbers of highly educated Jews, these restrictions shaped their specific social intelligentsia milieux. Strong bonds and high educational levels led to a disproportionally high success rate among Jewish Russians in post-Soviet business structures.[50]

When rich Russians talk about the roots of their post-Soviet fortunes, they often cultivate an image of rags-to-riches billionaires who can lay claim to humble beginnings and to having made it without enjoying any advantages, neither the cultural and social advantages they got from their parents, nor the vital social networks they enjoyed during their university years. Instead, they often cherry-pick elements of their work biographies. Fridman got his start running a window-washing business and a theater-ticket purchasing system, which he organized while doing a degree in physics and employing fellow university students. (In 2017 he was in possession of assets worth $14.4 billion.)[51] German Khan, an oligarch and partner in Alfa Group (who, in 2017, had assets worth $9.3 billion) started off his path to enrichment with selling T-shirts and jeans at a market during his student years in Moscow.[52]

If we look more closely, however, their trajectories do not really qualify as rags-to-riches stories. Khodorkovsky's parents were educated members of the Soviet intelligentsia. Fridman's father, an engineer, was awarded a USSR State Prize for developing military air traffic control systems. Khan's father was a well-known scientist specializing in metallurgy. No matter how powerful the drive that individuals like Fridman and Khodorkovsky got from being considered second-rank because of their Jewishness, the head starts they had through their favorable connections to the elite and their parental backgrounds helped them succeed in the marketization to come.

The influence of parental background was closely interlinked with the educational paths young people took. Study at prestigious universities during the perestroika years increased their access to important social networks.[53] Highly educated graduates with science degrees were overrepresented among the winners. Some were scientists in the military-industrial complex; others worked in research institutes.[54] Thus when Russia's billionaires started off with street markets, they did so not because street trading was their inevitable way of existence, but because such ventures during perestroika and the early 1990s were a gold mine compared to their previous or envisaged academic jobs.

The Educated Elite

While ignoring the head start that their backgrounds offered them, many interviewees acknowledged the importance of Soviet education for their later careers. In explaining the phenomenon of new money to me, the billionaire Boris Mints reflected: "None of us has inherited anything," and paused for a second before adding, "except for education." The financier and art collector Igor Tsukanov stressed his intellectual curiosity, while he left out his early entrepreneurial endeavors.

After finishing his university studies in mathematical economics in 1984, Tsukanov worked for the prestigious Institute of World Economy and International Relations, which was affiliated with the Academy of Sciences of the USSR. The number of institutes and management structures within the Academy was so enormous that alternative ideas and dissident voices could easily find a shelter in its laboratories and centers. When Tsukanov started working for the Institute in 1984, its director was Alexander Yakovlev, who later became one of the main ideologues of perestroika and a senior advisor to Gorbachev. Tsukanov's department dealt with the US economy, calculating economic models and conversing with US economists. "It was the most interesting time of my life," he said.

The years of perestroika were extremely exciting. Nobody understood at first where things were heading. It was a time when everything was changing and we were in the frontline of everything. I worked with Yegor Gaidar, Maxim Boycko, etc.—all these people and others like them, who, together with Anatoly Chubais, expedited the privatizations. . . . The later years were also interesting, but those were easily the best. Without too much effort you could change something in the lives of people.

No matter how active a role Tsukanov took in dismantling the Soviet system when working together with the most influential reformers, he has great respect for the quality of Soviet schools. Tsukanov went to the famous school No. 57 in Moscow. This school for gifted children had high admission standards and accepted children primarily from privileged intelligentsia families. Tsukanov transferred to this school when he was fifteen, as he felt that a normal school was not good enough for him. It had a decisive influence on his later career as a researcher.

Helen Yarmak is one of the rare women in this generation of scientists-turned-entrepreneurs. She was at the forefront of research at a cybernetics institute, but in the early 1990s her career took a U-turn. She became a fashion designer and soon gained an international reputation. Her furs and jewelry appeared in Hollywood productions such as *Sex and the City* and *The Devil Wears Prada*. Her showroom in New York is at the corner of Fifth Avenue and Fifty-Seventh Street, in front of the headquarters of Louis Vuitton and next to Tiffany's. "*Playboy* used to be in our building; it's a famous place in New York. Why there?" she said, preempting my question. "To be honest, I have not the slightest idea why. Like all Russians we completely improvised."

Looking as glamorous as her clients, in flashy clothes and red lipstick, Yarmak constructed a direct link between her past as a mathematician and her subsequent career as a designer, although she did so in a slightly peculiar way:

> For me it was a big advantage that I was a mathematician because I didn't understand anything about fashion. After all, mathematics is logic. I had to find an entirely new concept for my design and the creation of my fashion house. Sometimes it's much better not to have much of a clue about what you are doing because it gives you more energy. I simply didn't know that it was impossible to do what we did.

Yarmak said that now she wanted to get on with design. She was at pains to stress how little patience she has for the business side of things or for money-making, which she increasingly leaves to others. If it was her, she would just give away things, which she claimed to do occasionally when potential clients are too poor to buy her fur coats.

Yarmak also accentuated her intelligentsia credentials. Her husband still works in a university. His company and the company of friends from his world are essential to Yarmak if she is to feel intellectually inspired, she said. Her daughter is a mathematician, basically taking up the science career her mother abandoned. Yarmak is proud that her daughter is following in her husband's academic footsteps: "Not for anything in the world would my daughter ever have anything to do with fashion," Yarmak said flamboyantly smoking thin cigarettes with a long filter. "She despises fashion. And she doesn't want to waste any second of her life on it."

Only in passing did Yarmak eventually mention her family background and, surprisingly, this was not the Soviet intelligentsia. Instead, she hails from a nomenklatura family with roots going back to the privileged strata of higher state officials in late Imperial Russia. Her great-grandfather owned a big square in Moscow. Her father was a high-ranking official who held nomenklatura positions in a Soviet ministry. Nomenklatura-ranked party officials, managers, and high-status members of the intelligentsia enjoyed an extensive range of privileges, including access to rare goods and comfortable apartments and dachas in exclusive areas.

Yarmak was reluctant to answer my follow-up questions about her high-powered great-grandfather: "I can't tell you more," she said resolutely. "This would destroy my PR strategy." She left me wondering whether this was because it clashes with her image of being self-made or because it does not harmonize with her intelligentsia identity. However, she added one brief remark about her family's modesty and her father's "inner" strength: "Even though my parents occupied high positions, especially my father, we were poor. His work would have allowed him to take huge bribes, but he never did. He has an immensely strong and impressive [*kristalno-chisty*] personality."

The Entrepreneur as an Ordinary Guy

The billionaire Oleg Tinkov (with assets worth $1.4 billion in 2014) was born in 1967. He started out trading in all kinds of products before brewing beer and producing *pelmeni*, Russian dumplings. Now he owns a bank and a cycling team that participates in the Tour de France. In his leisure time he cycles around the Alps. According to his own account, his initial motivation to get going in business was libido-driven. As he told an audience full of Russian-speaking students at University College London in December 2014, he was primarily inspired by the desire to be able to take out his sweetheart at college (who later became his wife), and for that he needed cash.

Tinkov has told this story many times. The sporty man with silver-fox hair and sea-blue eyes is Russia's answer to the British billionaire entrepreneur Richard Branson, Tinkov's role model and friend. He presents himself as one of the more open and down-to-earth men (albeit with film-star looks), who runs an entertainingly honest blog. *I'm an Ordinary Guy* (*Ya Takoi Kak Vse*) is the title of his autobiography.[55] Witnessing him speaking to an audience in his often endearingly clunky, ladish manner, it is easy to believe this ostentatious understatement. And indeed, he is the son of a Siberian miner. Such as a working-class background makes him a rare exception among the many intelligentsia sons. Tinkov sees himself as belonging to a small group of twenty to thirty "pure" entrepreneurs in Russia, who did not grow rich from state connections but from "proper" entrepreneurship.

One of his fellow entrepreneurs from the early 1990s, who has since become a billionaire, is Alexander Svetakov, born a year later than Tinkov, in 1968, to a legal expert and an economist. He studied technical engineering at the Moscow Institute of Electronic Technology in 1988 after returning from his military service. He made his first money from importing calculators and other electronic goods from Singapore. Calculators were a gold mine because they cost less than $10 in Asia but up to $50 in Russia.[56] Svetakov set up his company Absolut in 1990, as well as a bank to finance his activity.

The bank's office was in the basement of his parents' apartment on Leninsky Prospekt, an address which in itself speaks to a background in the Soviet intelligentsia. The façade of the prestigious semicircular Stalin-era apartment block with a private courtyard looked onto Gagarin Square. The house was home to several members of the Moscow *beau monde*; for instance, Konstantin Ernst, the head of Channel One, lived there ("From the window of my room I could see into his room"), as well as the family of Andrey Makarevich, the lead singer of a very famous late Soviet rock group called Time Machine. "Andrey and his brothers are all trained architects," Svetakov said, alluding to how centralized Moscow high society was (and still is). "They studied with my uncle, who taught at the Architecture Institute."

While Tinkov and Svetakov were already some way along the path to becoming rich in the early 1990s, their subsequent rise to the *Forbes* list of billionaires occurred after the 1998 devaluation of the ruble. Svetakov followed a very cautious approach, which helped his bank weather the storm of August 1998 much better than others, and quickly advanced up the list of top banks. Svetakov sold the bank in 2007. His wealth exceeded $1 billion by 2008 and reached $3.3 billion in 2017.[57]

Because merit in neoliberal narratives is often associated with risk-taking and élan, the admission that one has benefitted from privileged family backgrounds or other personal ties can diminish the claim that one's success is merit-based. Accordingly, many interviewees not only claimed to be self-made but also presented themselves as simple and ordinary, regardless of the degree of privilege or social connectedness they enjoyed. Curiously, they seemed to have convinced themselves of their own "lowbrow" narrative.

The telecommunications entrepreneur Yury Pripachkin, a former army commander, initially emphasized his working-class origins: "I'm a simple man. My family goes back to workers and peasants," he said, adding: "I can't say that my upbringing was particularly strict. I actually brought myself up in the courtyards of military towns." His parents taught him simple values "such as being honest to people." This also includes being honest to women, he added with a laugh, because "a woman is also a human being."

Later in the interview, Pripachkin changed his tune. Although far from the privileged echelons of the Soviet system, he now accentuated that he did not come from nowhere: "My great-grandfather was a famous man in Moscow," he said. "He sat in the prerevolutionary Moscow duma and owned seventeen houses in Moscow, as well as a restaurant at the Kursk Railway Station." Then the Revolution took place, followed by Stalin's purges, and Pripachkin's grandfather was caught up in these events. The family had to move to Kalinin (which has now reverted to its historic name of Tver), a hundred miles northwest of Moscow.

After the war, Pripachkin's parents had to work very hard to climb up the Soviet ladder, but managed to do so. Pripachkin himself graduated with a degree in radio engineering from the prestigious Moscow Aviation Institute (MAI), an incubator for the young Soviet elite. He stayed on to do a PhD in technical science, and for some time he worked as a research fellow. Next, he pursued a military career in the army's rocket division, one of the most prestigious sectors. But then, from 1985 onward, the faltering Soviet economy forced Gorbachev to radically strip down the country's defense industry and in 1989 to withdraw Soviet troops from Afghanistan. The formerly massive Soviet Army suffered drastic cutbacks. "I ended up on the street, even though my career had not been at all bad," Pripachkin said. This career disruption did not last long. In 1992, together with some friends, he set up a business trading in computers, while also taking part in the creation of the Moscow Interbank Currency Exchange. The same year he started his telecommunications business. He became a close business partner of Viktor Vekselberg, the oligarch who gained fame when he purchased nine Fabergé Imperial Easter eggs from the *Forbes* publishing family in 2004.

A similar pattern appeared in my interview with Andrey Korkunov. This wholesome, rotund, chubby-cheeked man with smiling eyes and an Elvis Pompadour, who was born in 1962, launched his eponymous A. Korkunov chocolate brand in the late 1990s. Prior to his confectioner career, he served for five years in the army. In our interview, he played with his down-to-earth image. With a boyish demeanor, he admitted gaps in his knowledge: "I completely depend on my wife in terms of cultural education. Funnily enough, this sometimes ends up with me picking up something and memorizing it." Giggling, he continued: "Then I might recall it when I'm among people, and everybody thinks that I'm really culturally versed. In fact, I don't know any more than the tip of the iceberg."

Like those of Pripachkin, Korkunov's parents, who both held university degrees, were actually quite successful. When Korkunov was growing up, the family lived in the small town of Aleksin, some 120 miles south of Moscow. As in many provincial Soviet towns, Aleksin's districts were built around big factories, and all social life revolved around them. Aleksin had two big factories, and Korkunov's father was the deputy director of one of them. Now speaking in a much more serious tone, Korkunov explained to me what forced him to put his nose to the grindstone at school:

> In a small provincial town, the director and the deputy director were the local elite who formed the worldview for everybody around them. This meant that everyone knew our family. All the teachers knew whose son I was. So I always had to work hard and study a lot. As the son of the factory's deputy director I couldn't possibly be a bad student. I had to conform to my parents' status. Moreover, I wanted to stay in this elite, both as a little boy and also later, when I was studying.

After initially presenting himself as simple and down-to-earth, Korkunov shifted the emphasis of his story to the disciplined work ethic which he got from his parents. Pripachkin's narrative took a similar turn. Both of them presented their relatively privileged backgrounds as the stimulus to work hard and achieve success through merit. They both grew up in the Russian provinces which makes these stories more credible, as the elite was concentrated in Moscow and Leningrad and children from outside had always had to make an extra effort, as they still do. Both succeeded in getting into prestigious universities in Moscow.[58]

TAKEN AS A whole, the Soviet upper class weathered the changes following 1991 very well, particularly in comparison to those in other countries in the Eastern bloc.[59] Only slightly less than one-fifth of those in Russia who were on their way up in 1993 did not hold somehow privileged positions five years earlier.[60] Before becoming rich they were most likely already to be part of the nonmoneyed Soviet elites, albeit in the second or third row. Nevertheless, their professional positions provided them with information, as well as access to the corridors of power and foreign-currency bank accounts. Statistically, the most likely winners of the economic transformation were highly educated men, primarily with a background in engineering and economics, and some with science careers. This resulted in a situation where the end of a centrally planned economy and the introduction of market reforms accelerated the careers of individuals who were already well on their way to success even before the collapse of the old system.[61]

In other words, although it did help in the climate of the 1990s to be aggressive, wily, and not overly principled (characteristics typically ascribed to the winners of that period), it was even more important for climbing the social ladder to have relatively privileged social origins. In Soviet society "real" (financial) capital did not exist. In such circumstances, symbolic and cultural capital become overwhelmingly important. The members of the early post-Soviet elite were largely recruited from the same social group that had dominated the Soviet Union for decades. Not least because of their educational background and their social connectedness, these people quickly worked out how to exploit the new rules of the game. They used the social assets they already had, were quick to recognize which parts of their expertise and skill sets were of no value in this period of turmoil, and learned how to realign their resources accordingly. Thus, paradoxically, the social inequality that existed before the transformation process both sharpened and established new socioeconomic differences, adding to and aggravating existing sociocultural ones.[62]

2

Becoming Bourgeois

ARKADY IS ONE of Russia's longest-standing businessmen. Born in 1959, he began his ventures in the late 1980s and now runs a large tech holding company. With his full beard and round spectacles, this earnest and thoughtful man from a Jewish intelligentsia background could be mistaken for an academic. He cares about his public image and is fully aware of the reputation wealthy Russian businessmen have in the West. "At first we tried to understand what money could do for us and what kind of opportunities it opened up," he said, alluding to his formerly more ostentatious lifestyle. "But now we don't think about that any more. We started to live in a different way. We started to think in a different way." The billionaire was dressed in a khaki-olive shirt and pants, reminiscent of a factory worker's uniform. He had just come back from a big-game hunting trip that very morning, so I assumed that he had not yet had the chance to change.

A couple of weeks later I met his wife for an interview in her office. Larissa is a petite, blue-eyed woman with the stature of a ballerina, and auburn, shoulder-length hair. On this occasion she was wearing a faded, worn-out pink tracksuit top. I start suspecting some conscious strategy, since I had previously seen her during her free time dressed in a chic riding outfit. A friend of the couple later confirmed that Arkady and his wife are extremely attentive to their clothing and Arkady's khaki-olive outfit and Larissa's worn-out tracksuit jumper were not unconsidered choices. Rather, they are aiming to present themselves in a studied, individual, and almost flamboyant new style—the reverse of glitz.

Arkady and Larissa are trendsetters. The couple's dacha is located in a new development to the north of Moscow. It was deliberately planned to be different in every respect from the grandiose palaces of the *nouveaux riches* built in the 1990s in Moscow's infamously glamorous suburb of Rublyovka, where Putin has his residence. The couple's dacha is built of wood, in a traditional style but with modern features; it is similar to contemporary wooden architecture in Scandinavia and Switzerland, albeit on a grander scale. The individual houses have no fortified walls, but disappear into the forest, thus ensuring their privacy and invisibility to any passersby. The adjoining golf club's fairways spill over into the sailing club grounds, which are full of boats, yachts, catamarans, and other craft. Arkady proclaimed proudly that there was "nothing comparable in the whole country. I think even in the West there are only very few such places." A trained construction engineer himself, he appreciated the contribution to this development of "the most renowned" architects, Russian and foreign. "Many dream about working for us," he added. After a day out at this dacha, he explained to me that his aim was to show me that his family had little in common either with ordinary Russians, or the "tasteless" rich.

The breakup of the Soviet Union in 1991 threw people into a new world in which little was familiar. Many of their assumptions about status, professionalism, and respectability no longer held true. The new rich of the 1990s had no established role models to emulate: All they had was money, sometimes ill-gotten and on display. In many respects Russia's *nouveaux riches* resembled Chicago's leisured class of the 1890s, described by the American economist and sociologist Thorstein Veblen. In Chicago at this time, private property had become the basis of esteem, and the new rich marked their social position by parading their untold wealth.[1] Conspicuous consumption ruled Russia in the same way in the 1990s and the early 2000s. Many craved and embraced superlatives in terms of size, quantity, and novelty, which they had felt deprived of in Soviet times.[2]

During the course of the 2000s, however, many began to distance themselves from this surfeit of glitz and glamour. We can see this trend in Kseniya Sobchak, born in 1981, the daughter of the first post-Soviet mayor of St. Petersburg, Anatoly Sobchak. The socialite and TV host became a household name as Russia's answer to Paris Hilton and the "It Girl" of the Putin era. (Incidentally, Putin is widely rumored to be her godfather.) The sexy blonde, who was frequently showing off her semi-naked body, was notorious for being involved in scandals, fabricating exciting escapades, and being ever more capricious in her moods and actions.[3] In the winter of 2011–2012, however, Sobchak became one of the faces of the opposition movement and joined street protests against the falsification of the 2011 parliamentary election results. During these months she dated the political activist Ilya Yashin, born in 1983. Yashin stood in stark contrast to the elderly rich businessmen she had previously chosen as boyfriends. In September 2017 she announced her intention to run for the Russian presidency in 2018. Still a media celebrity, she now enjoys prominence as a journalist and political activist, rather than as a glamour queen.

A similar evolution can be seen in Mikhail Prokhorov, formerly Russia's richest man, the owner of the NBA's Brooklyn Nets and the stereotypical playboy oligarch: A six-foot-eight giant of a man, he was born in 1965 into a nomenklatura family. In 2007 Prokhorov spent the New Year holiday in the French ski resort of Courchevel, a mecca for many rich Russians. In order to entertain a group of male friends during the trip, he brought along twenty hand-picked female students from St. Petersburg University; these beautiful young women had been through a very thorough selection process. After customs discovered a binder containing photos of twenty young women in the luggage of one of his aides (and perhaps after a tip-off from a business rival in Russia eager to damage Prokhorov's reputation), French police suspected that the women had been procured for sexual services. Prokhorov was detained, but no charges were actually brought against him (indeed, the French later apologized).[4] One of his personal assistants was also arrested and spent a few days in detention. I met the personal assistant shortly afterward. He swore that the young women were not prostitutes: "They were highly educated, many of them students at St. Petersburg State University. They just liked the idea of a luxury skiing holiday in the Alps. But they were not paid." They would, however, receive expensive gifts. For example, he would persuade the assistant in the fur coat store in which the young women were shopping to close the store to the public and give them the peace and privacy to choose what they wished.

The Courchevel incident did not do any harm to Prokhorov's image. On the contrary, it triggered a storm of outrage among the elite back home against the French authorities. Many were offended: They perceived the allegations as an attack on their country. As a consequence, they called for a boycott of Courchevel and of French ski resorts in general. Despite this support, Prokhorov changed his public image quite radically soon after this. He launched the media project *Snob*, with which he endeared himself to upper-middle-class intellectuals, and ran for the presidency in 2012. The projection of this new and mature image was vastly enhanced by his highly articulate sister, Irina Prokhorova, founder of *New Literary Observer*, the main intellectual journal and publishing house in Russia, who supported his election campaign. This beautiful and charismatic woman—who, when I met her in her office, was wearing no makeup but had perfectly manicured red nails—now leads Civic Platform (Grazhdanskaya platforma), the party set up by her brother, as well as the philanthropic foundation named after him. Although still something of a party animal, Mikhail Prokhorov's new public persona is firmly shaped by his sister's serious vision of modern Russia.

Contentious as Sobchak and Prokhorov might be, they reflect a shift away from an endless party lifestyle to more discerning and cautious tastes, values, and interests that are less directly related to money. Many other rich Russians have now adopted this more subtle approach: They present a refined, mannered, and cultured image, which is sometimes called "new modesty."

This "new modesty" does not necessarily mean a more frugal lifestyle. For Arkady's wife, Larissa, a great reader almost exclusively of Russian nineteenth-century classics, it means a longing for some sort of human decency. She elaborated on her idea of modesty while we were driving from her residence to the private community's club restaurant, housed in another stylish wooden building: "What is modesty? Modesty can express itself in many things. I can't quite say that I live ascetically." As she spoke, her tiny hands, which looked as if they had never experienced any household chores, were steering her black Porsche 911 through the woods. "I think that modesty is the antonym to ruthlessness, and ruthlessness is absolutely the worst thing you can find in a person."

Cultural Omnivorousness

For present-day visitors to Russia, conspicuous consumption might still seem omnipresent. Ostentation, for which the *nouveaux riches* are famous, has not disappeared from the scene; after all, new money thrives on visibility. Moreover, newcomers who became rich in the 2000s on the back of high oil prices, especially from resource-rich former Soviet republics and Russia's provinces, have kept Russia's glamour culture flourishing. Further, conspicuous consumption has trickled down the social ladder. Thorstein Veblen and his contemporary the German philosopher and sociologist Georg Simmel argued that new fashions, introduced via the elite, would pass down through the status hierarchy.[5] Aspiring middle-class groups in Russia have acquired an obsession with certain branded clothes, expensive cars, and glamorous leisure-time activities. Due to their visibility, these groups are still the most prominent in the public consciousness and have been the focus of popular stereotypes.

Seeking distance from the attributes associated with *parvenus* is one way of building up refined tastes, social distinction, a legitimate self-image, and eventually a bourgeois identity, but it can also be an expression of enduring status anxiety. Therefore, even though one might still encounter people holding on to the glittery displays of the nineties, one is equally likely to encounter people who conspicuously exaggerate their new understated civility. Not very self-assured representatives of the new bourgeoisie might be particularly anxious not to look anything like rough and crude *parvenus*, while more confident and class-assured members are usually very relaxed about their ostentatious past.

High-status groups tend to participate more frequently in many different kinds of leisure activities, even "poor chic"—a recreational and temporary consumption of poverty.[6] Maxim, an oil businessman who had previously trained as a lawyer, was born into a family of scientists. His father was an economist and his mother a chemist. This chubby, round-faced young man rejects some forms of ostentatious behavior, but indulges in others. He likes gambling in casinos, going to strip clubs, and indulging his extravagant eating habits.

Yet in some respects Maxim behaves in a manner that could be described as a flamboyant reversal of these norms. During our opulent dinner this father of two (his older child is thirteen) reached for his wallet and pulled out a Metro card: "I can waste money on 'deluxe' hotels but I can just as readily take the Metro." Maxim travels by the Moscow underground every day. "I even have a monthly travel card. Have a look! My friends always make fun of me."

Maxim talked of shopping at cheap street markets, which is also a kind of inverted snobbery:

I can buy myself a shirt for $1,000 but I wear a shirt costing 100 rubles [just over $1.50], because that's not important to me at all. For my wife it's a little more important, but not fanatically so. She likes comfortable clothes, and the problem is that comfortable clothes are usually branded clothes, which are expensive. Just recently she took ages looking for a pair of glasses. In the end she bought Gucci glasses, which were incredibly expensive. She didn't buy them because they were from Gucci but because they really fit well. If she had found suitable glasses for 500 rubles, she would have bought them. By the same token she can buy shorts for the kids at the market for 250 rubles and shorts in a boutique for 250 dollars. . . . These jeans, I think I bought second-hand.

There is no guarantee in Russia that the people Maxim encounters possess enough of an expert eye, or sufficient "symbolic capital," as Pierre Bourdieu would have called it,[7] to be able to evaluate, let alone recognize or appreciate, his "new simplicity." The entrepreneur is aware of this, and so are others, which is why they often combine their "simple" clothing with carefully chosen luxury items that are more conventional status markers. These are primarily shoes, perfectly manicured hands, and watches.[8] Maxim uses an ultra-expensive mobile phone, which is "the only little thing" that is important to him. It is made of gold. "I don't like expensive watches," he said. "But sometimes in meetings it's necessary to let people see a phone like this, which is more expensive than an average car. This will put your opponent in the right place." The advantage of using a phone as a status marker is that it can remain invisible if the owner wishes.

As well as using the Metro and buying second-hand clothes, Maxim sends his children to Pioneer camps (Soviet-style summer camps) and admires Stalin. Yet he also upholds some liberal and left-wing views and openly defends gay rights. Social distinction does not necessarily exclude eclectic tastes and cultural "omnivorousness."[9] Taken on their own, Maxim's willingness to use the Metro when it suits him, or his selective "poor chic" approach to fashion, appear as random, but they reveal a common pattern of strengthening his individualism while still relying on familiar elements of ostentation.

Adornments: Sartorial Signs and Trophy Women

Changing tastes and social hierarchies are visible in how people dress. Simmel wrote that fashion is an excellent means of achieving individuality and, at the same time, a group identity.[10]

Since the days of Peter the Great, fashion has been a crucial marker of group identity and individual worldview for the Russian elite.

Eighteenth-century boyars who shaved their beards and wore shirts made in Germany and Hungary both displayed their distance from lowly Russian peasants and demonstrated their affinity with Peter's modernizing mission. Yet in the mid-nineteenth century, after Russian aristocrats had mastered European elite culture, ennui set in. Tolstoy documented this fatigue with dressing *comme il faut* and, in an echo of Rousseau's idealization of the rustic life, aristocrats embraced the traditional tunic of the peasant. Such "dressing down" was first and foremost an intellectual statement and only appropriate for rich aristocrats.[11]

This elite aristocratic trend in intellectual history and culture acquired the name of Slavophilia. It emerged in tandem with the rise of a similarly aristocratic Westernizer current; writers such as Alexander Herzen and Ivan Turgenev preferred French fashions and mores. Yet Westernizers' and Slavophiles' tastes were not mutually exclusive. Slavophiles also traveled in Western Europe in expensive suits and enjoyed French fashions, and Westernizers could equally idealize Russia's *narod* (people) and dress down if they chose.

A more recent historical factor that has shaped a certain mentality in relation to dress codes is the relative scarcity of everything in Soviet times, including clothes. Those who could afford to be well dressed showed their privilege at every possible opportunity. Foreign visitors to the Soviet Union who chose to dress elegantly for one occasion and casually for others often aroused astonishment and irritation among Russians. Soviet Russians were not accustomed to people who could afford elegant clothes wearing things that looked casual and maybe even cheap. Conversely, to a Western observer, Russians could look overdressed for many occasions—the more money they had, the smarter and the more expensive-looking their clothes. In the new millennium, things have been turned upside down. Currently, foreigners in Moscow are easily identifiable by their "inappropriateness," a barman in a flashy nightclub explained to me, while confidently pointing out to me the foreigners on the dance floor. For example, Russians would not dream of going to certain upmarket nightclubs in suits, but Westerners do so when they come straight from work without getting changed.

Already in 2009, the Russian fashion historian Alexandre Vassiliev observed that "glamour is out."[12] A new trend was emerging in its place, he explained: " 'new modesty', with fashion becoming intellectual." When today's bourgeoisie wear rustic-style clothes, there is an unmistakable parallel with the Slavophile dress code.[13] Yet the rules of today's new modesty in fashion are more complex: First, one should avoid being overdressed (and preferably be slightly underdressed); second, one should dress appropriately for every specific situation, which involves frequent dress changes.[14] Dressing down does not mean spending less money on clothes; neither does it make dress codes more relaxed. It requires daily decision-making about aesthetics, which can be overwhelming, and it definitely reveals one's taste. Getting it wrong can damage one's image.[15]

Although some highly successful females as well as fashion icons do it as well, dressing down is generally more of a male phenomenon. In particular at semiformal events such as private receptions, it is not unusual to see some male guests in their best suits while others are sloppily attired, but often accompanied by young model-like women in designer dresses. Fashion choices seemed to reflect the status hierarchies of the guests at a preview party hosted by Sotheby's, which took place in Barvikha, the central district of Moscow's luxury suburb Rublyovka. The scruffily dressed guests were all big names—owners of large publishing houses, famous art collectors, and wealthy businessmen. For the most part people knew that those they were dealing with were aware of their superior position. Here, conspicuous understatement was as much a hierarchy marker as a group marker.

Dressing down is not uncommon among privileged circles in many cultures and nowhere more so than among English aristocrats, of whom there were a fair number at a gala opening in May 2013 of a high-profile art exhibition staged at a beautiful English country mansion. Prince Charles was the exhibition's patron. His helicopter was met by the host's wife, who was dressed in what one of the guests called pajama trousers and a vintage blazer. The former model, twenty-three years younger than her aristocratic English husband, later joined a table of her similarly dressed-down friends. Their informality stood out among the other guests, who, with the exception of some artists, had stuck to the rules and dressed smartly.

Meanwhile, the exhibition sponsors queued up for an introduction to the royal patron. Among them was Alexander Lebedev, the owner of *The Independent* and *London Evening Standard* newspapers. The Russian ex-billionaire was in white high-top basketball shoes, a tight-fitting tailored jacket, waistcoat, pencil-thin tie, and super-skinny black jeans. His casual attire signaled a different message: Although his upper body was just about worthy of a royal audience and handshake, his overall looks and demeanor were one of merit-based success, emulating the I'm-my-own-man style of

Bill Gates and Richard Branson, in contrast to the I'm-above-the-dress-code of the English aristocrat.

Lebedev was accompanied by his wife, Elena Perminova, a model twenty-six years his junior. When appropriate, she can dress down, too. She is frequently cited in trend stories for wearing bold prints, pajamas, and a turban or a scarf. Yet on this occasion Perminova was wearing a long, low-cut, very tight dress that showed off her slender figure and stressed her femininity. Clearly, the youth and exceptional beauty of the wives both of the English host and the Russian guest were assertions of their husbands' status. Yet while the casual clothes of the host's wife demonstrated that she was "at home," Lebedev's wife was the perfect foil for her cool husband.

A strong accentuation of femininity and physical attractiveness was characteristic of post–Soviet Russia and was taken to a new extreme. The economic meltdown of the 1990s caused a re-evaluation of personal relationships, resulting in a commodification of women's bodies and female sexuality that was unprecedented in Russian history.[16] This process was intensified through the "trade" some women engaged in, seeking material security and financial benefits through marriage or living as a mistress, thus making a "good deal."[17] One of my interviewees, Ignat, a businessman and politician in his late thirties, commented on this form of "mercantilism," as Russians often call it: Flaunting stunningly beautiful wives and mistresses, dressed in the most elegant, expensive haute couture and adorned with jewels, was a substitute for buying yet another Mercedes that nobody would notice anyway. Ignat himself sought distinction by rejecting such a lifestyle and being demonstratively faithful to his wife. (He held to this up to the point when he had to acknowledge to himself that nobody appreciated his approach to refinement.)

Ostentation through female companions is one of the most durable features of modern times and throughout history in general. In the late nineteenth century Thorstein Veblen, and later his fellow sociologist Werner Sombart, linked the first conspicuous form of property to the "ownership" of women. In Veblenian terms youthful wives and mistresses are "trophies," not only suggesting that they provide sensual pleasures, but also that they show off a man's success.[18] Young women's bodies in particular symbolically increase the status of men, radiating an image of exceptional virility.[19]

But even with respect to female companions, quantity and sensational beauty have become less important for social distinction in Russia.

Indeed, the businessman Arseny asserts that socially inferior women, regardless of their beauty, might today even undermine one's standing in society: "The fashion to go out with, and maybe even marry, models has disappeared here in Moscow. It has moved to the provinces and to lower social strata." He stressed that while it goes without saying that women must be attractive, now they must also be sophisticated, well educated, and cultured. Some of my interviewees affirmed that a long and stable marriage, particularly if predating the acquisition of wealth, had become a distinctive and distinguished social marker.[20]

Modes of Transport

The French sociologist and comparativist Jean-Pascal Daloz, who researches elite distinction, reminds us that private jets, helicopters, and the best cars are not only status tools but they also satisfy practical needs. They increase privacy and protection from observers and provide convenience for frequent travelers—a minibar or a satellite telephone; tinted and, if necessary, bullet-proof car windows.[21]

Practical use is true for most means of transport, except for yachts. Yachts are black holes in a budget with running costs of at least $1 million a year.[22] Curiously, they have gained some practicality with the introduction of sanctions. For Russians whose travel has been restricted by the European Union, yachts offer mobility through many Mediterranean ports where border controls for short-term visitors are lax.[23] For others, however, yachts serve as anti-symbol ("While Abramovich collects yachts, I collect paintings," a businessman told me). Nevertheless, every Russian yacht I have been on was about to be sold by its owner so he could get a bigger one.[24]

The continued popularity of yachts is an example of how even "advanced" representatives of the new bourgeoisie have shown quite enduring patterns of taste over the last two decades. One thing people did after the breakup of the Soviet Union, once they had some money, was to travel the world. Even though the excitement of traveling has long evaporated, they still have a tendency to give an inventory of their foreign travel (a very Soviet habit), assiduously counting destinations even if they run into the dozens. Many of my interviewees also doggedly stuck to the luxury travel routine to which they became accustomed in the 1990s. When a yacht is not an option, five-star hotels provide a safe haven; however, as

Maxim sighed, they are very boring. For some, a sense of monotony has set in; they feel that they have already seen everything. As a result, they have stopped traveling. "I can't be bothered," said David Iakobachvili. "I don't like discovering new things for myself. I don't want any more. I've seen a lot." The billionaire, however, does have a passion: "When I've got the time, I just ride my motorbike."

As for luxury cars, traditionally the quintessential status symbol,[25] they can have great emotional value. Andrey Korkunov, the "chocolate tsar," recalled a childhood memory of the 1960s:

> Back then a black Volga was an important status indicator. It was a sign that its owner had achieved something. You had to be a boss or a director. I always wanted to be a director and drive a black Volga. It was the smell of this car. My father often took me on business trips to Moscow. You had to get up early. Then you had to wait for this car to come out of the factory gates. The town was still asleep, so you could hear the car well before you would see it. Then we hit the road; all those magical conversations in the cocoon of the car. It's a memory so vivid and close, as if I was that little boy again. Now I've got many cars and no longer any Volgas. But, sadly, the excitement has gone. Everything becomes mundane. But it is exactly these feelings of youth and these desires that can move and motivate a person to achieve something in life.

In theory, ordinary Soviet citizens could buy Volgas, but as only a relatively small number were produced, to drive one's own Volga was probably the greatest dream of many. KGB officers and other privileged members of society used chauffeur-driven black Volgas. During Korkunov's childhood, the highest ranks of the leadership traveled in Chaikas. These black seven-seater limousines were produced in small numbers at the Gorky car factory after 1958, exclusively for the highest-ranking state and party officials.[26] Chaikas and Volgas were status markers visible to everyone, and they were convenient, as are today's versions—the Bentleys, Lexuses, Hummers, Range Rovers, and Toyota Infinitis.

This was something Nikolay realized quite quickly. As an act of reverse "poor chic" snobbery, the young politician drove a Zhiguli (Lada) for a while. Driving his own Zhiguli was definitely less practical than using a service car with a driver or driving one of the other fast and comfortable cars the politician had at home. Not only could he not make use of the time spent on the road, but he also had to devote time to finding a parking space. This could be especially time-consuming, because Nikolay occasionally felt embarrassment over his modest car and so eschewed his right to leave it in an official duma parking space. His constituency initially admired his choice of car, but then found it rather odd. He soon gave up this foible.

Cars are a public reminder of social hierarchies—in contrast to homes, which are carefully hidden behind high walls or in gated condominiums. Automobile hierarchies are, however, to some extent equalized when people are collectively stuck in traffic. This was particularly acute in the mid-2000s in Moscow, where road infrastructure struggled to cope with the increase of the volume of traffic. The pecking order was quickly re-established, at least for high-ranking officials who were afforded privileged road space via street closures.[27] Lesser elites abused special number plates that permitted the use of express lanes and speeding as well as sirens and flashing lights, allowing drivers to race down the wrong side of the road.[28]

These motorcades, constant closures, and abuse of fake sirens became such an issue that, in 2010, road users took to the streets. This protest campaign was directed against both uncouth upstarts who aped the earlier behavior of the new rich and hot-blooded members of the established elite, who continued to enjoy privilege irresponsibly. It was a harbinger of a new mood of opposition within Moscow cultural circles.

Parallel to these new trends, Moscow's Metro came back into the picture. The art critic and philosopher Boris Groys describes Stalin's grandiose project, with its beautiful stations, as both utopia and hell. It is hated with particular ferocity by those who can afford to travel by other means.[29] It is, nevertheless, one of the most brilliantly designed underground systems in the world—not always pleasant to use but quick, efficient, and the most rational option to beat Moscow's endless traffic jams.

As expected, for most of my interviewees, the idea of using the Metro was utterly absurd. On one occasion I found myself walking along the High Line in Manhattan for at least half an hour and my feet started hurting. I had expected to be sitting in some office rather than being taken on a long walk. Although I had opted to wear low-heeled shoes, they were still not meant for extended walks. But Victor was determined to press on. The fifty-something-year-old billionaire always did this when visiting his two children, who study at Columbia, as a means to fight the flab accumulated around the midriff of an otherwise sporty physique. He seemed to relish moving around freely without any bodyguard, even occasionally braving the subway. I asked him whether he also walks a lot in Moscow, which made him stop and frown at me with a mixture of confusion and irritation: "I've got my driver," he retorted. As Victor appeared to be relaxed and casual, I pressed further and asked him whether he occasionally uses the Moscow underground transport. The reply was brisk: "No, I never use the Metro. My children? No idea!"

Even among some of my younger interviewees, matters were not dissimilar. Twenty-three-year-old Nikolay, the son of a businessman who had set up the second largest company of its kind in Russia, told me:

> By the time I went to the kindergarten, I already had a driver. I only used the Metro at weekends to meet up with friends when the driver had a day off. Public transport is very unpleasant, it's stuffy, and oh . . . the queuing! The Metro is simply abominable.

All the same, some people are slowly changing their minds as Moscow's traffic jams have begun to make it impossible to travel by road. Ivan, an oil businessman in his early sixties, lives in Surgut, an oil-rich city in Siberia. He tries to avoid using the road when in Moscow:

> In Surgut I go by taxi, in Moscow by Metro. I simply can't stand the traffic jams in Moscow. I'd go completely mad. . . . I know, I'm an absolute exception. Nobody else goes by Metro. I love that my life is so different from that of my contemporaries.

Ivan is not actually as exceptional as he might think. Alexander, an investor and trained aeronautical engineer, who is also in his early sixties, started using the Metro again after two decades of abstinence:

> In the early 1990s, I stopped using the Metro. But a few years ago when these crazy traffic jams started, I started using the Metro again when I had to get somewhere quickly. . . . I'm not scared to go down there. I actually enjoy going down there. The Metro works very well and there aren't that many people. . . . You can see normal people there and I like watching their faces.

At this point of the story, Alexander became pensive: "But how much poorer people have become!" Compared to Soviet times? I asked. "Yes, what unhappy people there are!" he replied. "And it's dirty, very dirty. The Metro I remember was definitely cleaner. My Metro is the Metro of the

1980s. My Metro represents Moscow." Dressed as he was in casual beige pants, a light blue shirt, and a vintage-looking brown jacket, I could see how he easily goes unnoticed in the Metro. However, I wondered how people reacted when he arrived at his destination by public transport. My question provoked surprise. "How would people know?" Alexander usually sends his driver on the long traffic jam route hours ahead of him, so that he can be picked up shortly before reaching his final destination.

Unlike Alexander, the billionaire Roman Avdeev speaks publicly about his public transport habits. It is logical to go by Metro, not modest, the banker and businessman corrected me. "Status symbols are neither good nor bad, but some of them get in my way and make life more difficult. I do whatever I like. If it's easier to take the Metro, I take the Metro." Then, sighing, he added a rare comment in a country that has learned to adore Stalin's achievements: "In the 1930s, during the collectivization, people were starving and yet they built these underground palaces."

Like Alexander, Konstantin Ernst, the head of Channel One, Russia's biggest television channel, also uses the Metro. "You can spot changes very early when you look at the people in the Metro," Ernst replied when I asked him what he did to keep abreast of the latest trends among ordinary Russians. He then laughed and said: "The other day I noticed that an elderly man was staring at me. I was about to get off the train, he came up to me, patted my shoulder, and whispered: 'Sorry to see you here. Did they sack you?'"

The Intelligentsia Ideal of the Bourgeoisie

The pressure to distinguish oneself from uncouth new upstarts does not wholly explain the speed of the shift toward more restrained patterns of consumption. This fast pace is also grounded in the cultural resources that the bourgeoisie inherited from the Soviet period. If they played down the head start their Soviet biographies gave them in developing their careers in the 1990s, in the 2000s it became appropriate for them to link themselves with the intelligentsia in social terms. The biographies of almost all of my interviewees corroborated the privileged intellectual and social capital they had received from their Soviet intelligentsia backgrounds.

My interviewees' claim to belong to the intelligentsia constitutes one of the most prevalent narratives in Russian culture. In his lectures on the Russian intelligentsia, Isaiah Berlin drew attention to the memoir of the aristocrat Pavel Annenkov, who described Russian society of the 1830s–1840s as consisting of two distinct groups: the intelligentsia, a tiny minority who possessed some formal knowledge, and the masses, who did not. In the decade that Annenkov chronicled (1838–1848), the intelligentsia was drawn largely from the aristocracy and was united in a way that is reminiscent of a medieval guild.[30]

With the expansion of university education in subsequent decades, an influx of nonaristocratic *intelligenty* from merchant and especially clerical backgrounds changed the composition of this group. Many of this younger generation advocated a progressive social program. This was the time of the emancipation of the serfs, which was passed by imperial decree in February 1861. In *Fathers and Children* (1862), Ivan Turgenev, one of the participants in the lively discussion circles of the 1830s–1840s and a close friend of Annenkov, provided a seminal account of the struggle for cultural dominance between aristocratic and non-noble intellectuals in the 1860s.

At the turn of the century the composition and values of the Russian intelligentsia evolved alongside the twists and turns in Russian history. Crucially, a split took place over the 1917 Revolution. While many within the progressive wing of the intelligentsia supported the Revolution, or formed part of the nonparty intellectual elite of the 1920s, others became the backbone of anti-Bolshevism. Many emigrated. Others, however, morphed into the Soviet intelligentsia, both through their professional and managerial careers, and through academia and literature. Many found work as "bourgeois specialists" (experts of all sorts who had been trained in Imperial Russia, especially as engineers and higher military personnel), over whom the Communist Party exerted vigorous scrutiny. Some joined the Communist Party. Stalin's purges eventually uprooted the aristocratic line of the intelligentsia, but they even more systematically liquidated the wing of the intelligentsia that had felt duty bound to serve and enlighten the common folk. Instead, a new Soviet intellectual elite came to the fore that specialized in technical professions.

After this period, the radical critique of the Russian socialist tradition had become a thing of the past. The Soviet intelligentsia elite lost its humanistic search for truth and its self-effacing devotion to serving the people.[31] At the same time, it continued to produce a steady stream of trends and fashions, some of which stood in stark contrast to mainstream culture and to the prevailing political atmosphere.[32] As the American Russian journalist Masha Gessen has noted, the late Soviet intelligentsia became particularly status anxious. Much like Annenkov previously, they sought to distance themselves from ordinary Russians.[33]

I met Pavel, a young banker, at a charity ball in London. He looked comfortable in his tuxedo, but he seemed rather bored. He told me that he was born into an intelligentsia family from a Jewish background. His grandfathers were scientists, which is why this banker and son of a billionaire businessman saw himself as part of the intelligentsia:

> In Russia there are two major social groups in society, the intelligentsia and the majority of the population. These two groups have no relation whatsoever with one another, except that they live in the same territory. The majority of Russians are totally different; I've got nothing in common with them.

This perception of Russia's social structure serves for Pavel as a reference point. He had difficulty, however, positioning himself in the class structure in the United Kingdom where there is no intelligentsia: "I've never thought about which social class in the UK I belong to. English society is very stratified, but I'm outside any strata. I don't like class society."

Pavel's view is the product of his post-Soviet upbringing, which coincided with the collapse in the position and prestige of the Soviet intelligentsia. Overnight in the early 1990s a chasm opened up between the new rich and members of the Russian intelligentsia who remained writers and academics. The impoverished intelligentsia tried hiding its envy by turning up its nose at the lack of culture displayed by Russia's *nouveaux riches*. The Russian literary critic Mark Lipovetsky has remarked on this envy:

> In fact, New Russians possessed everything that a Soviet *intelligent* was deprived of and dreamed about. New Russians had power, money, and freedom from moral norms and social limitations. Unlike the pauperized intelligentsia, New Russians represented that segment of society which enjoyed the fruits of perestroika and glasnost, economic reforms and the politics of openness—the ideals cherished and cultivated by the intelligentsia for decades.[34]

Rather than linking itself to the shabby post-Soviet intelligentsia which has now fallen on hard times, the Russian bourgeoisie has found it more useful to articulate its place in Russian society by reference to the elitist brand of the earlier Soviet intelligentsia. Vladimir, a short, thin man in his mid-forties with a round face and dark bushy hair, sees himself as being not only outside any strata, but "outside society" in general. He hates commoners, if not people in general, but makes an exception for the Russian intelligentsia. "It has almost disappeared," he sighed, sipping latte with soya milk in a newly opened organic whole food cafe. "Only a very small layer of what used to be called the Russian intelligentsia is left," he said. Still, if he is to be ascribed to any group in society, "then it is to these one hundred to two hundred intelligentsia people who are left in Russia." He peered over his large green spectacles with a glint in his eyes and added with a wry grin that his family was in fact exactly that: intelligentsia in the purest form, "the actual elite, who would never sell their souls and never work with any power structure."

I asked Vladimir whether his parents and uncles were dissidents in Soviet times. "Gosh no," he waved me off, showing this dismissive attitude toward dissident activists that I have often encountered among the well-off offspring of the intelligentsia. "My family has an incredibly solid internal culture," he explained, as if this contradicted the tenets of dissident activism. Vladimir's father, his two uncles, and three younger siblings have done very well in post–Soviet Russia, running businesses and arts projects and making money from both. Vladimir is the only one who is not in the art world. Although allegedly not involved in any power structures, Vladimir's father was superbly well connected, which enabled him to secure his son a high-powered job as a political speechwriter in the 1990s—definitely not the most ethical field one could work in in those years. Vladimir has since set up a successful PR and lobbying company.

Karina and her husband, a wealthy businessman, live in the Moscow luxury suburb Rublyovka, a conglomerate of villages with the most splendid mansions and showy villas along the Rublyovskoe Highway, which has been reserved for the elites for centuries. It is where Lenin, Stalin, all of the subsequent general secretaries as well as grand literati, composers, and actors had their dachas. "Financially, we belong to the upper class. But we'd certainly like to consider that we came out of the intelligentsia, beginning with our grandfathers," she said. Karina has lovely olive skin, black silky hair, and dark eyes, all of which point to her partly Central Asian family background. The forty-seven-year-old mother of three had entered Moscow's high society through marriage. She met her future husband, an engineering student, when he was working in Uzbekistan; there was a Soviet tradition of sending students to help on construction sites all over the Soviet Union. After that summer, he took her back to Moscow, where they lived very modestly, but within Moscow intelligentsia circles. These were the crème de la crème, whom people from all over the Soviet empire aspired to join.

This cultural significance has repercussions up to the present day: "Of course, there are artists and writers in our circle. That's a must!" In case I thought she came across as a little too frivolous, Karina quickly expanded upon the worldview appropriate for a Soviet intelligentsia family. "You can also place us in the intelligentsia in terms of our attitude to life and our moral and spiritual values, such as support for others, friendship, love, and mutual understanding," she said. "The most important values are certainly integrity, propriety, and good manners, as well as high ethical and aesthetic standards. But of course, without money it's all difficult."

Pyotr Aven, an oligarch with assets worth $4.6 billion in 2016, the son of a professor of computer science and a former scientist himself, considers himself to be intelligentsia, but he does not think many of his fellow bourgeois are. From the researcher's perspective things look different. Many of my interviewees combine intelligentsia and bourgeois identities in an effort to emphasize their cultural credentials, even though in many cases their parents were not as high-status and intellectually blessed as Aven's.

Aven might see as an exception Ilya Segalovich, cofounder of Yandex, the world's fourth-largest search engine and Russia's equivalent to Google. To ask for an interview, I sent this IT multimillionaire a message on Facebook. He replied the next day out of an innate respect for scholarship and said he would give me an interview if I promised to use it for academic purposes. We met at a simple cafeteria next to a Metro stop. When I arrived, I nearly missed him. Segalovich sat at a tiny table in a corner. The setting seemed appropriate as he described the values he thought his parents bequeathed to him:

> A certain distrust toward money, respect for labor, respect for honest achievements, distrust of everything superficial, respect for what is within a person. That is, my parents always took external achievement as something trivial and bad. Our values have always been to work a lot and to be honest.

Segalovich's parents were geophysicists: "They did groundbreaking work in engineering back in the 1960s," Segalovich told me: "My father received a state award for what he had discovered and his name was entered into one of the republic's encyclopedias."

Segalovich was the antithesis of the corrupt, lavish businessman and crook whose morals had disappeared long ago, and hence he was an idol for many urban youth and some members of the intelligentsia. Thoughtful and highly intelligent, he seemed to care about the weak in society. In 2011 he appeared on Russia's *Forbes* list at position 159, with a net worth of $0.6 billion. In the same year he joined the anti-Putin demonstrations, mingling with the crowd instead of with the liberal celebrities on the speakers' stage or in the front row.

After the interview, Segalovich gave me his wife's phone number so that I could also arrange an interview with her. I met Maria in her city center flat, a large bright place with high ceilings packed with bookshelves, randomly collected furniture, and an old coffee machine. Her mother met me at their front door, which was ajar, quite extraordinary considering the fortresses the Russian superrich usually inhabit. On the floor sat Maria's baby daughter playing with a young woman. She was an orphan who had been taken in by them and now worked as their nanny. Maria would sadly soon become a widow. Segalovich died from an aggressive form of cancer in 2013, before he had even reached the age of fifty.

Kulturnost

The notion of *kulturnost* provides us with a good handle with which to understand post-Soviet trends. *Kulturnost,* or culturedness, is the social glue between cultural resources and material goods, a behavior code that guides civilized consumption, tastes, and manners. Scholars have used the term to describe the values and practices of Soviet distinction.[35]

Kulturnost dates from the mid-1930s, after a period when thousands of peasants had flocked to the cities as a direct consequence of forced collectivization. *Kulturnost* for the new urban poor meant a certain standard of personal hygiene, which was vital in the cramped housing conditions they lived in. They learned to be clean and neat, brush their teeth, wear fresh underwear, and dress smartly, albeit in a dour Soviet style. It worked. Although the cities were bursting at the seams, the young generation of those years was the healthiest ever in Russian history.

Meanwhile, Stalin nurtured new patterns of consumption: access to cinemas, spectator sports, and consumer goods, including perfume and makeup for women, shaving kits for men, and Soviet champagne produced in Crimea. For people in those groups of Soviet society that were treated to these new pleasures, *kulturnost* embodied above all a need for cultured norms, good manners, and a minimum knowledge of high culture. Even for ordinary party members, by the late 1930s, it had already

become unacceptable to be indifferent to the classics of Russian literature, Pushkin in particular. The higher up the social hierarchy, the more
important it was to expend significant time and energy on self-education,
on cultural events such as visiting the cinema and exhibitions, on having
relatively refined diction, and on being well read in contemporary Soviet
fiction, poetry, newspapers, the works of Marx, Engels, Lenin, and Stalin,
and in the classics of Russian and foreign literature.[36]

The historian Catriona Kelly wrote that the brilliance of the *kulturnost*
ideology "lay partly in the fact that it was a fusion of two value systems
previously thought incompatible, those of the bourgeoisie and the intelligentsia."[37] Citizens at the higher end of the newly differentiated social
hierarchy could enjoy some modest, conservative comfort, while at the
same time feeling themselves to be highly cultured.[38] Mingling with the
new Soviet *beau monde*, established party members developed a sense of
themselves, if not as intellectuals (*intelligenty*), then certainly as people of
culture.[39]

After the Second World War, in the late Stalin era, the administrative
elites were amply rewarded for their loyalty to Stalin. They had access to
special retail outlets where imported high-quality consumer goods were
legally on sale. Those who wanted to live up to the tenets of *kulturnost*,
however, abstained from being too acquisitive. *Kulturnost* taught them
that if they showed their prosperity too overtly, they would be considered
vulgar. A cultured person of the late 1940s and early 1950s learned to skill-
fully encode brash status markers. This was particularly important for the
offspring of the first generation of party leaders who reached young adult-
hood in the early 1940s. Many of them were keen to dissociate themselves
from their parents' dirty party work and the pursuit of power and privilege. Instead, they aspired to become part of the intelligentsia.[40]

Having long turned away from revolutionary politics, the Soviet intelligentsia emerged as a carrier of the former values and refinement of
Russia's prerevolutionary aristocracy. There was a parallel between the
Soviet intelligentsia of the 1930s and the Russian intelligentsia in its for-
mative years, the 1830s–1840s, that Annenkov had recalled. The implicit
assumption of the Bolshevik elite was that Russia's literary tradition was
pioneered above all by aristocrats, such as Pushkin and Tolstoy. By promoting Russia's literary heritage, for example on the centenary of Pushkin's
death in 1937, the Soviet regime began to champion Russia's aristocratic
legacy in a shift away from the earlier rejection of prerevolutionary culture
in the 1920s.

A clear undercurrent in many of my interviews was an expression of nostalgia for the culture of reading that had characterized their youth, and reminiscences of a private culture of bookishness. Sitting in his architect-designed minimalist house in Kensington, in west London, the financier and art collector Igor Tsukanov remembered the uniformity of most Soviet apartments and their interiors: "It was difficult to distinguish oneself with fine taste in furniture or paintings." The only thing that allowed educated people to express themselves was the choice and range of books on their shelves: "We had a big library at home and I grew up on books. It's a typical Soviet story. We had nothing else except education and books." As Tsukanov summed up with a hint of nostalgia, "We all read a lot in our childhood. Now that's all changed. I was lucky."

Continuing our conversation on her intelligentsia background, Karina, the Rublyovka resident originally from Central Asia, also spoke of her childhood: "Both my husband and I did so many different things in our childhood. It was very diverse. We took part in an amazing variety of things." Karina told me this while picking on a salad in the Cafe Margarita, named after Mikhail Bulgakov's book *The Master and Margarita* and located right on the corner of Patriarch's Pond, where the opening scene of that book is set. "And we read a lot," Karina sighed. "The amount we read! Oh, how much we miss this today!"

"Isn't there some irony?" moaned Karina's elder daughter, who dropped in briefly to say hello. "You guys in the 1990s had absolutely no time for reading because you were so busy with all kind of other things, making money for example. And spending it! Now you are the first ones to complain that your children don't read enough." I was impressed by the young, cheeky woman with a slim face looking out from under long, silky dark hair. She dashed off a second later to meet her boyfriend outside. "Well, she's got a point, of course," her mother admitted, as we watched her daughter walk off. "But she is also exaggerating. We always encouraged our children to read, even when we had no time to do so ourselves."

Yevgeny, a flamboyant businessman and art collector, also alluded to the elite distinction of his youth. We met at the Moscow art gallery Garage, which back then in 2009 was still in a former bus garage. The original 1927 building, the Bakhmetevsky Bus Garage—designed by the Constructivist architect Konstantin Melnikov, while the roof was the work of his fellow architect engineer Vladimir Shukov—is an avant-garde landmark, thanks to its parallelogram-shaped floorplan. Dasha Zhukova, Roman Abramovich's third wife, had turned this 8,500-square-meter space into a contemporary art center. That evening, Zhukova opened an exhibition of work by Antony Gormley, who is highly popular among Moscow's bohemian set.

Yevgeny, who is fifty-nine years old, was wearing an olive green shirt, a bright tie spattered with red, and a dark-blue cord suit. I commented on his dapper attire. He explained that he has clothes made for him by his favorite French tailor whom he visits every time he goes to Paris. That city is also one of the potential locations for a museum he is planning to set up. The museum will be concerned with the soul of the Russian people, though Yevgeny is not sure if this soul exists anymore. He finds it instead in the past, in the period when the Soviet intelligentsia and their reading and educational traditions were blooming:

> I was socialized by the '68 epoch. That is to say literature, art works, bards, Galich [the dissident singer-songwriter]. This was a spring, a proper, real spring! It was the Beatles! It was an incredibly interesting period. I was sixteen/seventeen. It was all an immense influence on me and on how my personality was formed. It was the spirit of free culture and free love in a philosophical sense, yet at the same time we were conscious of ourselves as being "at one" with the people.

By referring to political awakening and rebellion, Yevgeny struck a different note than his peers and I wanted to hear more, but he was distracted by the arriving artists and fellow collectors. Another time he would tell me more, he promised me.

In fact he never did do this, but he had provided me with enough clues. Many entrepreneurs have, like Yevgeny, turned into people of culture and now spend most of their time on art projects. Bourdieu reiterated that the fundamental advantage gained from membership in a privileged class is distance from economic necessity. This has resulted in some Russians becoming dismissive of their own involvement in business. Yevgeny's wife has taken over business matters so that he can devote almost all of his time to art. He explained why:

> I belong to the professional intelligentsia. My business is just a means to an end. I'm interested in dealing with global

cultural projects. I belong to the part of the intelligentsia that seeks answers to eternal, philosophical questions [ishchushchaya intelligentsiya].

Yevgeny sets the tone for those members of the bourgeoisie who no longer need to concern themselves with money-making, but are free to pursue their individuality. With their closeness to the intelligentsia, individuals of the kind I have analyzed potentially set the parameters of la classe dominante: a social class dominating not only the economic and political sphere, but also culture and society—the embryo of a new elite class that in key respects models itself on the Russian aristocracy. From this perspective, it is significant that the present-day elite vindicate their claims of just how special they are by referring back to the Soviet intelligentsia, though they superimpose onto this model their own qualities and leanings.

Being Difficult as a Marker of Superiority

In a very short time, upper-class Russians have changed the criteria for what is considered distinguished. They have traveled the world; taken on board a whole new range of symbols, styles, and tastes; and modified some of these to their liking and rejected others. However, when it comes to certain aspects of social interaction and demeanor, they seem to strongly reject foreign styles. Different behavioral norms may be found in the ways people display their power and relate to social inferiors. American elites treat their social inferiors with a combination of easiness, warmth, openness, and friendliness, but still, however subtly, put them in their place.[41] British elites tend to be similar.

Russian elites have a different approach. As a relic of both Imperial Russia and Soviet times, social relations in Russia are typically hierarchical and paternalistic. People are happy to openly display their superior position in society and are not concerned about hiding their arrogance and dismissiveness. Chrystia Freeland recalls in Sale of the Century that, when dealing with Russian men, she had become accustomed to having to go through several months of "courtship," during which she was "alternately patronized, dismissed, and softened up with a barrage of sexual innuendo."[42]

A good number of the upper-class Russians I encountered had little concern for creating an atmosphere of ease and comfort. They would make it clear if they felt that the conversation was intruding too much on their time. Some of them became tight-lipped and were reluctant to respond to my questions. Sociologists locate the phenomenon of reluctant respondents around the top and bottom of socioeconomic hierarchies:[43] It is a weapon used by those at the bottom of the hierarchy to make their refusal clear without having to go through the trouble of actually articulating it. This works equally well for those at the top of society.

The easiest way of refusing to interact with me was simply to remain elusive. Even after I had convinced someone to give me an interview, planning it remained difficult, as hardly anybody would agree on a date more than three days ahead. The next hurdle would be to avoid having the scheduled interview cancelled. If a prospective interviewee decided to refuse to meet me, they would usually stop answering my calls before we got to the point of making final arrangements, while others simply stood me up. Some repeatedly reconfirmed their willingness to give me an interview but then continually deferred the meeting.

This could turn into a long-term game, as it did in the case of Maxim, the golden mobile phone man. This young businessman kept me waiting for over a year, although I pursued him relentlessly. He would agree to a meeting then not answer the phone, so that we could not arrange a place and time. I kept chasing him both because he repeatedly gave me hope, and because I was very keen on this interview, as, from the gossip I had heard, Maxim promised to be slightly different from most of the other entrepreneurs I had encountered. Eventually, after a year, we agreed on a time, but when I called to confirm the place, he did not answer. Later that day he sent me a text saying that he would call in a minute, which he failed to do. Finally, after I had been sitting around for twelve hours trying to get this interview scheduled, I received a text message ordering me to go to a restaurant in a casino: "Get something tasty for yourself and find out if they have got the snails which I ordered the other day. Don't be shy." The interview lasted three hours and was accompanied by a great deal of food. Maxim presented himself as a down-to-earth, easygoing, warm, and generous host. It nearly made me forget that he had subjected me to a yearlong game of hide-and-seek in which he playfully demonstrated his power.

Among the rich Russians I encountered, invariably, it was the more established and wealthier interviewees who were the most fickle and self-absorbed, playing out their foibles and moodiness with a complete lack of inhibition. Vanya, a youthful fifty-something, was the most aloof guest at a dinner party a hundred or so miles outside Moscow. While everybody else was sipping champagne, he was knocking back vodka. This slim, tall man with dark silver-streaked hair and a slight belly, dressed in a plaid shirt, jeans, and fancy dark-framed glasses, took sporadic notice of the people around him, including me once in a while. The first question he directed at me was about my age. I was used to people telling me they thought I was at least half a decade younger. Not so Vanya. He nodded and remarked: "Yes, that's about the age I thought you'd be." The next question was whether I was married. I said no and the conversation dried out.

Later that evening the host of the dinner party asked Vanya to give me a lift back to Moscow. Once in the car, Vanya asked me who I actually was. I replied briefly and returned the question. He hummed and hawed and finally muttered that he was an entrepreneur, "or, let's say, a businessman." We came to the entrance of the gated housing complex. For no apparent reason he asked the driver not to hand back the estate entry pass to the security guard but to pass it over to him. Vanya then turned on the light and held the pass in front of him so that the light shone on it and I could see what was written on the card. It was his name. I had to smirk at this convoluted way of making me aware of his identity. He was a famous oligarch.

During the one-and-a-half-hour journey, odd things happened. We talked about football, his family, the Russian mentality, and what he disliked about Russians—he actually used the word "hatred." I asked why. His reaction was strange: He leaned forward and put his head in his hands, as if he were feeling sick or dizzy. I asked whether he was alright, but there was no reply. He then seemed to fall asleep. I became worried and felt quite helpless about how to deal with the situation. Illness was already on my mind because the party guests had been discussing all sorts of medical issues related to ageing. All of this talk (and his odd behavior) had me wondering if he was having a heart attack. All of a sudden, however, he came back to life and opened the window (he smoked, so it was stuffy in the car) and, more surprisingly, replied to my question (which I had asked ages ago) concerning what he disliked about Russians. I wondered whether he had just taken a rest to think. Or maybe he had dozed off, which would not be surprising given the amount of vodka he had consumed at the dinner party. In any case, his odd behavior had its effect: While I was initially oblivious of the social difference between Vanya and me, and had felt comfortable asking the odd cheeky question, I was now pretty much disarmed, especially when he did this strange head-in-the-hands thing three times. With this behavior, consciously or not, he accentuated the power imbalance between the billionaire and the researcher.

Leonid was more straightforward in his condescending and patronizing behavior toward me. Born in 1940, this elderly heavy industry businessman was in total control from the moment I stepped into his office, which overlooks the Moscow River and the Cathedral of Christ the Savior. Leonid made clear that he had very specific expectations about how the interview would proceed, how long it would last, and what we would talk about. Although Leonid preferred to pursue his own agenda rather than reply to my questions, he nevertheless took things seriously and wanted to give me the information he considered important. He also had his own ideas of what would happen with the interview material, and was perplexed when he learned that I would not base my empirical data exclusively on the one-and-a-half hour interview with him.

During the interview, Leonid occasionally tried to test my knowledge. This is in his character: The former scientist turned entrepreneur had given lectures at higher education institutions, and now he was lecturing me about science and the philosophical theories he had elaborated. Although he appeared at times to be slightly tired, he repeatedly put forward authoritative statements. "The big bang is proven. Of course, there has to be a God," he told me while walking through his office. Looking down his nose at me, he continued: "Darwin's theory is absolute nonsense. I can assure you of that, as a professor who has published more than a hundred works."

Challenged by no one and presumably subject to no criticism, constructive or otherwise, this man appeared detached from the world and slightly off kilter in his self-assessment. Leonid was proud of the many things he had accomplished in life, but he was particularly pleased with his writing talent. In his opinion, his fiction is on a par with that of one of Russia's greatest short story writers, Anton Chekhov. Nonetheless, he did accept that Chekhov enjoyed quantitative superiority: He had written more than two hundred pieces, whereas Leonid had written only one work of fiction. Leonid made sure that I would receive a copy through his secretary. In due course I met him two more times; the second meeting was arranged specifically so that I could collect the DVD of a documentary in which he had starred and that had been broadcast on a Western TV channel.

Some interviewees appeared nervous when I spoke with them. While waiting for an interview with a famous fashion designer, I met Polina, a journalist. A few weeks later she took me to an interview with Fyodor, a former KGB officer turned industrialist. When we entered his office, Fyodor, a big, broad-shouldered man with a squashed nose, was visibly uneasy and tense, to the point that his hands were shaking.

He calmed down quickly when he met me and the interview proceeded very well. When we left, Polina asked me whether I noticed his shaking hands at the outset. She explained that this was because he knew he would be meeting a Western journalist (this is how Polina had introduced me), and that this kind of insecurity and suspicion was not untypical for his generation and his professional background.

Admittedly, these examples might not be typical. However, many of the people I encountered seemed uneasy about small talk and basic communication. Something that people from different cultural backgrounds, especially British and American, perceive as straightforward can be tiring and exhausting for Russians. Status, for them, does not necessarily involve communication skills in social encounters. Indeed, it can mean the opposite: It relieves people from the obligation to keep a conversation going. Arkady feels he is at a stage in his life where he can expect people to engage and entertain him, rather than the other way around: "When I meet new people, I want them to be interesting. . . . I don't want to talk myself and keep everything going. I've done that for twenty years."

SOCIAL DISTINCTION FORMS part of the package of how to be rich, together with the gravitas of family history, merit-based achievements, exclusivity in lifestyles and possessions, art philanthropy, and care for the less fortunate. The sociologist Pierre Bourdieu regarded distinction as the seemingly natural expression of social worth—something he ascribed to a well-established and stable bourgeoisie such as the French. The discrepancy between 1970s France and post–Soviet Russia could not be greater, and yet Bourdieu's concepts work for Russia as well.

The contemporary Russian bourgeoisie has grown out of twentieth-century history and therefore contains tensions and contradictory features. Its members have generated and established their own character, among other things, by creating distance between themselves and others, especially from groups with features that they used to exhibit themselves but have now rejected. Many of my interviewees, in one form or another, have converted their abundant economic resources into cultural and symbolic ones. They have learned not to show off their money but to embrace more cautious, discerning, and refined tastes. Ostentation has turned into a more moderate and private affair. However, tastes change first in external signs and in items that can be consumed and reconsumed; changes in manners, demeanor, and intrinsic tastes take longer.

3

The Quest for Legitimacy and Superiority

IN HIS BOOK *Capital in the Twenty-First Century*, the French economist Thomas Piketty is scathing about the idea of a "moral hierarchy of wealth." According to this idea, ingenuity and sweat justify great fortunes, while exploitative profit-making and inheritance do not. Piketty dismisses the distinction between the deserving and nondeserving rich because, he says, any such hierarchy obscures the structural factors that perpetuate social inequality.[1]

The American sociologist Rachel Sherman has investigated how this idea of a moral hierarchy of wealth is implemented and how the conflict about how to be both wealthy and morally worthy plays out in practice. Interviewing wealthy New York City families, she found that the "good" rich pursue a set of strategies to set themselves apart from what they consider to be the morally deficient and unworthy rich, who are greedy, profligate, lazy, and self-indulgent. They want to think of themselves as hard-working and socially responsible; they encourage their offspring to have an awareness of their privilege, act as if they were no different from others, and not demand special treatment or seek to show their superiority.[2] This is in line with Max Weber's idea that the holders of power and wealth want to believe that they "deserve" their good fortune due to their superior qualities in comparison with others,[3] and they want everybody else to believe this, too.[4]

For a rich elite to be secure in its long-term position, it must possess moral authority. For that to happen, people need to respect how society is organized. For society to live with class-based disadvantages and inequalities, a significant number of people must believe them to be acceptable and possibly even just. As Bourdieu argued, these beliefs must not be overt, but must be perceived as run-of-the-mill, taken-for-granted practices and ideas—something he called false beliefs, or méconnaissance.[5]

The quest for legitimacy is surely a great challenge for Russia's rich, given that the large majority of Russians regard the elite accumulations of wealth in the 1990s as highly illegitimate.[6] Yet it is not an acute challenge in the current political climate. Russia has parliamentary and presidential elections, but the vertical organization of power means that the bourgeoisie are not really subject to the scrutiny of society, but primarily to the scrutiny of the Kremlin. Putin can tap into widespread popular opposition against Russia's rich elite if it suits his interests, but he can also shore up their position by using his authority to protect their property rights. Hence to avoid the fate of persecuted oligarchs such as Berezovsky and Khodorkovsky, the rich need to identify which superior qualities are part of a narrative that can enable them to reinforce the image of themselves as deserving (and not only because of how cunningly they have outdone others), both for public consumption and to remain in the Kremlin's good books.

The Legacy of the 1990s

Soviet propaganda had it that under capitalism the gains made by the few (the "capitalist sharks") inevitably lead to the suffering of the many.[7] The crude dog-eat-dog reality of the 1990s confirmed the Soviet propaganda position. Unlike the Western bourgeoisie that actively pioneered industry in the early nineteenth century, capitalist wealth accumulation in 1990s Russia went hand in hand with the halving of the country's GDP between 1990 and 1997. Russia's 1990s capitalism was the catalyst for a sharp fall in the living standards of ordinary citizens and the fastest ascent ever of a new wealth elite.[8]

The former *Financial Times* journalist and now Canadian politician Chrystia Freeland observed the early wealth accumulators, the 1990s oligarchs, over many years. She found that they "believed that they triumphed in the brutal Russian capitalist contest of the 1990s because they were the strongest, smartest, and most daring six men in Russia, and possibly in the world." They saw their strengths as having the instinct to seize opportunities, and the tenacity and determination to pursue their aims without shying away from high-risk challenges.[9] Back in the 1990s, then-oligarch Mikhail Khodorkovsky boasted to Freeland: "We all took the risks to get there, and not everyone is able to take such risks." The implicit note of self-congratulation was even stronger in his follow-up remark: "If a man is not an oligarch, something is not right with him. Everyone had the same starting conditions, everyone could have done it."[10]

At that time Khodorkovsky felt that his success provided its own justification for his personal biography, regardless of his contempt for the rule of law and the living standards of ordinary Russians. After ten years in prison, however, he publicly conceded that he bears significant personal responsibility for the political situation that emerged in Russia, having prioritized economic reforms at the cost of the population's social well-being in the 1990s.[11] Not many other members of the elite, most of whom have not shared his experience of incarceration, have explicitly engaged in self-criticism.

Pyotr Aven, the head of Alfa Group, which includes Russia's largest private bank, is a liberal figurehead among the oligarchs and a darling of the Western media for his beautiful collection of fine art and his ability to move in Western high society. He accepts that he cannot personally become a moral authority because his name is too closely linked with the rapid 1990s enrichment.[12] Nevertheless, he retains his neoliberal thinking. In 2000 he encouraged Putin to resort to Reaganomics with dictatorial control, as implemented by the former Chilean dictator Augusto Pinochet, to push through radical economic reforms and fulfill his promise to make Russia great again.[13] More than a decade later, in 2013, Aven still openly expressed his admiration for Pinochet and his model of dictatorial neoliberalism, but acknowledged that there had never been the possibility for a leader like him to emerge in Russia: "For a Pinochet to appear, there need to be some preconditions in society. First, the elite must not be corrupt. Second, a law-abiding spirit must be at a high level."[14]

Aven is no exception among Russian market liberals in his admiration for Pinochet. This makes sense; Pinochet was anti-communist and neoliberal. At a public event I asked Aven's 1990s market reformer peer, the former deputy prime minister Alfred Kokh, who had overseen the controversial 1995 loans-for-shares auctions and the 1997 privatizations in alliance with Chubais, what he would do differently if he had the chance to repeat 1990s history. At first he did not respond, but after a while he admitted that he would change one thing: He would base the privatization program around pension reform, modeling this on the one implemented by Pinochet (which was basically a fully private retirement system; it has been increasingly criticized for failing poorer Chileans).[15]

In the 1990s, Russia's market reformers' strong advocacy for rapid neo-liberal reforms and their deep hatred of communism, together with the absence of a critical and socially oriented intelligentsia, gave them the freedom to explore their neoliberal agenda without many restraints. The lack of a vibrant civil society meant that other than Putin's executive power after 2000, there was no regulatory force in society that could tame the rich with regards to both their business practices and their self-righteousness.[16] The civil society initiatives that erupted during perestroika and the early years of transformation did not gain momentum beyond a tiny percentage of the population. This was partly related to the fact that after nearly seventy years of Soviet authoritarian and Stalinist totalitarian rule, Russia's population had no great tradition of civic participation to fall back on.[17]

The legacy of this lack of civil society is aggravated by widespread irresponsibility. While Khodorkovsky appears to have changed his views during his years in prison, others, including young entrepreneurs, continue to cut corners. Artyom, a young oil and finance entrepreneur, told me, while we drank cocktails at Claridge's in London's Mayfair, that if his status does not help him to get his way, he lies. He does this a lot, several times a day, "for the benefit of others," he assured me. He appeared to be half absent, readjusting the cuffs of his tailored dark-blue suit jacket that sat perfectly on him. "Although I'm very good at lying, I don't like it that much," he said, turning his attention back to our conversation. "No, I don't feel any guilt." He glanced at me with a smile, showing off his perfect white teeth. The end justifies the means of successfully performing his nerve-wracking job: "Otherwise, you don't get anywhere. The more hostile your environment, the more you will lie." Nothing in Artyom's appearance betrayed how merciless he must be when dealing with business matters. He revealed his recipe for keeping calm: "Do you know what the one important thing about our conscience is? It's quite flexible and resilient. You need to conclude a big contract once and for all and not start renegotiating it time and again."

Artyom was socialized in the practices of the Russian business community in the 1980s and 1990s, a time in which individual initiative, audacity, and brutality were rewarded. It was also a period in which one had to be a chameleon, able and ruthless enough to switch from one moral code to another. Being two-faced was a strategy for survival and had been used extensively throughout the Soviet period. People had one face when they swore allegiance to the Communist Party line and a very different one in their homes when surrounded by their closest friends and family.

Automatically switching from one to the other and fusing together different, often opposing values became the norm—and this was not necessarily false and cynical opportunism.[18]

"My biggest concern is freedom," declared twenty-four-year-old Pavel, a banker and the son of a super-rich businessman. Pavel's agenda has clear priorities. "Poverty and misery" do not feature in his "top-ten worries about Russia," he said: "Poverty is actually not really a big deal." He paused for a second: "Well, maybe there is poverty in Russia, but I'm not really bothered about it. Poverty is more the consequence of all the other real problems we have; the lack of freedom, the isolation, and the lack of openness to the world—that's what bothers me." Pavel is annoyed that the majority of Russians do not share his list of priorities, which he considers to be yet another major problem. "There is total apathy."

Vladimir, a PR entrepreneur in his forties, combines his neoliberal views with individual adventurism. He considers himself to be less a businessman than a member of a tiny group of Moscow intelligentsia. At one point in our conversation, he told me that when he was little, he wanted to be like Robin Hood. This surprised me. "Ah," I retorted, "that means you wanted to take money from the rich and give it to the poor?" Vladimir stared at me and then started laughing out loud: "No, I wanted to go into the woods and shoot with a bow and arrow," he said, referring to the medieval hero's active male attributes. Vladimir took advantage of my hesitation to clarify his view. "I didn't think about the poor back then; in fact, I don't think about them today either." He sees them as being responsible for their own fate: "Yes, social inequality in Russia is horrendous, but I'm not against this inequality. I'm not a socialist. In my view, everybody can earn money as long as they aren't ill and are physically intact. I don't see any reason to help these people." Then his eyes hardened: "They will help themselves—well, as long as they are not lazy or idiots—then they'll go figure something out," he said, adding defiantly: "This applies to women as well!"

Genes

Yekaterina, the wife of a billionaire, became impatient with me when I asked what she thought her parents had passed on to her that has helped her to be successful: "Listen, I got genes from my parents. Of course, these genes allowed me to develop myself and all the qualities that led to success." She turned away from me to get the attention of the waiter, who on this Monday afternoon in summer on the rooftop of The Standard in New York seemed in no particular rush to respond to a Russian woman's energetic waving. Yekaterina was wearing a sharp white trouser suit and, at almost sixty, looked absolutely stunning, if somewhat daunting. She finally managed to place her order—three mojitos, one with very little sugar for her, normal ones for me and for her husband, Gennady, who was standing by the glass fence overlooking New York's Hudson River and smoking— and softened a little. She explained in more detail:

> I don't have any noble roots. My parents are reasonably simple. They are also self-made. All they achieved, they achieved because of their own capabilities. They graduated from university despite the few opportunities life had offered them. My father is from a family of ten children, from a rural place. He became a professor and a great scientist in his field. My mother is from Ukraine. She made it into university in Moscow on her own efforts, right after the war. She practiced science all her life. She held a doctorate and worked as a senior research fellow, quite successfully.

Yekaterina is convinced that it was her parents' genes that gave them their willpower and strong characters and were responsible for their fast-moving careers and social mobility:

> You can see, they hadn't had their paths laid out for them. They possessed natural and biological resources, which they managed to make the most of, despite this being very difficult at that time. Well, they had a thirst for education, culture, and a certain lifestyle, both of them. And I inherited it. That's actually really wonderful.

It works well for Yekaterina's self-legitimization to see her parents' rise from humble origins in the immediate postwar period as a result of genes, rather than as a part of postwar mobility facilitated by an education system geared toward mass social advancement. It is particularly significant that Yekaterina's narrative revolves around her thirst for education and her work ethic, which she believes she inherited from her parents. Her husband, who had by now joined us at the table, confirmed what she said. Gennady told me about one of their sons, an exceptionally gifted young man who at the age of fifteen received an offer to study at an Ivy League university: "I wouldn't say he's got special talent, but he is very gifted.

Well, Yekaterina is very gifted, too." Turning to his wife, he asked: "Have you told Elisabeth that you graduated with a Red Diploma from a very prestigious university?" Not waiting for a reply, he continued: "In physics, where there are usually only two females among a hundred males." Playing with his cigarette box, he added in a lower voice: "Well, I'm probably a bit gifted as well."

Gennady was wearing beige linen trousers and a blue shirt. A Panama hat covered his head; I assumed he was going bald. The billionaire was somewhat socially awkward and there was something Soviet in his demeanor, as he presented himself as humble and grateful ("Our son is much better than I am"), although there was a hint of pride about his own role in his son's success.

Unsurprisingly, Gennady chose not to mention other factors that very likely helped develop the son's talent: that he had grown up in very privileged circumstances—an extraordinarily affluent family from a hugely aspiring and socially privileged intelligentsia background. Instead, Gennady—despite being a self-declared atheist, and in whose family everybody of his parents' and grandparents' generation had been a Communist Party member—identified two reasons for his family's outstanding talent, both of which are beyond the sphere of rational questioning or criticism: "This is thanks to God and thanks to genes."

Genes and God were the most frequently cited reasons for success, and the people I spoke to sometimes identified themselves as "chosen ones." Such assumptions replicate ideas implicit in Protestant thought. Calvinist ethics speaks of individual predestination due to God's divine will, though the individual has to pursue his or her vocation. In the same spirit the Russian bourgeoisie speak of their own innate entrepreneurial vocation and merit. God's divine will dovetails with genes, as it is through their DNA that they inherited their God-given capitalist drive.

Ivan, an oil businessman from the Siberian oil town Surgut, reflected on the relationship between individual merit, genes, and the will of God while we were having a late lunch in a Moscow restaurant: "I don't like it when people say, for example, I'm proud of being Russian or I'm proud that my shoe size is 45. After all, that's from above, from God." This physically voluminous oilman, with an equally voluminous baritone voice, said that individual effort was his motto: "Be proud of what you've done yourself in your life." He applied this logic to his family history: "My ancestors are from the Polish gentry [*szlachta*]. My surname was first mentioned in 1280. In my family a genetic refinement has taken place. But . . ." Ivan paused for a second for effect, and poured more vodka into our glasses: "I'm not proud of it!"

Nevertheless, Ivan takes genes very seriously. He even believes that his political attitudes derive from his genetic inheritance. He sees himself as a sort of oppositionist, somehow more liberal than the Kremlin clan, and in any case not one who can easily be subordinated to the authorities' will: "My political conscience is 98 percent genetic. It's from my mother." He recalled an episode from 1943:

> After Ukraine was occupied, my mother was taken to Germany. She was eighteen back then. She worked in a factory in Mannheim. When she came back to Ukraine in 1943, a guy working for the NKVD [the predecessor of the KGB] made a pass at her. She went to get advice at the women's department. She took a form and wrote a statement addressed to the NKVD chief saying that she was a virgin and that this guy had offended her.

Ivan is still in awe of his mother: "Imagine, a twenty-one-year-old woman writes a complaint to the highest NKVD officer about his colleague! The officer forced his subordinate to apologize to my mother," he said. Then he got lost in his memories: "She was very beautiful. Very, very beautiful." After this digression, he sat up straight and announced the story's conclusion: "Obviously, it's something genetic which I have got from her, this willingness to protest."

Ivan is probably very aware that being brought up by his mother and having her as a social role model were just as important in the development of his views of the world and his preferences as were any genes. He might even agree with the notion that making ethical choices is part of what makes us human, and that this does not fit well with the assumption that everything is genetically predetermined. Nevertheless, what first came to his mind was the matter of genes.

Although justifying success by reference to genes is in many ways ad hoc and improvised, it is not random. This kind of essentialist reasoning is strong in Russia, not because everybody is obsessed with genes, but because it offers a convenient justification for inequality. What is supposedly grounded in nature is difficult to argue against. In addition, secular ways of "naturalizing" the social and the historical have a strong tradition in Russia. This is despite the fact that Marx considered consciousness to be determined by being.

Soviet traditionalist ideology had by the 1960s and 1970s long dictated that everything was in the place allocated to it by "nature," such as respect for traditional family and gender roles, with an emphasis on motherhood for women. That these ideas extended deep into the intelligentsia was partly related to the fact that in Soviet academia science was prioritized at the expense of developing the social sciences. It was further strengthened by the conservative nature of Soviet dissent.[19]

A consequence of this was that, at a time when in the West critical thought, especially feminist thinking, demonstrated that repressive hierarchies imposed on society were the result of human action and not nature and biology, the Soviet intelligentsia held a strong attraction for politically conservative views, which they merged with biological interpretations of history and human behavior. The American historian of science Loren Graham observed in the Soviet Union in the early 1980s that the "naturist viewpoint enjoyed uneven but surprisingly widespread support across a complex and contradictory spectrum of academic geneticists, literary avant-gardists, dissidents, anti-Marxists, ethnic specialists, conservative nationalists, and police administrators."[20]

Many of my interviewees, raised in this spirit, had adopted a similarly biologically driven perception of the world. This thinking outlived the Soviet period and continues today. Putin's conservatism and the rising influence of the Russian Orthodox Church have not significantly intensified biologically driven views, but neither have new ideas emerged to question, for example, the "naturalness" of patriarchal gender characteristics or of ethnic traits.[21]

The Russian elites' obsession with genes is not unknown among their counterparts in North America. According to several studies by the social psychologist Michael Kraus, high-status individuals in the United States tend to endorse essentialist views and are convinced that their success is due to their talents.[22] However, as social inequality intensifies, most of them are sensitive enough to promote a different language, at least in public. This is a crucial difference between Russian elites and their Western equivalents: The latter make use of a more elegant public narrative that is readily "digestible" by the wider public as opposed to the blunt and unpolished Russian style.

Although less focused on genes per se, the narrative of rich Russians who have spent time in the West still entails naturalist elements in the sense that they see entrepreneurialism as something biological. "Entrepreneurialism is a talent. It requires a very specific set of skills. Fast thinking, courage, willpower, and more," the multibillionaire Pyotr Aven explained to me. He did not have those skills himself (he was rather more suited to becoming a scientist, he said), but he managed to successfully apply his academic skills to his business activities. "Every society has a certain percentage of naturally born entrepreneurs," he said. However, he also granted a role to nurture: "Whether they can develop and apply their skills depends on the environment they grow up and live in."

A few of my interviewees stressed the role of luck. "Of course, genes decide a lot in life and determine personality," noted the billionaire Roman Avdeev, "but I've simply had a lot of luck, rather than special qualities." After returning from his military service in 1988 to study at the Moscow Power Engineering Institute, he traded in decoders and then set up a bank. Today he owns Moscow Credit Bank, one of Russia's biggest in terms of assets. His wealth in 2014 was assessed at $1.4 billion. As the economist Robert H. Frank points out, in a winner-takes-all society, luck decides who, among a pool of talented, gifted, well-equipped individuals, moves on and reaches the top.[23]

Freeland's close observation of the 1990s oligarchs concurs with Frank's analysis, that a good part of their success comes from luck. This is not only about being at the right place at the right time but also about "reading the one book or having the single conversation that allows you to spot a nascent opportunity in a fast-changing world."[24] The social entrepreneur Veronika Zonabend admits that she and her husband were lucky "to live in the right place at the right time. Our strength was the ability to adapt very quickly." Zonabend sees adaptability not as her individual character strength but as another lucky overlap in age and era: "We were lucky to be at the right age, when one is most flexible, at a time when all the new opportunities opened up when the systems were changing."

Such analysis may sound reasonable, but was an exception among my interviewees. Luck rarely featured in their narratives. This is not difficult to explain. Acknowledging chance as a key element in their path to riches would diminish their version of success as deserved. This is particularly the case when fortunes are too clearly associated with illegitimate activities, be they criminal, corrupt, or nepotistic. Again, rich Russians are not alone in overlooking luck as a crucial ingredient in their success. Frank argues that a large majority of fortunate people around the globe tend to disregard luck as an explanation for their superior talent, intelligence, and discipline.[25]

Religiosity

The many references to God alongside references to genes reflect a specific post-Soviet take on religious belief in Russia. Soviet upbringing was, as a rule, atheistic. Within some families, religious traditions lived on throughout the Soviet period, but people in the Soviet elite—Communist Party members, army personnel, prosecutors, KGB agents, among others—tended to adhere to Soviet atheism. Against the background of a post-Soviet value vacuum and Putin's conservatism, many elites, despite their atheist Soviet upbringing, began to embrace a newly discovered religious faith.

However, this process is not straightforward. The billionaire Boris Mints told me that he cannot become religious because faith comes from one's mother's milk, or maybe as the result of some epiphany. Since he reached his fifties, he has considered himself to be an agnostic rather than an atheist, and religion has become a part of his life through his Judaism-related philanthropic engagement. Mints is actively involved and holds an official position in the plenum of the Russian Jewish Congress. "Before that, I read everything; the Old Testament, the Torah, the Koran, but I've always been more interested [in Judaism] from a theological, philosophical point of view." Mints grounds his philosophical engagement with religion in his need for intellectual and spiritual growth: "I've matured and spent a lot of time with rabbis, who've taught me a lot." Several times around Passover he has gone on desert trips to Israel where, together with a group of fellow Russian Jewish billionaires, he was taught the rules of Judaism.

This kind of religious renaissance is not standard among the Russian elite, and neither is it clear-cut among the younger generation. In the 1990s, Ilya's father made quick money in the oil business and became one of the top five hundred richest people in the world. Later he moved to Israel, together with Ilya's mother. Ilya and his sister went to the United States to study. Ilya has worked as a banker, a journalist, an artist, a tech entrepreneur, and an angel investor, buying up tech startups in Israel and the United States. The family have always been atheists: "I'm not religious. No one in my family is. I'm actually totally anti-religious. I'm not only indifferent to religion, I'm actively against it."

Turning to Russian Orthodoxy, we find that things are equally complex. According to the postwar historian Eric Hobsbawm, Christianity in

Eastern Europe is in many respects indistinguishable from nationalism and can be described more as a bastion of national identity than as a confession.[26] This reconciles the first upper-class generation, still socialized into Soviet atheism, with a post-Soviet conservatism that is heavily reliant on a renewed form of Russian Orthodoxy.

I was sitting with Dmitry Kiselyov, "Russia's chief propagandist," as *The Economist* called him,[27] in his office in the All-Russia State Television and Radio Broadcasting Company (VGTRK), a building that up to 1956 hosted the Interior Ministry's Gulag administration headquarters. This media manager told me that he had not adopted any faith: "I am myself not religious, but I certainly know that I'm not a Muslim or a Buddhist. I support the Russian Orthodox Church a lot, out of tradition." He explained why, with a slightly apologetic air: "My socialization was not the slightest bit religious. My father was no longer religious. In the early 1920s massive repressions were carried out. My grandparents didn't want their children to be religious because it was too risky."

Kiselyov supports religiosity in and with his family and cultivates the elite connections he has built up in the church. He seems in awe of Patriarch Kirill of Moscow, primate of the Russian Orthodox Church, whose lifestyle he humbly admires: "Kirill is an absolutely outstanding man, a proper personality. He rides a motorbike and goes skiing. He is one of the great philosophers of our time." Kiselyov is proud of their close acquaintance: "He baptized my youngest son. He suggested it," he said. "I like people of his stature. People who are passionate about what they do and yet are role models for their children." Kiselyov's comments on religion were highly gendered. While the patriarch is an appropriate male role model, Kiselyov sees women as having a different religious identity, with more everyday duties: "My wife is, of course, a believer."

Kiselyov has been married several times. He was married for the third time by the age of twenty-two, and the Communist Party criticized him for his weakness and lack of discipline. Kiselyov holds a grudge against the Soviet Union in its final years because his career was blocked as a result of his multiple marriages, which prevented him from traveling abroad or becoming a member of the Communist Party.

Today Kiselyov is very public in expressing his ultra-conservative views, for example with regard to homosexuality.[28] He lauds the early Soviet period—despite official Soviet atheism and the fact that both his grandfathers were killed during the purges. He told me that he considered the Stalin era as the most important period in Russia's history: "There were many fewer problems than now. Drug addicts, homosexual marriages, and so on. These things have never been welcomed by Orthodoxy from the outset. I regard them as a Protestant-Lutheran compromise." In applying his conservative Orthodox values to Stalin, Kiselyov highlighted the overarching conservative ideology that underpins his position, linking Stalin's legacy to Russian Orthodoxy.

Such glowing praise for Stalin is in tune with Putin's ascendancy and the rise in patriotism. In a national survey conducted by the Levada Center in March 2016, 54 percent of respondents said that Stalin had played a positive role in the country's history, compared to 42 percent in 2006. Fifty-seven percent considered Stalin to have been a wise ruler who had made the Soviet Union a powerful and prosperous country, compared with 47 percent in October 2012.[29] While Kiselyov does not claim to offer a model of Orthodox belief for public consumption, his comments on Stalin, seen through the prism of present-day Orthodoxy and broadcast on his media outlets, are an influential factor in shaping the outlook of Russian television viewers.

Social Inequality and Soviet Nostalgia

Chrystia Freeland recalls that until the early/mid-2010s, one could talk extensively about poverty at global gatherings or conferences put on by international organizations, but talking about social inequality was taboo. Poverty has usually been seen as completely separate from inequality: That is, it has not been seen as an issue strongly interlinked with the unequal distribution of resources. Talking about social inequality, in turn, has the disturbing implication that the legitimacy of those in possession of wealth might be questionable. However, after the continuous rise in inequality in recent years, it has become a hot topic, at least among the more enlightened and farsighted representatives of the international business and political establishment.[30] This is not yet the case in Russia, despite the fact that at no other time or place throughout history has social inequality increased as rapidly as it has in Russia since the collapse of the Soviet Union.

Georgian-born businessman and art collector David Iakobachvili is now involved in the energy sector but is better known as the founder of food processing giant Wimm-Bill-Dann, a manufacturer of dairy products and beverages. According to the *Forbes* list, he was worth $1.2 billion in 2014. He cringed when I asked whether he was concerned about the social threats that accompany the growing gap between rich and poor: "Misery in Russia bothers me. But certainly not social inequality! Talking about social inequality only leads to revolution; nobody needs that! No, no, no!" Still looking slightly uncomfortable, he said that he categorically wished to see "a strong state that can help its citizens live under humane conditions. I just want people to live well."

While I assumed that Iakobachvili was uncomfortable with my question because it concerned the relationship between inequality and revolution, and, presumably, Russia's history of social upheaval, other interviewees thought this link was exaggerated. Pyotr Aven, the multibillionaire head of the Alfa Group, does not see any risk "whatsoever" of social protests erupting in Russia because "the population has become a lot richer in the last twenty, thirty years." He provided a perceptive comment about the isolation of Russia's richest: "There is a problem of social inequality, but the group of very rich people is very small and lives separately from the rest," he said. "Even though social inequality is vast, there won't be any social protests for that reason." Nevertheless, he finds it alarming that inequality in Russia equals that of the United States. The solution to this problem lies with the state, he argued, not with him: "It's a question of social policy. Social mobility must work. There mustn't be any nepotism."

The London-based art collector and former financier Igor Tsukanov thinks the impact of inequality should not be overrated: "Most got onto the *Forbes* list through their own strengths, not because they inherited wealth. Most rich were born poor. As we speak, new poor people are born who'll be rich one day."[31] In contrast to Piketty, Tsukanov considers that inherited wealth is decreasing important in wealth accumulation. As for society in general, he argued that the existence of super-rich individuals actually benefits disadvantaged groups in society: "Well, look at them, those on the *Forbes* list, they started giving everything away. In the States there are huge projects where the rich give half of their wealth to charity." Tsukanov insisted that the key to success is education, which he seemed to think is accessible to all. "If you don't have money, get a scholarship. At university nobody cares whether you are wealthy or not."

Veronika Zonabend, entrepreneur, graduate of the prestigious Moscow Aviation Institute, and former engineer at the Research Institute of Avionics, is also convinced that many successful people come from the lowest rungs in society. In her philanthropic work within the educational sector she strives to provide opportunities for children who demonstrate great abilities regardless of their socioeconomic background.

> We need equal opportunities for all, rather than social equality. People are born with different intellectual abilities and they are born with different social opportunities. It is essential to create a diverse environment where all participants can learn from each other.

Seeing one's own privilege as grounded in talent and, therefore, seeing society as open to social mobility does not remove the problem of growing poverty in Russia, and some do feel uneasy about it. Alexander Svetakov, in 2016 the 595th richest man in the world, assesses the number of those living under the poverty line to be 22 million. The billionaire is happy about the rising number of people who are ready to help the poor, although that provides little comfort. "The number of those who need help is increasing three times faster. The situation is pretty grim right now."

If Russia's rich are to achieve sufficient authority to ensure stability and perpetuate their own social position, they will have to promote a socially orientated image of themselves and demonstrate their social responsibility. Boris Mints admitted that few people "talk about this [social responsibility], especially in Russia." The billionaire made it clear that people with political power have "no right whatsoever to take decisions that cause a deterioration in the conditions of the common people, who elected them to those positions." He also called businessmen to account: Their responsibility is simple and straightforward: "to create workplaces; our main task is to create workplaces!"

While Mints deplored the lack of social responsibility among Russian businessmen, Irina Sedykh, the wife of an owner of a metallurgy empire, was relieved that not even the post-2014 ruble decline caused any major social tensions in the cities where her husband's businesses are located, even though unemployment has increased significantly since then. Both Sedykh and her PR person talked about how up to the eleventh hour they tried to save their business projects, whether or not they were profitable. "But then, when the crisis hit harder, it was just looking too bad," the young PR manager said.

Sedykh's foundation has tried to mitigate the consequences of layoffs, she emphasized, assuring me that "the state is helping as well." In a reference to nineteenth-century Slavophile discourse on social harmony, Sedykh concluded that "historically in Russia we have always been concerned about finding a balance between commerce, production, economy, and society." She has taken steps to translate her compassionate sentiment into action in the towns where her husband's factories are based. The work she has done to increase respect for her husband's business empire makes her highly regarded in her community and among her peers.

When searching for possible solutions, some interviewees looked back to their own Soviet past. Fashion designer and former mathematician Helen Yarmak alluded to a collective Soviet-grown sense of obligation: "Social responsibility is important. We are the progeny of the Soviet Union and we were raised to care about other people." In commenting on social responsibility Andrey Korkunov, famous for his chocolate brand, explained: "That attitude comes from our Soviet past. We've got it in our blood. It's our obligation and I bear this cross."

I met the investor Stanislav in his office, a large gloomy room filled with intimidating heavy dark-brown furniture and stuffed animals. Stanislav is one those interviewees who have a picture of themselves with Putin hanging on the wall. Awards that his company received from the journal he owns are also on display, together with photos of his family at home and abroad. The elderly financier is a staunch anti-communist. Nevertheless, he is resolute in his conviction that communists "should have a right to exist. They are a counterweight to capitalists and fascists. If there are no socialists, there are no social programs. They should exist as a party. . . . Why am I telling you that?" he asked as if he had just read my mind: "As someone socialized into socialist society, I reason in social categories."

References in the narratives of the super-rich to Soviet morality reflect a certain unease about how society is developing. Although being careful not to glorify the Soviet past, Yury Pripachkin nevertheless made it clear that he deplored the moral decay in post–Soviet Russia: "Of course, it then turned out that we had double moral standards in the Soviet Union. But today we have not only double moral standards but triple moral standards." The technology entrepreneur and business partner of the Fabergé egg-owning oligarch Viktor Vekselberg believes that post-Soviet capitalism has had a destructive character. "You know, the capitalist system destroyed the value system," he said: "The socialist, communist system required that workers lived decently, that science was developed, that medicine was developed, and that culture was developed." In Pripachkin's view, the loss of socialism resulted in "a loss of philosophy per se" because, he explained, "the world can't live without competition in philosophy between capitalism and socialism." He complained that the result of this loss of "philosophical competition" was that there was no need to develop anything. He concluded that "also in this sense we have totally destroyed everything we gained from socialist society."

Pripachkin, Stanislav, and Yarmak are all of a generation and professional background that might explain their Soviet nostalgia. Others, however, exhibit no obvious features that could have given away their nostalgia for elements of the Soviet past. The billionaires Ziyavudin Magomedov was born in 1968, and Roman Avdeev in 1967. Avdeev made his money in banking, and Magomedov in banking, oil and gas, port logistics, engineering, construction, and telecommunications. Both seem textbook examples of modern entrepreneurs easily navigating the capitalist world.

It was already dark when I arrived at Magomedov's family office. I was led in after a security check and had to leave my phone and computer with the two scary-looking guards, whose presence made me slightly ill at ease in the otherwise beautiful and serene surroundings of the elegant Moscow building. Magomedov, tall, athletic, and smartly dressed, looked completely at home among the fine antique furniture and leather-bound editions lining the bookshelves.

Magomedov grew up in Makhachkala, the capital of the Soviet republic Dagestan, on the shores of the Caspian Sea. Though he was not from one of the centers of Soviet intellectual life (which were, for the most part, Moscow and Leningrad), he is proud of his intelligentsia background. His parents were a brain surgeon and a teacher of Russian literature and history, professions that placed them at the top of Dagestan's intellectual elite. They were Avars, one of the predominant ethnic groups in the region between the Black and Caspian Seas. They brought Magomedov up to be bilingual, stressing the cultural importance of the Avar language to their family. An aunt was married to Rasul Gamzatov (1923–2003), the most famous poet writing in the Avar language.

In line with the best Soviet intelligentsia tradition, Magomedov's family was uncompromisingly atheist, and as a boy, Magomedov was only exposed to the Sunni Muslim culture of the Avars during his summer holidays at his grandparents' place in the mountains. After attending "the best school in the North Caucasus," he studied economics at Moscow State University, where he started his quest for wealth (accumulating $1.4 billion by 2014). When I commented on his background, suggesting that he hailed from a "classic Soviet intelligentsia family," this instantly produced a broad smile, softening the effect of his strict Marine Corps hairstyle.

So far, nothing unusual, until he outlined his views on social policies. As my recorder had to stay with the guards, I had to rely on my memory when writing up the interview, but a few things stuck in my mind: Magomedov said that he thinks that under the Soviet regime people had everything apart from private property: peace and friendship between the peoples, excellent Soviet education for all, strategic planning, and a deeply ingrained social spirit to support those in need of help. He is keen to bring up his children in line with these values.

Avdeev spoke equally warmly of many Soviet-time values, which, he said, he would like to pass on to his children:

> Khrushchev said at one plenum that we have now founded a new people, the Soviet people. It's difficult to say what that is exactly. I very much share my parents' and grandparents' values. There is something in them we have in common. . . . Humanistic values were very important for Soviet society.

Avdeev spoke very quickly. He clearly found me too slow when I had to search for the right words to phrase my questions. He became fidgety and began readjusting his suit jacket, though there was nothing wrong with it, and then decided to answer my questions before I had actually finished asking them. But when I asked him whether he could name me a philanthropist, from Russia or elsewhere, historically or in the present day, whom he particularly admired and saw as a role model, he fell silent for what seemed like a very long time. "Someone I see as my role model?" he finally asked, with some hesitation. I nodded with relief—but another long pause followed. Then he said: Karl Marx. "Of course, there is a lot of utopia in Marx, but utopian ideas are not so bad after all."

Carrying on at his previous speed, Avdeev explained that Marx had formulated a number of demands in relation to capitalist society, among them an eight-hour working day, the right to paid holidays, the right to organize unions, and the right for workers to take part in a factory's management. "All these demands have long been realized in capitalist society," he said. He was positive about the realization of these reforms, but said that one important demand had never been implemented:

> The abolition of inheritance! This last point has a lot to do with philanthropy and I've thought about it a lot. They are now introducing a high tax on inheritance, which I think is very correct. Everybody should achieve on their own merit.[32]

RICH RUSSIANS WJ1HO explain their privilege by reference to genes and God draw a veil over the possible structural advantages they have enjoyed in life: those which they derived from their parents, or which they seized illegitimately. In typical neoliberal manner, they often present themselves as deserving of their wealth by emphasizing their belief in upward mobility, both in their own cases and those of other people. If everybody has the potential to become wealthy, then those who do become wealthy can congratulate themselves on their success, which they supposedly achieved through fair competition, while the failure of the less fortunate can be attributed to their lack of merit. Rich Russians' articulation of a belief in the survival of the fittest allows them to fashion an interpretation of biology and religion in their own neoliberal image. This has worked in Russia, not necessarily because everybody strongly believes in rich people's natural right to privilege, but because they collectively lack alternative concepts and explanations.

This is, however, by no means an entirely successful hegemonic project. Although Russia's rich are trendsetters in fashion and ideas, they are as yet incapable of (directly or even indirectly) transmitting more universal everyday ideologies to society that could buttress their rank. This is partly because the earlier cutthroat pursuit of wealth destroyed the possibility of developing a common ethics in Russia that could bind the population together. This vacuum has been filled, to some extent, by recycled Soviet templates—that is, primarily intelligentsia values filtered through Soviet experience. My interviewees would have been unlikely to have acknowledged the Soviet legacy in the 1990s when the survival-of-the-fittest mindset was at its crudest. They do so today, however, because they are ready to refashion a more widely acceptable ethical system, having developed a more complex, albeit at times contradictory, narrative about their own success.

To me, as an outside observer, it seemed reasonable to suppose that Russia's rich could theoretically outsource the job of legitimizing privilege to thinkers within the intelligentsia, in whom they take pride and whose friendship they cultivate. After all, in the West rich elites have left this task to others. In Victorian and Edwardian Britain, commentators such as Charles Dickens, John Galsworthy,. and E. M. Forster famously made scathing remarks about the elite, whether these be aristocratic, mercantile, or colonial. They sought in their writing to reconcile the advantages of money-making with a more harmonious and ethical vision of Britain's future. By contrast, Russia's intelligentsia has not done anything remotely similar, at least not in a sufficiently subtle way, and thus has yet to convincingly endorse bourgeois superiority. In the few cases where such redemption has arisen, paradoxically, this has been thanks to President Putin. In part by criticizing selected oligarchs (and thus asserting his own authority),

Putin acquired the clout to support what he presented as the just demands of a "legitimate" bourgeoisie. This raises the question as to what the bourgeoisie will do in a post-Putin Russia, when they will no longer be able to use his legitimizing image to shore up their own position.

In the meantime, there is another obstacle to legitimization, which flows from the fact that Russia is a country with a dark and silenced past. This concerns not only the Soviet period, but also the 1990s. Konstantin Ernst, as head of Channel One, almost certainly has more insight than anyone into the process of transmitting the values of the bourgeoisie to the wider Russian population. In addition to deciding not to show a film that he himself produced of that troubled decade (*An Alien Girl*), despite the fact that he has the necessary institutional means to do so (as mentioned in chapter 1), Ernst also omitted the 1990s in the opening ceremony of the 2014 Winter Olympics in Sochi, which constituted an overview of Soviet and Russian history, because those years are still too close and painful to show on television.

This is not an issue unique to Russia. In Austria today, hardly anybody has heard of the film *The Sound of Music*. This reflects the attitude of the Austrian nation toward its twentieth-century history. At the time of the film's release in the 1960s, Austrians were either ignoring their recent past, or clinging to the idea that Austria was the first of Nazi Germany's victims, an idea that some parts of the elite still hold. Obviously, it is not only the bourgeois elite in Russia that is slow to expose its less than glorious role in history, in this case in the 1990s. This goes hand in hand with the fact that many ordinary Russians do not want to be reminded of this demoralizing and traumatic period in their lives.

In sum, a key to the legitimacy of the bourgeoisie does not lie in a harmonious narrative of post-Soviet history, but in their birthright. So far I have highlighted the importance of their narrative about their genes as an explanation of their individual success. In chapter 4 I will broaden the focus to chart how their family origins are essential to the status of their class, despite the upheavals of their country's history in the twentieth century, which make the link between family history and class identity particularly complex.

4

Family History

BOURGEOIS RUSSIANS HAVE become increasingly conscious of the need to legitimize their social position by constructing a distinguished past. Some seek to retrieve their earlier family history, especially in relation to previously forbidden roots and family members who were repressed in Soviet times. This new search is not purely a way of canceling out Soviet distortions. Rather, it is in itself a reminder of how the retrieval of the past is a creation of the present, as scholars into memory research reiterate. In the words of the historian Catriona Kelly, memory is dependent both upon what one is told one should experience, and what is fashionable at the time.[1] The first big fashion among the rich in post-Soviet Russia was to find some privileged family members from the past, preferably "blue blood." By now, the fashion has moved on, shifting the focus onto the Soviet intelligentsia. This chapter considers how upper-class Russians view their family backgrounds from their present-day, post-Soviet perspectives.

Resuscitating Prerevolutionary Family

Valery Babkin, a chemical industrialist and art collector, born in 1941, was raised solely by his mother. His father, a pilot, died in the war. Babkin had carved out a successful career well before the Soviet Union fell apart. He was a Soviet enterprise manager, in charge of a large combine called Ammophos. Through privatization, he succeeded at turning around all thirty factories under his control; from being "basket cases," they were transformed into thriving enterprises.[2] (Later this giant phosphate-based fertilizer producer was bought by Andrey Guryev, the billionaire who today owns Witanhurst in Highgate, London's second-largest private residence after Buckingham Palace.)

Babkin said that his mother did not pass on the family history to him. She was scared that her son, when he was a little boy, might talk too much in front of people whom she would prefer not to know about his background. Ignorance of his immediate family history became increasingly problematic as Babkin gained more of a public profile. He was a people's deputy under Gorbachev, then a duma deputy under Yeltsin, and later the organizer of the industrialists' faction, which actively supported the policies of the young reformers Yegor Gaidar and Anatoly Chubais. "The whole nation was listening to me, and I brought the truth to everyone," he boasted.

After the collapse of the Soviet Union, when an interest in a bolstered family genealogy became risk-free, crafty historians, who had barely subsisted on their meager university salaries, set up agencies offering family history research to well-funded clients. They attracted rich customers, among them Babkin. He found out that his family came from Russian noblemen who were later impoverished.

> My great-great-grandfather was in the Izmailovsk regiment under Empress Elizabeth [who reigned from 1741 to 1762]. As a token of gratitude she elevated the regiment to the nobility. We've got a coat of arms. But he was a noble even before this. And on my grandmother's side, there were also noblemen. My great-grandmother was married to one.

In Babkin's life as an engineer, the humanities side did not always feature prominently, something which, as an art lover, he has always regretted. He should not have allowed this to happen, he said, given that most of his family had a background in humanities:

> We've got teachers, we've got scientists, we've got artists. . . . What's more is that in our kin there is a certain General Kolabin who organized the first settlement in America. He was a famous navigator and a famous scientist.

Babkin is very pleased to have "good people" in his "clan." "No doubt, there was a certain genetic code passed on to me," he said with conviction. After a brief pause, he added: "I nearly forgot about the most important person: The playwright Viktor Rozov is related to us."

Viktor Rozov was a little boy at the time of the 1917 Revolution. When he came of age in the 1930s, he was initially blocked from entering a prestigious educational institution. However, during the Second World War, thanks to the urgent need for propaganda writers, he was able to put his literary talent to the service of the state. After the war, his plays became hits on the Moscow stage. Some of them were turned into blockbuster films, most famously *The Cranes Are Flying*.

Dropping Rozov's name brings Babkin some of the kudos he seeks. Babkin has engaged in the arts in his spare time to make up for not devoting his professional life to the humanities. He has assembled a collection of Dutch paintings, as well as owning a gallery in Moscow and a fine art foundation in Montreux in Switzerland. As for his storyline about his family history and its adaptation to fashions, Babkin is in tune with post-Soviet trends: His initial search for his family history coincided with a moment in post–Soviet Russia when it had become very fashionable to find some blue blood in one's family lineage. In the 2000s, this fashion shifted toward combining—if not replacing—noble ancestors with intelligentsia ancestors.[3]

Many still hold on to the 1990s fashion of stressing blue-blood ancestry. On a Saturday in late spring I interviewed Tatyana, the glamorous wife of an entrepreneur. She had cancelled a few times and finally suggested to meet somewhere near her place. Her driver picked me up at the Park Pobedy Metro station, and from there it was a direct drive along an unclogged motorway into the forests to the west of Moscow and then the luxury suburb of Rublyovka. He delivered me to the restaurant where Tatyana would meet me.

Tatyana was already waiting for me in a corner of the dacha-style restaurant. I met her previously at a party where she was very glamorously dressed. Now the thirty-eight-year-old brunette, who stressed that she socializes with all of Moscow's "classy" rich people, was casually dressed in jeans that were too wide for her and a washed-out striped shirt. We quickly got through questions about her husband's business, about the boutique she set up with his help, and about her experience of being a mother (something she liked at first, but then quickly lost interest in). When I asked her more about her husband's family, the floodgates opened.

Her husband is from what she considers to be "good stock," she said. He can boast a gracious, noble lineage that goes back to the fourteenth and fifteenth centuries, as well as to the Polish gentry of the eighteenth century. "You could spot their refined demeanor a mile away," she boasted.

"His grandmother was very well turned out; her hands, her hairstyle, the posture of her head. Like a woman from a portrait; her manners, everything. And she was an extremely engaging conversational partner." Both this refined demeanor and the physical appearance are, in Tatyana's view, the result of lineage and (biological) inheritance: "He also has this beautiful command of the language; you can feel it in his intellect, the breadth of his knowledge and interests, his aristocratic appearance. He is tall. His grandfather was a Polish Jew."

Tatyana is less taken with her own family history. I had to prompt her to talk about it. This was strange, because her family might actually go back to higher-status circles in nineteenth-century Russia. Her great-grandmother was an Armenian princess, born in the 1850s. During her education she became close to Narodnaya Volya, or in English, the People's Will, the radical revolutionary organization famous for the assassination of Tsar Alexander II. The princess eventually married a revolutionary. Tatyana added: "That was fashionable at that time," as if apologizing for her great-grandmother for marrying down.

Indeed, the fashion to marry down and take a lower-class radical for a husband was also culturally significant. The aristocracy lost the necessary prestige to maintain the purity of its ranks and protect it from outsiders after the emancipation of the peasants in 1861, when the landowning aristocracy became bankrupt, both financially and intellectually. This also radicalized many of their youth, who felt angry about the tsarist autocracy. Some of them joined the People's Will, which attracted activists from various social backgrounds.

Although her great-grandmother displayed idealism, Tatyana did not present her family legend as something to boast about. That she could still produce it after my prompting suggests that it is part of a shadow canon of narratives that she picked up previously and has retained somewhere in the back of her mind. This makes sense as the grandmother's idealism and her link with the People's Will movement were considered honorable and politically correct throughout the Soviet period and would have justified preserving and passing down the memory of their family's aristocratic heritage. What confuses the issue is that in post–Soviet Russia her great-grandparents' social backgrounds changed their relative positions, with a sharp drop in the prestige of the revolutionary great-grandfather and a rise in that of the princess great-grandmother. That Tatyana seems not quite sure what to make of the story is an indicator that narratives are still in flux and ideas about what makes an ideal family history have not yet settled.[4]

Resuscitating Soviet Family

Albert was in nuclear science in Soviet times. In the 1990s he went into trade and then real estate. We met for a late breakfast in one of those overpriced restaurants in a business complex in central Moscow. Albert was dressed casually in brown trousers, a green turtleneck jumper, a washed-out denim jacket. His glasses with massive frames looked as if they hailed from Soviet times. He put five spoonfuls of sugar into his black tea with lemon. His paternal grandfather was from a very poor family. They were "slaves in a factory," Albert said referring to the bonded labor that remained a common reality after the emancipation of the serfs in 1861.[5] "The Revolution made a man of my grandfather as well as a lifelong passionate supporter of the Bolsheviks." He worked his way up from bonded laborer to the director of the Institute of Red Professors, where he prepared cadres for the party.

While Albert's grandfather is a classic example of someone who benefitted from Stalin's 1930s modernization program to recruit a new Soviet intelligentsia from lower sections of society, the family members of some of my other interviewees were not so lucky. After the 1917 Revolution the government's policy was to undermine the power of formerly privileged families (which included the aristocracy, wealthy merchants, industrialists, state officials, and the clergy). Aristocrats had to give up their estates and merchants their assets, and after 1922, members of the clergy were forced to abandon the church. To apply for a job, a place at a university, or membership in a party organization one had to write "file autobiographies" or "file-selves."[6] Applicants from "wrong" backgrounds naturally sought to hide compromising details in their family history and present themselves as being of exemplary humble origins. In response, the state engaged in campaigns to expose authors of false or misleading file autobiographies—as happened, for example, during the years of collectivization, with people from an affluent peasant *kulak* background, and later with whole swathes of citizens during Stalin's purges. As a result, Soviet citizens quickly became very cunning at concealing elements in their family history or biography that were not "suitable" in order to survive.[7]

Tatyana and I were still having lunch. She had hardly touched her roasted fish when she sauntered off to say hello to some friends. One of them came over. Svetlana, who is forty-nine and a neighbor of Tatyana's, was dressed in a tracksuit. I naively assumed that she would be heading to the gym later. In fact, she was simply adjusting her attire to fit in with that of her "hipster" daughter, with whom she was having lunch earlier. She took the place where Tatyana had been sitting and, after checking me out, delved into her family history. She also laid claim to noble blood, in the form of her highborn great-grandmother, who married a Bolshevik. However, rather than marrying down, like Tatyana's great-grandmother, Svetlana's great-grandmother married into the new post-1917 elite, after the old ruling elite had been swept overboard.

She explained her great-grandmother's move as a pragmatic choice: "She had two sons from her first husband, a general, nobody even knows his name." When the Bolsheviks took power and the civil war broke out, anti-communist forces, represented by the White Army, tried to regain power by fighting against the Red Army. The White Army was in retreat from 1920 onward, and Svetlana's great-grandmother sensed that things might end badly for her.

So to save the family, she gets married to a Kremlin *kommandant* [a senior Kremlin official] and she brings her two children into the new marriage. They have another son together and everybody thinks that all three children are his. That was also what they told everyone. Later it came out that he had adopted the children and given them his surname.

Through her marriage, Svetlana's great-grandmother managed to integrate smoothly into Soviet society and avoided suffering any repression on account of her social background and previous anti-communist liaison. Indeed, she even married up. "As you can see, she didn't choose a simple chap," Svetlana said, acutely aware of the social significance of this new bond with the Kremlin *kommandant*. His status left its mark on all subsequent descendants. Proof of this may be found in their last resting place, Novodevichy, Moscow's most famous cemetery. Novodevichy's residents are a pantheon of Russian greats: Anton Chekhov, Nikolai Gogol, and Mikhail Bulgakov; the filmmaker Sergei Eisenstein; the composers Sergei Prokofiev and Dmitry Shostakovich; and the First Secretary of the Communist Party of the Soviet Union Nikita Khrushchev. "Yeltsin is buried there. All our relatives lie there," Svetlana said.

I heard recurrent stories from my interviewees about a blue-blooded grandmother, most beautiful when she was young, who saved the family by winning the heart of a senior Soviet official and "marrying away" her background, as Svetlana's great-grandmother had done. The politician

Dima told me about his noble grandmother, who got married to an officer in the secret police, a *chekist*, to escape suspicion from the very same secret police. The businessman Arseny had a noble grandmother who also married an officer in the secret police. "She assured me that she really loved my grandfather. Being an NKVD officer meant that he was in a position to save her."

The example of Svetlana's family points to the long-lasting resources the privileged prerevolutionary strata had in their possession. Such families were no longer economically part of the social class they had belonged to prior to 1917. Deprived of their economic assets, they were limited to the transfer of cultural capital. However, this concentration of culture—which was generally cultivated before 1917, in noble, intellectual, merchant, and clergy families—was precisely their strength. Elder family members continued as best they could to inculcate their social norms when bringing up the next generation, who accordingly had the benefit of a home atmosphere that encouraged broad erudition, a knowledge of the arts, the ability to speak foreign languages, and the development of artistic abilities, good speech, and manners. As a result, the cultural resources they inherited helped them find ways to circumvent the obstacles that the Soviet regime imposed on them. Many of them adapted their skills to the Soviet job market to advance their careers. Often the wife's cultural background fostered the offspring's talents and the husband's powerful positions opened up career channels.[8]

Between 1928 and 1931 Stalin orchestrated a wave of purges against the old intelligentsia. This weakened it so decisively that it became fully subordinate to the Soviet regime. By the mid-1930s the mutual hostility between the old prerevolutionary intelligentsia and the Communist Party softened, and the two groups were merged into one. More and more representatives of the intelligentsia became Sovietized and took up party membership.[9] In newly established salons the cultural world and the party leadership mingled with one another: secret police, high-profile party officials, writers, journalists, artists, and theater directors.[10]

In the 1930s, while still lambasting what he considered to be reactionary aristocrats, Stalin began to revive prerevolutionary history, drawing the refinement of aristocratic or otherwise privileged heritage into the public sphere. The centerpiece of this shift was the revival of Pushkin as a kind of literary saint. The new Soviet elite appropriated the function of the nineteenth-century aristocracy in claiming legitimacy due to their stewardship of Russian literature. This enabled the Soviet elite to claim continuity with Russia's prerevolutionary history. Thereby, the formerly privileged strata contributed their cultural resources to the new identity of the Soviet elite.

This cultural policy helped turn many members of formerly privileged strata into compliant intellectuals. (For example, the noble grandmother of the politician Dima later became a university professor. One of her daughters became a Red Director, a factory manager.) Intellectuals from privileged backgrounds played an important role in implementing the government's educational program, which was designed to promote the children of peasants and workers. An example of someone who benefitted from this policy was Albert's grandfather, born into a very poor peasant family, who had the chance to rise in Soviet society due to this new access to education.

The Paradox of the Purges and the Rise of Soviet "Good Society"

The purges of 1937–1938 were directed against whole swathes of the Soviet elite: veteran members from before the Revolution, Old Bolsheviks who had taken part in the Revolution and the ensuing civil war, people who had simply witnessed those events, and those who had made their way up in the new regime. Millions of Soviet citizens, branded "enemies of the people," were repressed and with them often their families. This included both the old intelligentsia and the new Bolshevik intelligentsia. The worst charges of counterrevolutionary "bourgeois sabotage" were leveled even at the longest-standing and most loyal party members.

The purges seem to have been the major cataclysm during the twentieth century in Russia for many of the families I have spoken to, much more so than, for example, the 1917 Revolution. They destroyed many of my interviewees' families who had come from aristocratic or otherwise "unsuitable" backgrounds but had survived the 1917 Revolution and its aftermath relatively unscathed. Several of my interviewees' grandfathers were executed or jailed.

I was still walking on Manhattan's High Line with the billionaire Victor. He liked talking about his paternal grandfather. He slowed down and even stopped twice when talking about him. His grandfather had a successful career until 1937:

> He was thirty by then and had excelled in the Soviet system. He worked in industry, not as a state official but as a hands-on manager. He was a factory director. But then he was put in prison for eighteen

years. They said he was a British spy, the usual thing. While in prison, he always maintained his innocence. They couldn't break him in any sense. He was a very strong person. This enabled him to survive.

Victor is critical about his mother's family, however. His other grand-father was from a poorly educated family. He earned his living by play-ing the violin. After losing his hearing in the civil war, he worked in the education ministry, then, from the 1930s onward, for the NKVD, the pred-ecessor of the KGB. After the war he was the police chief in a district in Saratov, a city on the Volga River. Victor does not have any particularly fond memories of him: "I remember that he went to the police station all the time to play cards there," he said, in a dismissive tone of voice. The relationship between the families—one of them constituting Stalin's ter-ror victims, and the other the perpetrators of the terror—was understand-ably bad: "My parents met in Perm [in the Urals], where they had sent my grandfather after he was released from prison. My mother was there because my grandfather worked there for the NKVD. No, they didn't really become friends with my father's family."

After his grandfather's release from prison Victor spent a lot of time with him as a little boy. He looked up to him as a role model. Despite the social intimacy and closeness he described, which echoes the stories of the people I referred to in chapter 3, he suggested that his grandfather's char-acter traits were passed on to him through genetic transmission rather than this intense interaction. "It's most likely something in my genes. Specific character traits and these internal characteristics my grandfather had. People say that I remind them of him."

In their retrospective view the descendants do not place much signifi-cance on the great injustice their family members experienced. What is more important to them is that their grandfathers and great-grandfathers had played a significant and high-status role, important enough actually to be repressed.

Media manager Dmitry Kiselyov, sixty at the time of this interview, introduced the story of his family's tragic fate by emphasizing their prerevolutionary role:

My mother's father was an outstanding military engineer. There was General Brusilov in the First World War and the famous Brusilov offensive. They came to Poland and my grandfather built wooden bridges for the army. My grandfather was a real hero.

Kiselyov did not pause when he moved on to his grandfather's deep fall from grace during the purges: "He was repressed by Stalin and shot in '37. We don't even know where his grave is. He was sentenced to 'ten years without the right to correspondence' [a euphemism for a death sentence]." Kiselyov's other grandfather suffered repression in 1937–1938 because he had been in business.

By the time Khrushchev carried out an amnesty during the Thaw of the late 1950s, 25 million Soviet citizens had passed through the Gulag system, which had a stigmatizing effect not only on their own careers but also potentially their children's. Nevertheless, this suffering was largely irrelevant to the families' later course, their outlook on life, and even their views of the Soviet state: "I wouldn't say that my grandmother hated the Soviet Union then or later in life, despite her heavy suffering," said IT entrepreneur Ilya Segalovich. His grandfather hailed from a family of a priest in Nizhny Novgorod, a city with a population of 1.3 million, about 250 miles east of Moscow. He had become an active Bolshevik in the 1920s and climbed the career ladder until the purges caught up with him:[11] "Like many people of his importance he fell victim to the first Nizhny Novgorod trial of 1938. He was arrested but not shot. He was in prison till 1956."[12] Segalovich's father did well. As noted in chapter 2, he became a geophysicist and laureate of a USSR state award for his discovery of the country's biggest chromite deposits.

Alexander Svetakov's family, like Segalovich's, contained priests, but also merchants and peasants. The billionaire's grandfather was a deputy minister and the constructor of seaports, a skill he had acquired in England in the 1920s. During the purges he was sent to a Gulag, from where he would never return: "They went for him in 1938. They accused him of being a spy for the English and Japanese. He eventually died in the Gulag the same year as Stalin died, in 1953." Nevertheless, the family did well after the war. The children went to university and made good careers as members of the Soviet intelligentsia, in academia, and in engineering.

The lack of bitterness may be in part due to the fact that many victims' descendants had very successful careers in the postwar Soviet Union, like Segalovich's and Svetakov's parents. Those engaged in intellectual pursuits enjoyed a level of comfort unparalleled in the Western world with, for some of them, special living quarters, luxurious resorts, superior-quality medical care, and their own restaurants.[13] Intellectual prowess, as long as it moved within certain demarcations, afforded not only material benefits but also significant prestige, especially when directed toward Soviet science and the military. Both were important pillars of patriotic pride. Many considered working in them to be a service to the country rather than the Soviet authorities.

The period of relative stability after the Second World War allowed for the stable transfer of cultural capital across generations within privileged families. Individuals from various elite backgrounds mingled within the Soviet elite. This provided the raw material for which the German-British sociologist Norbert Elias employed the German term *Gute Gesellschaft* (good society). "Good society" denotes "a specific type of social formation" of centralized circles consisting of groups who have maintained their position in society for at least two generations. Elias considered that most dictatorships were too young and too unstable to generate "good societies." However, he saw the basic elements of a "good society" emerging toward the later part of the Soviet era, formed by the nomenklatura elite and the intelligentsia.[14]

After the Second World War, Soviet "good society" blossomed. The synthesis of cultural resources that were strong among different elite groups was bearing fruit. In many ways, it provided the children of former members of the prerevolutionary privileged strata with the ideal means to advance in Soviet society. They appeared as factory directors, state officials, and members of the Soviet intelligentsia—especially in academia. The higher nomenklatura members did particularly well in transmitting privilege across generations. They ensured that their own sons and daughters went to the best schools, filled the best positions, and married the children of other high officials.[15]

Even though they were stigmatized as enemies of the people after both their grandfathers were repressed, Dmitry Kiselyov's family also smoothly integrated into Soviet "good society." Kiselyov's father was the ninth surviving child of a peasant family in the Siberian province of Tobolsk. One of his sisters succeeded in moving up through marriage:

My father's sister was married to a very famous man, the notable Russian composer Yury Shaporin. Shaporin was the president of the Union of Soviet Composers of the USSR. He wrote an opera—*Dekabrist*—which was performed at the Bolshoi Theatre. He was not a party member. He was a nobleman. He graduated from the St Petersburg conservatory before the Revolution. And my father's sister was his wife.

Yury Shaporin was awarded the Stalin Prize three times for his composi-
tions, including a patriotic piece in 1941 at the outset of the war and, after
the war, his opera *Dekabrist*.

The first time Kiselyov's father entered "this world of poets, composers; very intelligent people" is deeply ingrained as a family legend:

> They embraced him wholeheartedly and he absorbed their man-
> ners and everything. He was a very smart, adroit, and bold man.
> Everybody remembers when he went to visit his sister and her hus-
> band Shaporin for the first time. He brought half a horse with him.
> "Well, I had to bring something," he said. There was almost no food
> around at the time. So he carried half a horse from the frontline
> [laughing]. He was such a resolute person, courageous. Everybody
> can remember how he joined this musical family with a horse.

Thanks to moving in Shaporin's circle, Kiselyov's father quickly lost his
peasant manners, without losing his charming character. His adaption
to the Soviet *beau monde* facilitated the liaison with his wife, Kiselyov's
mother, who hailed from a noble family, despite their contrasting social
backgrounds. They met in 1943 in a theater when he returned from the
war. Today, this microcosm of Soviet *kulturnost* allows Kiselyov to present
himself as having roots in the Russian people as well as the refinement of
the aristocratic milieu in Soviet "good society."

With their cultural weight living on in Soviet "good society," children of the former aristocracy grew up as members of the intelligentsia.
Arseny was acutely aware and proud of this, considering himself "amaz-
ingly lucky to have two strong family lines, intelligentsia and aristocracy." Arseny's father who, as mentioned, was the son of the baroness
who married an NKVD officer, became a famous rocket scientist and
one of the main designers of the Soviet space shuttle *Buran* (the Soviet
Union's first reusable spacecraft), to this day a great source of pride as
well as suffering for his son. Arseny became animated when talking
about his father.

> His construction of *Buran* was simply the best that existed at that
> time on the planet. Actually, the *Challenger* is feebly constructed. It
> is a weakling now just like then. When *Buran* was unceremoniously
> dumped just after its hyper-successful launch and space flight, my

father—one of the principal designers, promoters, and construc-
tors of this amazing machine—suffered his first stroke.

Sitting in his bright, massive office, the walls of which are decorated
by contemporary artwork and the corners by modern sculpture, Arseny
recalled his father's funeral: "In the speeches, he was called by different
surnames, depending on where his disciples lived: by his noble name
and his title or by his Soviet pseudonym, that of a secret scientist." Both
the grandfather's noble identity and his Soviet intelligentsia identity were
similar in that they had both been cultivated within an era in which dedi-
cating one's life to the service of the state was part of the general ethos.[16]

THE LACK OF bourgeois family tradition was not an issue in the 1990s
when the new rich were obsessed with acquiring as much wealth and
power as possible. Back then, they did not feel the need to reflect on
how their family history could bolster a bourgeois identity, except for the
early 1990s fashion for claiming aristocratic roots. Now, as the interests
of the bourgeoisie have moved on from money-making to more refined
pastimes, chapters from their Soviet intelligentsia heritage, which were
sidelined in the 1990s, appear more relevant. Traceable descent from the
Soviet intelligentsia provides an ideal provenance and cultural legacy. If
before, in Soviet times, they were intellectuals and scientists as well as
state functionaries (who secretly aspired to bourgeois models), now they
are members of a bourgeois class that aspires to reconnect with its non-
bourgeois idealistic intelligentsia narrative.

The new demands of making it in, and into, bourgeois society require
bourgeois Russians to reinterpret their family backgrounds and establish
continuity with Soviet norms and clichés. Despite their strong identification with the intelligentsia, they do not equate the intelligentsia with the
bourgeoisie as a whole—for them the intelligentsia stands for work ethos,
family life, and literary culture, rather than anything related to their entrepreneurial activities. As such, although the Soviet intelligentsia steps in as
a reference point and a substitute for the lack of a bourgeois predecessor,
this identification does not challenge their capitalist existence.

5

Rich Russians' Philanthropy

THE ANCIENT GREEK word *philanthropia* means "love for mankind." Not even the ancient philanthropists, however, demonstrated benevolence out of pure love for mankind. In fact the reverse was true: Philanthropy was to become a part of philosophy and religion because the elite considered it practical and advantageous.[1] This holds equally true today: Philanthropy boosts the benefactor's image and underscores his or her high status. Asserting this status requires a certain degree of restraint and a recognition of responsibilities: noblesse oblige (which the philosopher Georg Simmel discussed at length when analyzing how social norms are constructed).[2] Unlike the payment of taxes, philanthropy provides benefactors with freedom of choice. People can live their individualism, influence politics and social affairs, and realize their own idea of citizenly participation. Philanthropy is also a way for the rich to atone for their sins. It alleviates possible guilt about having built their fortunes at the expense of others, which often also helps minimize the risk of having their recently accumulated riches questioned and challenged. The French nineteenth-century anthropologist Marcel Mauss set out an idea of gift exchange: that gifts make the recipients indebted to their benefactors. In some ways today, against the background of sharpened social inequality, the reverse is true: The wealthy are indebted to the people because they have allowed the rich to live so differently from the rest.[3]

IN THE EARLY 2000s, Russia saw an extraordinary growth in philanthropy, partly thanks to huge profits due to high oil prices. This charitable spending by the rich did not decrease significantly after the 2008 global financial crisis, and even shot up in the 2010s.[4] The *Coutts Million Dollar Donors Report 2014* identified some 126 charitable donations in

Russia worth a million dollars or more in 2013, and totaling over one billion dollars. This constituted a dramatic rise from 2012 when there were only thirty-five such donations, amounting to less than a quarter of a billion dollars. Individual gifts made up more than half of the million-dollar donations.[5]

The growth in philanthropy stemmed not only from the fact that the rich had excess money to spend but was also due to their increasing desire to improve their image and adapt to globally acknowledged bourgeois norms. If they did not establish some system of giving to show care and compassion for less fortunate Russians, they would never get rid of the reputation, which had stuck to them in the 1990s, of being ruthless and selfish.

Yet another reason for the growth in philanthropy is that rich Russians have not much choice but to give. Putin made it clear from early on in his presidency that he expected those who accrued a certain level of wealth to help fill the vacuum left by the withdrawal of the state. Already by 2006 almost 90 percent of donations in Russia went to state-run bodies, stepping in where the state had failed and helping to finance health care, nursery homes, orphanages, and cultural institutions.[6] This places an element of coercion on Russian philanthropy. If wealthy individuals are national players, the Kremlin will make them "contribute." If they are regional players, their governors will request assistance. Mayors and local authorities will "look after" the noble deeds of the local wealthy. Being proactive can be advantageous: It can protect rich people from being required by the authorities to undertake disagreeable projects.

Reviving the Tradition of Russian Elite Philanthropy

Irina Prokhorova, who runs her brother's Mikhail Prokhorov Foundation, recalled the reappearance of philanthropy in the 1990s: "People quickly took up all kind of things from before Soviet times." Prerevolutionary role models—art patrons and collectors like Pavel Tretyakov, Sergei Shchukin, and Savva Morozov, alongside impresarios like Sergei Diaghilev—served as a basis for reviving the prerevolutionary past and Russia's cultural heritage. Even though the memory of their philanthropic past was kept quiet in Soviet times, they were still mentioned in Soviet textbooks. Parents and teachers used to take children from an early age to the Hermitage Museum and the Tretyakov Gallery. Consequently, as Prokhorova points out, "People had some idea about prerevolutionary philanthropists. In the 1990s their historical memory was refreshed."

In prerevolutionary Russia, philanthropy was initially confined to the aristocracy. Charitable activities had to be sanctioned by the tsar. Philanthropy became a major public activity for the ladies of the court, who founded their own philanthropic societies. Controlling the exercise of philanthropy, the Imperial family themselves generously contributed to philanthropic causes, providing an example for courtiers and statesmen to follow.[7]

Beginning in the 1860s radical intellectuals, often from a clerical background, founded cooperatives. Many of them were influenced by Nikolay Chernyshevsky's novel What Is to Be Done? (1863). Chernyshevsky drew upon three sources: first, French utopian socialist visions of collective labor to help the poor; second, the self-help movement in Victorian Britain inspired by the work of Robert Owen; and, third, the American practice of forming voluntary associations as a training platform for democratic self-management.[8] Yet public and nongovernmental organizations were regarded with suspicion in Imperial Russia, not least because they nourished the opposition movement of the Narodniks.

The authorities did support an expansion in philanthropy on the part of Russian industrialists, financiers, and merchants who had accumulated sufficient wealth to divert some of it to charitable causes. Many prerevolutionary philanthropists were religiously motivated or connected to religious groups, including Jews and Old Believers, who played an important role in Russia's industrial development. This philanthropy covered a wide range of areas, from cultural institutions and the arts to social trusteeships and social welfare. Benevolence was a channel for upward mobility and a prerequisite for obtaining nobility status.[9]

These prerevolutionary philanthropists are widely celebrated in Russia today. Veronika Zonabend, an entrepreneur herself as well as the wife of an entrepreneur, wants the bourgeoisie to return to their prerevolutionary predecessors, "who understood that it was their duty to look after their country's fate."[10] Irina Sedykh, the wife of a metallurgy tycoon, considers the desire to help one's neighbors, and not turn a blind eye to suffering, to be in Russian blood ("It's something historical, cultural, and genetic"). She is proud of her country's philanthropic history. "In Tsarist Russia philanthropists provided for 80 percent of the social sector," she said, and regretted that "Soviet power put an end to all this."

After 1917, philanthropy was officially forbidden. The Soviet state formally considered it a demeaning, capitalist undertaking. In practice, however, it established various charitable institutions, albeit operating under another guise. Ilya Segalovich, the late cofounder of Yandex, Russia's biggest search engine, explained that during Soviet times there was no charity as such, but trade unions, the *Komsomol,* and other Communist organizations had departments that took care of "this work, which today we would call charity." His former wife was in charge of patronage work (*shefskaya rabota*) in the university faculty's *Komsomol* committee, of which Segalovich was a member. The university where he studied supported an orphanage close to Moscow. He went to visit the children: "We were shocked at the state of these orphanages and the atmosphere there. It was similar to a prison environment, claustrophobic. You know, that wasn't just after the war, but at a time when society was actually quite wealthy," Segalovich remembered. "They were mainly the children of alcoholics. It was all very gloomy."

The newly wealthy Russians' post-Soviet reconnection with charity was initially used as a form of advertising and a way of improving their negative image—getting their names into the press, buying the goodwill of important people, sponsoring high-profile projects and literary and artistic prizes, and restoring churches. These were usually one-off activities. However, most of them failed to boost their image. Polls showed that the public at large associated the concept of a "charitable" or "philanthropic" foundation with shady money.[11]

This negative perception receded over the years, although this was not because philanthropy had become more ethical in nature. According to the Alfa-Bank board member Oleg Sysuev, many state-affiliated companies, whose number has gone up as a consequence of the 2008 economic crisis, funnel money into social projects in the sort of public relations and corporate social responsibility activity that characterized philanthropy in the 1990s. He explained:

Let's take Russian Railways or Rosneft or Sberbank, they also call it philanthropy. The authorities tell them: "Give money to the Russian Olympic team." They take company money and give it to this kind of cause. Then they include it in their social report and call it social responsibility. In fact, what they do is waste the taxpayers' money. And a lot of it! When Russian Railways support the football club Lokomotiv, this is also from the state budget fund, that is, taxpayers' money.

Sysuev thinks that taxes should be distributed according to democratic mechanisms, not the whim of a state company boss or a bureaucrat. "If you want to call it philanthropy, it should be your own money," he said. Sysuev suspects that some Alfa-Bank shareholders might give money in response to pressure from the government: "But, nevertheless, it is their own money, you see, not taxpayers' money."

Informal Networks

In many Western countries, particularly the United States, elite philanthropy is institutionalized and strongly related to prestigious organizations. Established nongovernmental organizations (NGOs) in the West function as social catalysts. They define who has made it into the deserving rich and thus control class boundaries. This is because many powerful recipient organizations are highly selective about the kind of elite members they wish to be associated with as primary donors. To be accepted requires both physical and financial long-term support for these organizations, but it is usually very much worth the effort. Being a trustee or a board member of the organizing committee of a prestigious NGO often results in a wide and useful network of contacts and increased status in society.[12]

In contrast, in Russia philanthropy is often channeled through the state authorities rather than NGOs. This is partly because of the state's dominance, partly because Russia's rich prefer to control the whole process themselves, and partly because of the legacy of utterly corrupt and fraudulent NGOs.[13] This legacy also facilitated the Kremlin's attack on, and containment of, foreign NGOs after the 2004 Orange Revolution. Putin accused them of being instruments of foreign influence with the intention of secretly undermining Russia's interests. While their activities were hindered or stopped, independent but Kremlin-loyal corporate foundations and organizations were established or, if they already existed, strengthened.[14]

Apart from closeness to the state, two other important features that characterize post-Soviet philanthropy are, first, the dominance of some very large foundations set up by the most powerful oligarchs and, second, great discretion. The latter feature is partly grounded in the Russian Orthodox approach to philanthropy, which instructs that almsgiving should not be overt. Christianity in general supports the understanding that charity should be a private act. The Gospel of Matthew states that when you give to the needy, you should not let your left hand know what your right hand is doing, so that your giving may be done in secret; thus the Lord, who sees what is done in secret, will reward you (Matthew 6:3). NGOs in the West are not greatly influenced by such biblical exhortations; they generally carry out networking very openly and directly, and see publicizing one's good deeds as setting positive examples to others. In Russia, philanthropists are expected to give "secretly."

Given the fact that elite philanthropy in Russia is supposed to be secret, my question about charity evoked a defensive, negative response from some of my interviewees. Indeed, it was the only question that one person, businessman and politician Sergey, refused to discuss outright. He leaned forward and lowered his voice so as not to be overheard by anybody in the lobby of Moscow's Hotel National, where our interview took place: "It's delicate; I don't want to talk about it." My perplexed look must have made him feel awkward. He mumbled: "It's something very personal. It's for one's own soul, not for self-PR." Charity should be a private self-effacing activity, he insisted, and it is good and ethical if it is done for oneself, but not to promote oneself.[15]

After this reaction from Sergey, I introduced my questions about philanthropic activities very cautiously with other interviewees. Most people would talk, but not without first telling me how very personal the topic was. The billionaire businessman David Iakobachvili agreed: "You don't discuss your charity projects with anyone. Never!" Arkady, another billionaire businessman, confirmed this: "We don't talk about it, neither with friends nor with anybody else." Larissa, Arkady's wife, looked startled: "Actually, you are the first person who's ever asked me about it. Honestly, nobody has ever asked me anything. Well, it's because we don't speak about it anyway." Some people were both reproachful and defensive. "I don't shout out about my philanthropy," said the businessman Vadim Moshkovich, frowning at me; "I don't ask for money. I do everything myself." Then he seemed to change his tune: "What should I hide? I don't sell drugs after all, do I?" He closed the topic by adding in a defiant tone: "I don't see my duty as being an example for others."

I found this somewhat confusing, but eventually realized that the imperative to be modest exists alongside the well-publicized promotion of charitable activities by celebrities. Charitable organizations are very keen to win over well-known faces to promote their causes and thus to increase donations. Valentina, the daughter of a high-ranking state official, who is involved in charity herself, joined me at my table in a cafeteria close to the Tretyakov Gallery. She explained to me this division of labor among different elite groups: "It's considered unethical to advertise one's own charitable giving. You are better off not mentioning it." Yet, she continued, celebrities are allowed to do so: "Actually, to a large extent they are expected publicly to support charity causes." This means that the tradition of modesty and self-effacement coexists with a professional charity PR machinery supported by celebrity glamour, as well as the PR carried out by some large oligarch-run foundations.

Only Ivan challenged the cultural imperative to show modesty. We had been sitting in a Central Asian restaurant for some time and the waiters were still bringing new plates of food to our booth (the restaurant consists of single booths, visually and acoustically separated from each other by heavy dark wooden barriers). Ivan is a sixty-year-old businessman who lives in Surgut in Siberia and is not integrated into the tight networks of the elite in Moscow. This may explain why he does not adhere to the rules about secrecy and privacy (despite our very private restaurant corner). On the contrary, he openly flaunted his projects in his oil town, where he is, according to his own assessment, "a famous person." Everything about Ivan is big, including his very deep voice. "I was sworn into the most ancient religious order in the world, the order of Saint Konstantin, the great founder of Orthodoxy," he said, laughing so much that his large belly was shaking. "No, I'm not a modest man. There are things I tell everybody with the greatest pleasure. I love talking about it."

As a rule, however, philanthropists increase their legitimacy by not breaking the taboo of discussing their charitable activities. Networks of friendships are particularly tight in Russia, and the information channels within them are powerful. The involvement of glamorous friends, such as celebrities and cultural figures, subtly ensures that others know about their benevolence, while their modesty raises their aura and esteem as word spreads. Although reaffirming the taboo nature of the subject ("Nobody talks about it a lot. That's not what you're supposed to do"), Victor, a billionaire, provided a simple clue as to how this worked: Every sponsorship is predicated on networking and dialogue among "important" people, and both those networks and dialogues make things run by themselves.

Philanthropy opens up networking opportunities for the rich. Playing by the rules facilitates smooth relations between the bourgeoisie and the state authorities. Andrey Korkunov, most famous for his A. Korkunov chocolate brand, hinted at the benefits of his engagement in good works: "Both in the Soviet Union and today in Russia, social and public work is essential to create certain administrative networks and resources. I can't even picture myself without all these social burdens." In sum, informal practices that are based on personal relations of trust determine who gives to whom in Russia, who is allowed to give, and who is allowed to receive. These practices have much the same effect as the more institutionalized networks in the West: They are a factor in deciding who belongs to which elitist circles. This is in line with Marcel Mauss's analysis that the giving and exchange of contributions that occur among donors create a special sense of social obligation and interdependence.[16]

Concerns about Civil Society

Alexander Svetakov, founder and chairman of Absolut Group, gave to charity "right from the beginning," once money appeared in his life; but he did this in a chaotic and unsystematic way, he said, and without carrying out any fundraising. "Now I'm thinking that might have been a mistake. Now I try to change people's minds and win them over. Not their money, but their time and energy." Svetakov is following a more general trend with his aim of strengthening civil society: "That should start at the kindergarten level. It's very difficult if you don't talk about it from early childhood. In America and the UK you can see that children are involved in charity from a very young age."

Irina Sedykh has followed this kind of route for several years: "We want to unite people and encourage them to take part in other people's lives. This is a way of helping develop civil society."[17] Sedykh and her husband's foundation OMK-Uchastie Charity Fund works on the basis of open "volunteer participation" in the provision of care for disabled children. "The number of volunteers is an important indicator of success. . . . Every year we have more volunteers, and now we have so many that we can't accommodate them," Sedykh said with a smile that showed how proud she was.

The shareholders of the charity Liniya Zhizni (Life Line) pursue another approach in their attempt to strengthen civil society. They are all super-rich, and yet they see their main duty as getting the Russian population not to volunteer, as Sedykh and Svetakov have done, but to scrape money together to contribute to the cost of surgery and other treatment for severely ill children, rather than paying for the operations out of their own pockets. Their goal is to enlighten and educate ordinary people to create over time "the social institution of charity" in Russia. Engaging in charity, they claim, should become a necessity for all Russians and "an everyday thing." All this might sound absurdly arrogant on their part, but the project has been largely successful. The Alfa-Bank shareholders came up with most of the costs in the first three years, but now pay only for the charity's administration; the fundraising pays for operations. Oleg Sysuev, who was among the original founders, is happy with how things have developed: "We have many partners, wealthy people. But when the number of small donors goes up, this is great. Sometimes people just trust us and send us money."

Liniya Zhizni presents itself as a "people-sponsored" initiative. This means that in addition to teaching common people how to become part of civil society, it has another quite different objective: to work toward "rehabilitating private property in Russia." Oleg Sysuev explained: "The relationship to rich people is complex here in Russia. There is still the widespread belief that big money is stolen." For this reason, Alfa-Bank kept its involvement in the charity secret for many years: "We thought that if Alfa was seen to be associated with Liniya Zhizni, a smaller number of people would volunteer and donate," Sysuev said.

As well as instilling a sense of civil society into the communities and rehabilitating private property, Alfa-Bank's president, Pyotr Aven, believes that philanthropists will also out-perform the state in areas such as research and development: "Where capitalism develops, private philanthropy will emerge and grow." Aven echoes philanthro-capitalists like Bill Gates, who run their charitable giving like businesses:[18] "Medicine, culture—everything will be financed by private money."

These specific civil society and property rights activities are Russia-focused, and so is philanthropy in general. Russian philanthropists, charity initiatives, small donors, and volunteers have almost exclusively concerned themselves with solving domestic problems. The authors of the *Coutts Million Dollar Donors Report 2014* expressed surprise that in 2013 nine Russian donations of $1 million or more were made to organizations outside Russia, including the United States, Israel, Germany, and the United Kingdom.[19] This was a novelty. Even a catastrophe on the scale of the December 2004 tsunami in Southeast Asia did not elicit substantial contributions by private Russian citizens to international humanitarian and relief operations.[20] The same goes for arts philanthropists. No matter how cosmopolitan they are, they see patriotism as their duty. The art dealer Anatoly explained to me that many elements in art collecting in Russia today are reminiscent of the late nineteenth century in the United States, when American collectors were keen to stimulate a patriotic spirit with their purchases.

Religious Philanthropy

Russian Orthodox Christianity originated in Byzantium, where the tradition of philanthropy as an ethically significant obligation of the rich had been passed on from ancient Athens. Byzantine society viewed the miserable and wretched as God's envoys and did not hold them responsible for their misery. They accepted poverty as an inevitability, and almsgiving was encouraged. In this way, the rich could purify their souls and achieve salvation. This tradition clashes with the cold practicality, rationality, and utilitarianism that are characteristic of the Western matrix, especially in the case of the Protestant-influenced Western model, according to which philanthropists should systematically support the poor in order to enable them to help themselves, which would eventually render charity unnecessary.[21]

Back in the late 1990s Natalia Dinello drew the conclusion that Russians had opted for philanthropy of a paternalistic nature, which claimed to contain more kindliness and true humility, rather than utilitarian Western models. This assessment was echoed widely in the interviews: "As soon as philanthropy gains a rational character, it is not philanthropy anymore," insisted the politician and businessman Sergey.

Some rich people use charity to atone for their sins and "enter heaven." Surgut oilman Ivan admitted this openly: "When you show mercy, you pay yourself off with God. You bribe God because you haven't lived as you should have, which torments me; I don't deny it." His solution is straightforward: "So I pay." The church has benefited profoundly from such guilty consciences. "In the 1990s many businessmen and bureaucrats employed not entirely Christian methods to accumulate their wealth. Many decided to wash away their sins by helping the church," Oleg Sysuev said. "I know of a lot of dirty money which went to the church, particularly for the construction of churches." Curiously, this is not limited to Christians. Jews and Muslims can also be found among the financial supporters of the Russian Orthodox Church, as well as plenty of atheists. "It is simply these people's primitive idea of their religious duty," Sysuev said, showing some disdain for his fellow Russians.

Some of the Jewish philanthropists I met claimed that religion was of minor importance to them, if not completely irrelevant. Despite the fact that Jewishness was an important part of his identity, the multibillionaire Pyotr Aven seemed quite agitated when he emphasized that he was "not religious at all, not the slightest bit, not at all." Irina Prokhorova was not happy with my account of the influence of religion on today's philanthropy: "Max Weber is too narrow." Her father was a Russian from Ossetia, her mother a Jew from Belarus, but she sees her parents as secret Protestants in terms of work ethic, discipline, and values—all characteristics reminiscent of the Soviet intelligentsia in general.

Whether or not Prokhorova is influenced by religion, her structured and thoroughly conceptualized approach is quite different from the sporadic heartfeltness of the Russian Orthodox Church. What emerges from my research is that the Jewish businessmen share a stronger commitment and more structured approach to their charitable giving than their Russian Orthodox peers. In Judaism, giving to the poor is viewed as an act of justice, righteousness, and fairness, rather than as simple generosity to passive alms-takers. Jewish giving traditionally emanates from the perceived need to repair a world full of problems, which results in an interest in social justice and a desire to volunteer. Giving is a "must," rather than a "should."

Such a strong sense of duty is evident in a statement by Ilya Segalovich: "I think that if you have the chance to change something around you, or at least to maintain it in a normal state, you have to make use of the opportunity." Likewise, the billionaire businessman Arkady, also Jewish, said: "You need to support who you need to support. It's an axiom. If you can, you need to help. That's how the world is constructed." These statements flag the gulf between notions of philanthropy among Jewish interviewees and those from a Russian background who said that philanthropy must not be rational.

Oleg Sysuev (Russian and areligious) agreed with my impression that Jewish giving is more organized and structured. The organization he supports, Liniya Zhizni, was the brainchild of the Jewish oligarch Mikhail Fridman: "Misha [Mikhail] used his success in business and applied it to charity: business technology, good management, motivated with clear tasks, audit, and control." Sysuev pondered the weaknesses of this approach: "What we don't have enough of are those emotional drivers, which come from the soul," he admitted. "But maybe that's also good. We don't give money if we can't control it to the end." As for the influence of Jewishness in Liniya Zhizni's and Fridman's approach, Sysuev thinks that "it's probably more business experience than Jewishness." After a brief pause he added: "Then again, big business in Russia is mostly Jewish."

Despite claiming to be areligious, many of the Jewish businessmen I talked to had given money to synagogues. There might be two reasons for this: First, they wish to strengthen their ethnic and cultural identity, and second, they place more trust in Jewish organizations. Giving to Jewish institutions affords a link to the tradition of mutual support within this social and ethnic group in Russia. The billionaire Victor, who runs his own foundation, also donates to one of the most important Jewish organizations in Russia. ("I'm not religious, but I think they do the right thing.") Arkady provides a synagogue with some of its equipment. ("I'm more of a nonbeliever than a believer. First, Judaism is a very specific religion. Second, my upbringing was absolutely irreligious; it was atheist.") David Iakobachvili supports one of the biggest Jewish organizations in the country. ("No, I don't have any religious motivations, not really, even though I'm a person who has a relative amount of faith. Well, to the extent to which I can comprehend it.")

Rich Russians put little weight on religious exclusivity. Vadim Moshkovich, the head of the agro-industrial holding company Rusagro, Russia's largest sugar and pork producer, supports the Jewish Center of Tolerance (as "a supporter of tolerance, not only Jewish tolerance"). Moshkovich is determined to get across that he is areligious: "I'm Soviet. I'm a product of the Soviet period. I wasn't brought up in any religious way." Alongside his support for this Jewish institution, he has donated money to the renovation of six churches in Belgorod where parts of his business are based. People of all backgrounds support religious institutions. For example, the billionaire Ziyavudin Magomedov stressed several times how atheist his upbringing in Dagestan was. Nevertheless, he built a mosque in his hometown, Makhachkala, as well as contributing to the restoration of the Kronstadt Naval Cathedral.

In some contexts religious education is seen as a lever of reform. The former financier Igor Tsukanov supports five to six Russian students a year to study at the Paris branch of the Orthodox Academy and at the Sorbonne. "When people have gone through this program, they become European and have the skills you learn at a European university," Tsukanov said, seeming to associate some enlightenment maxim with the scholarships. He is in principle very critical of the church, but nevertheless hopeful of change: "At the top of the Russian Orthodox Church are very odd people who have nothing in common with religion. But these young people are a totally different matter. So the pyramid is based on really good people who will eventually work their way up."

Supporting Children

Ninety percent of all Russians making charitable contributions give to causes that support children.[22] Children are considered trustworthy in Russia, a society that is largely based on distrust.[23] "We don't really believe in the honesty of adults," said the businessman Gennady. "That's why we help children." Charity primarily goes toward those who are helpless through no fault of their own, as in the case of orphans, children with diseases, and children who are terminally ill, whose claims to charity exist independently of the motives of the giver.[24]

In response to my question as to whether he was prepared to look after groups that were not so popular, such as migrants, homeless people, drug addicts, ex-prisoners, or the long-term unemployed, the Surgut business-man Ivan generously announced: "I never say no when people ask me for help." Then he paused for a moment: "Should I help drug addicts, you mean? No, no, no, no way." His voice was changing, getting even deeper than it was before, but markedly raised in volume: "I wouldn't give any-thing to them or a medical center that deals with them. Never!" When he had calmed down, he added: "To people who look after prisoners maybe, but not through an organization. Well, the organization could send me a list and I'd say, 'This one yes, this one no.'"

His insistence that he would not help drug addicts highlights how peo-ple who have supposedly caused their own misery are not seen as deserv-ing of the mercy of the rich. Widespread social-Darwinist reasoning (see chapter 3) partly explains why there is little interest in some quarters in helping those who have already ruined their chances in life. Supporting children, on the other hand, is seen as an investment in the country's future, the impact of which is multiplied if the best of the best are sup-ported. Anatoly, an art dealer in his mid-sixties, put it bluntly: "It's nec-essary to help healthy and normal children. I've got a strictly biological outlook. One needs to help the very best." For Anatoly and those like him, the country's future is best served helping the healthy and the normal, even if this means that there is less focus on other groups in need, such as physically and mentally disabled children.

Philanthropist Vadim Moshkovich's approach is very different, even if the outcomes of his project might well agree with Anatoly's. Moshkovich's education project promotes excellence. His aim is the development of a cadre of highly educated Russian youth. His school for exceptionally gifted children handpicks its students. They live on campus together with their teachers. The whole area is a mini-town on vast grounds of nearly a hundred hectares with a river and a forest. It took the billionaire (with assets worth $2.3 billion in 2016) $50 million and five years to prepare everything. He traveled the world looking at top schools in Europe, America, and Asia. In the end, he opted to model his school after the Anglo-Saxon school system. "Within five years, the school will acquire the reputation of being one of the best," he said confidently. An endowment fund of $150 million will help keep things running.

Moshkovich wants to foster the best of the best. His stance on the question of nature and nurture is, however, slightly unusual. He deems all children to be talented, but thinks their motivation varies widely, and that motivation is more difficult to influence; it is "determined by a combination of upbringing and nature." Moshkovich's aim is not only to foster the best but also to give something back to his motherland. In Soviet Russia the entrepreneur, born in 1967 to parents who were a doctor and an engineer, was able to attend one of the best schools of his time, the mathematical school No. 57 in Moscow. He went on to study at the Moscow State Institute of Radio Engineering, Electronics, and Automation. "My education helped me a lot in life," he said. Knowledge is an important value for him: "I want knowledge to increase in Russia."

In addition to this elite school, Moshkovich finances many local schools ("the best schools in our region") in Tambov, Belgorod, and the Far East, the areas where his agricultural businesses are located. He has built up an internal structure in his company to look after this, and he is personally heavily involved. He has devoted many hours of his life to understanding in detail how schools work, and his company's strategic planning meetings take up a good part of his working week. Moshkovich also supports a couple of universities: the Higher School of Economics in Moscow ("A clear example of a successful university with a professional management structure") and Belgorod National Research University ("Now that we have started dealing with genetics and selection, we set up a center there") to enhance his agricultural business.

Instead of promoting the best of the best, Alexander Svetakov looks after the weak and ill: "Our society likes the strong and healthy. It doesn't like the weak and infirm. Hence, nobody wants to help disabled children." The billionaire owns several hundred thousand square meters of real estate and twenty thousand hectares of land. His portfolio includes a school for mentally disabled children. Twenty of them are boarders, while eighty attend day school. There is a wide variety of children in his school. Many of them are physically disabled, others are the children of alcoholics. "It's not something many are comfortable with, you know," Svetakov shrugged. When I asked whether he thought that he had become an example to others, he laughed: "No, I didn't win any admirers among the people around me or beyond, certainly not." With a sad smile on his face, the billionaire property developer recounted a story that illustrates the attitude of Russians to disabled children:

Just before the opening two years ago an important politician came up to me and said: Why do you need that? Let's do a school for gifted children. We can have a quota of five percent disabled ones and you show those off. But why on earth a whole school for disabled children?

Svetakov would probably get along well with Maria Yeliseyeva, an artist, who with her charity Deti Marii (Maria's Children) has always focused on empowering orphans with mild mental disabilities. "The most important thing is not just to put food into their mouths, but to help them develop while they are little," she said. Her late husband, the cofounder of Yandex, Ilya Segalovich, had been excited by the results. For example, before one of their trips to Italy, the children had to learn Italian and rehearse a play that they would perform for Italian children in hospitals. "It was terrific," he said. "These are children nobody believed would ever learn Russian, let alone a foreign language."

Arts Philanthropy

Patronage of the arts is the most direct way to convert financial resources into cultural credentials, offering its participants a good chance to live beyond the grave.

More immediately, patronage of the arts and art collecting are ideal ways for high society to network.[25] In Russia it is relatively easy for an art patron or collector to join exclusive art circles, not only as an open purse, but also as someone who commands respect. Russia's art world is young and the market still relatively new, which makes it accessible to outsiders and newcomers. "In Europe, everything is static. There, you can join thousands of troops," said Kirill, a banker and contemporary art collector in his late forties. "Here, you belong to a tiny circle of people." Guarded and earnest, Kirill has pursued serious aims with his arts engagement: to influence society and artistic tastes. He has succeeded: "Today contemporary art is fashionable and has a different image; I've played a role in that," he declared as we sat in the Moscow Hyatt Hotel rooftop café on a chilly summer afternoon.

Private collectors in Russia have moved into what has traditionally been the domain of public museums, curators, critics, and historians.[26] They create private museums, set up art foundations, showcase their private collections in their galleries, and sometimes simply act as mediators. Lyudmila Lisina, the wife of the steel tycoon Vladimir Lisin, runs a small gallery that displays forgotten twentieth-century pieces from private collections. The owners are unlikely to entrust anybody else with their art, but they trust her.[27] Her mediating role allows for hidden artwork to be displayed.

Making art available to the public is every collector's duty, Igor Tsukanov said firmly. Many others agree with him. The art collector and gallery manager Alexander Shadrin insisted that art must not be kept in boxes, but made accessible. ("One has to show it; it's not your property.") "I agree with Tsukanov that it's the collectors' duty to show their art," said the art patron and collector Stella Kesaeva, the wife of Russia's biggest tobacco retailer, Igor Kesaev (with assets worth $3.7 billion in 2014).

In the mid-2000s her plan was to set up a museum in the Novo-Ryazanskaya Street Garage, designed by the Constructivist architects Konstantin Melnikov and Vladimir Shukhov in 1926 in the shape of a hammer and sickle. The bus garage would have to be relocated somewhere else, but the Moscow City authorities were reluctant to agree to this. Plus, the soil beneath the garage was soaked with fuel down to 55 feet and would have to be cleaned out. "That wasn't really very realistic," Kesaeva acknowledged. All the same, "I used to doggedly pursue the idea [of opening a museum] as long as there wasn't a proper museum of contemporary art." However, she later abandoned the idea for other reasons: "Everybody is setting up a museum these days."

Kesaeva clearly has a point. The oligarch Roman Abramovich's third wife, Dasha Zhukova, runs her Garage Museum of Contemporary Art. Russia's richest person both in 2016 and 2017 (with $18.4 billion), Leonid Mikhelson, spent $150 million on a new contemporary art gallery,[28] and Boris Mints renovated a building for $16.5 million to turn it into a museum to show his art in a public space. David Iakobachvili has so far spent over $50 million on a museum to exhibit his collection of self-playing instruments. Viktor Vekselberg's Fabergé Museum in St. Petersburg opened in 2013. Pyotr Aven contemplates setting up a museum in Moscow or Riga to show his collection of avant-garde art. The businessman Yevgeny's concern about Russia has inspired him to set up a "museum of the Russian soul," which will cover a space over twenty-two thousand square feet.

I met Kesaeva in her foundation in the center of Moscow. She is as elegant in real life as she is in her photographs on the Internet: tall, with silky, wavy hair. That day she was dressed in a striking dark-green dress. Kesaeva, born in 1965 to a geologist and an engineer, came to art when she was traveling the world with her husband. "While he had his business meetings, I went to museums," she said, emphasizing her high level of *kulturnost*: "Not shopping, but to museums!" She gathered inspiration from all over the world, especially New York. When she came back to Moscow, she found contemporary art to be in a bad state. For the first show she put on in 2003 she brought Warhol, Wesselman, and Basquiat to Moscow. "There were also fantastic Russian artists, but they were hidden in basements," she remembered. "In the 1980s there was a whole movement of Moscow conceptualism, but it was underground art, and the attitude to contemporary art in general was a bit sneering." Then things moved quickly, and everything changed. "In Russia this goes in massive steps. Contemporary art is now at its peak of popularity. Patrons are the fuel of the machine."

I was lucky to get hold of Kesaeva. She spends only a couple of days per month in Moscow. The day prior to our meeting she had received a prize from *The Art Newspaper*. Her daughter now goes to school in England, and so Kesaeva moved there to be with her. She divides the rest of her time between Spain, the Maldives, and Germany. Nevertheless, she loves her motherland and aims to make Russia's contemporary artists "as famous as Malevich," she said. "For artists to become famous, someone needs to invest money in them so that people know about them. Hence we need people who love these artists to expose them to the world." Kesaeva's role was soon officially acknowledged. She was appointed the commissioner of the Russian Pavilion at the Venice Biennale three times in a row, most recently in 2015. In the tradition of those aristocrats who were aware that their status came with duties, as Simmel recorded in the early 1900s, Kesaeva stressed the "great responsibility" she took on: "The whole world is looking at you. It's a big burden," she sighed, suggesting that engagement in art can be a tiring business, as well as pointing to the amount of hard work and spiritual investment she has to put in to achieve results.

This display of responsibility is in line with Soviet intelligentsia tradition and contrasts with the approaches taken by her less cultured peers, many of whom are only at the start of their journey toward becoming bourgeois. She told me a story about a friend bringing a group of wealthy young women to her to be trained in how to open a gallery and "do their own art thing." She refused to provide them with a basic introductory course (*likbez*). "I couldn't do that because in my case it came from inside, from my soul," she said, alluding to aesthetic standards typically ascribed to the intelligentsia. These standards are perceived as almost innate and yet they require constant discipline and hard work. If you want to collect art and be a proper patron, Kesaeva continued, an internal desire and urge is crucial: "You need to really want to define, search, and discover yourself [*poznat sebya*]."

Most of the art collectors claim to have higher aims—aims far beyond money-making—and some are not short of confidence. Alexander Shadrin asserted that the world history of Dali can be divided into two parts: the story prior to the art collector's project, and the story afterward. "We found so much archival material that Dali's story has to be rewritten," he pronounced boldly. "Had I not financed the project, they [a Dali museum in Spain] would have never found this material." With a grin, but with a slight expression of guilt because of the extra work his involvement created, he added: "They had to redo everything." In addition to Dali, Shadrin mainly collects Picasso. "Dali [who had a Russian wife] and Picasso are very important to Russia," he said. "Dali had many complexes and anxieties. He was slightly schizophrenic and mad. Here in Russia we're surrounded by the very same surrealism Dali portrayed."

Yevgeny's ideas are almost spiritual, as well as a kind of nostalgic throwback. He plans a museum of the Russian soul. While conceding that this soul might actually be a myth concocted in the works of Dostoevsky and Tolstoy, he still holds onto this idea, and deplores the fact that it is in decline: "We used to be proud of this myth, but now with the market economy even these myths start dissolving. They disappear and we forget about them. We can no longer be proud of being a very sensitive nation."

Yevgeny came of age in the 1960s at a time when liberal ideas were popular as an alternative to the communist system and the planned economy, but without the actual dominance of the market that has since eroded this generation's liberal ethos. His youth was one of excitement about literature; in fact, most of his generation's critical, intellectual life revolved around literature, epitomized in the cult status of *Novy Mir*, a monthly literary magazine.

Yevgeny was at pains to emphasize that his art activities are not about him, although he is aware of the fact that what he has done is "a big thing, a big story." His intelligentsia identity demands modesty and the suppression of personal vanity: "No, to be famous or to find a place in history doesn't flatter me in any way. No. It's more important to me to create something, to create a place where people can grow, live their emotions, become better." He considers his motivation to be purely altruistic: "It's about doing something for others in a spiritual, humanistic sense. That is important. Money, power, and ambition; that's not for me," he said.

This mental emancipation from economic necessity is the ultimate privilege of upper-class belonging, as Bourdieu emphasized. The Soviet version of intellectual detachment from money placed its stress on internal freedom and spiritual independence. In identifying greed as the enemy, Yevgeny evokes the classical Soviet intelligentsia feature of *kulturnost*.

Whether this idea will spread among the bourgeoisie depends to a large extent on whether a Soviet intelligentsia brand of distinction will experience a revival of sorts among exclusive bourgeois circles. From what it looks like today, the ingredients for post-Soviet distinction will be somewhat similar, but also differ in some key respects from earlier practices of *kulturnost*. The current competition among members of the bourgeoisie illustrates this: To compete one must display individualism and caprice, intellectuality and intellectual creativity, and pretend convincingly not to be interested in personal rewards (despite all the money, time, and effort invested).

New Meaning to Life

Making money and being successful in financial terms were the main concerns of the rich in the 1990s. In the new millennium, with people becoming accustomed to the opportunities money could buy, many started to feel the need to find something that provided more meaning to life. Financial well-being should now serve to enable people to engage in activities that they perceive as more meaningful.

What many of the art collectors and patrons have in common is boredom with what they have been doing for years, and the desire to find something that will make their lives more exciting and multifaceted. For Igor Tsukanov, art collecting is a new style of life: "I've worked a lot in my life. I think when you turn fifty, you can either go on doing what you used to do or do something new. It's like having another life ahead of you." Engagement in the art world itself holds no age barriers. The art dealer Anatoly, who has already long passed retirement age, told me:

I love holding masterpieces in my hands. I love smelling them. I love looking at them. It's a special profession. There are no time or age limits. You can be a hundred years old and you only get better. No, I'm not going to retire. Why should I?

Kirill, the earnest banker I interviewed on the Hyatt roof terrace, lost some of his stiffness when he described his thriving art activities to me. He gave me about six different business cards. Besides establishing his own contemporary art collection, he set up the first international festival in his field, organized art festivals, published books, taught at art school, and founded a young collectors club that brought international curators to Moscow. He told me how captivated he is by the dynamism of the contemporary art world in Russia: "The artists here are very experimental; everything is fluid and in motion. They take up themes you're living through right now. That's why it's so fascinating."

Kirill's entrance into the art world happened by accident. "I didn't have any aims, I was just interested," he said. Art has now become his big thing; it functions as a counterbalance to his work in the finance sector. "I've got absolutely no art background or training. I'm from a pure finance background. It started with me going to places and looking around. Then I bought something and became totally hooked," Kirill continued, becoming increasingly animated.

Art provided Kirill with the opportunity to immerse himself in the young and bustling art scene: "In business, you mingle with one kind of person, then you switch to art and you mingle with a completely different set, from a different society. You become part of this society. It engrosses you, it carries you away, and it becomes part of your life." Kirill moves within the epicenter of business–culture–politics, where people share similar lifestyles and tastes. Moscow offers the perfect platform for this: The city is particularly centralized, both in terms of its social hierarchies and the geography of exclusive places, which are all contained in the center of town. It is at arts events, among other things, that different elite groups often mingle.

Although charity organizations and the civil society sector in Russia are predominantly run and staffed by women,[29] it is usually rich males who initiate large-scale projects. This is partly because philanthropy is a new ingredient in Russian elite culture. People were not brought up in homes where charity would have played an obligatory part, determining a family's division of labor. "It wasn't part of my culture. As a person, I don't take part in charity, even though I could," one businesswoman admitted to me. "It's not a question of time. One could find time for it. But I don't feel an internal desire to do so. But no question, it's a very good thing." Her husband looks after both the company's and the family's charity projects.[30]

Accordingly, when husbands take a step back from work to devote their time to art, their wives or their children may take over, or at least maintain, their business functions. Igor Tsukanov's wife, to whom he has been married since 1992, runs her own financial advisory firm in Moscow, helping clients make investments outside Russia, while he organizes exhibitions. The banker Kirill's increasing involvement with art was the catalyst for his wife's return to work: "We're now setting up a few business projects. My wife's been a housewife; she's been bringing up the children. But now she'll be the manager of these businesses." Yevgeny's wife looks after his business, an activity that he found increasingly boring. Thus, paradoxically, the masculinization of art patronage and art collecting has allowed women to access business terrains that are normally dominated by men.

Immortalization through Arts Philanthropy

Philanthropists, and in particular art collectors and art patrons, have a chance to live beyond their death. "The idea of disappearing is frightening. That's why this is a very strong motive," gallery manager and former

Putin advisor Marat Guelman stated. He explained what triggered these emotions:

> Immortalizing yourself is one of the collectors' main objectives. Conserving the memory of yourself is worth more than all the gold in the world. So far it's the only chance we've got to extend our lives. People start thinking about this when they attain a certain level of affluence and wealth. In Russia this still isn't very obvious because none of the oligarchs have died yet. They haven't yet grasped that they can't take their money to the grave.

Back in 2008, when I met Guelman in his gallery in Moscow, his own ambitions were to "create a legacy and an inheritance for our time."

Kirill did not express his aims in quite such a grandiose way, but he admitted that he would love to achieve fame through discovering new artists. After all, patronizing young unknown artists is a somewhat hazardous test of one's tastes and judgments. The outcome of this test will only be revealed in the future, possibly even after one's own death. Yet postmortem considerations and the hope for posthumous fame are part of the appeal:

> When I buy the work of ten contemporary artists, they might become famous one day. However, the important thing is that they reflect our era. If in fifty years people ask what artists thought about at the beginning of the twenty-first century, my collection can answer this question.

Money nevertheless counts as an indicator of success. "Well, of course, everybody wants their own collection to be worth millions," Kirill admitted. "It would be prestigious because it means that you discovered something new back then."

Thinking about the fate of his collections after his death led Kirill to talk about his two children. The unpredictability both of the future of his collection and of his children's life choices makes him uneasy:

> When you've done these things for so many years, you start thinking that it is for your children, your descendants. But then again, what if they won't be interested in it? That's why I try not to think about the future and I don't plan ahead. If my children become

interested in it, they will be able to cherish it. And they will be telling my grandchildren about it. That would be nice. But it's also
possible that they will take one piece of work after the other to an
auction house in order to sell it.

The banker comforts himself with the idea of self-sacrifice: "Well, if they
need to do that for a living, I won't complain."

Alexander Shadrin is not ready to do this. "I told my children that they
mustn't sell the collection or split it up. It's my oeuvre. It's like a third
child to me. It's my work and it should be preserved," he said. The thought
of losing control distresses him. The risk of this happening is, however,
very low. His children are already heavily involved in their father's projects. His son, a lawyer, helps organize his father's exhibitions. His daughter will return to his foundation once she is back from maternity leave.
Nevertheless, Shadrin has taken precautions: "If they can't retain the collection, they have to hand it over to the state. It's gone beyond being for
my own personal satisfaction. It is no longer my own pleasure in art that
matters; it's the enrichment of civilization, world civilization." Shadrin is
in favor of having his collection under state control, as he thinks that "big
collections should belong to the people and be managed by the state and
accessible to the people." That does not mean that he thinks exclusively of
Russia. Another possible location is China.

Igor Tsukanov plans to hand over his collection to an institution at
some point ("Why should my children have it?"). He referred to Baltimore
sisters Claribel and Etta Cone, who collected works by Matisse and
Picasso, which ultimately laid the foundation for the Cone Collection in
the Baltimore Museum of Art. "Russians will do the same," he said. "They
have only two choices. Bring it to Russia to be stored at some place, which
is very risky, or do something here [in the West]." Tsukanov's plan is to
form two more collections and then set up an art center in London. "This
is not going to be a museum. Museums are something more academic.
It's not even going to be a Russian center (nobody needs a Russian center right now), but some thematic center where there will be a Russian
contribution."

IN SOME SENSE, the new philanthropists form the "aristocracy" of the
new bourgeoisie—aristocracy in the (metaphorical) sense that having
become economically secure they seek to leave a legacy for future generations by engaging in activities that lie outside of business. This is true

for art collectors and for art patrons in particular. Yevgeny's passion for rediscovering the Russian soul in art, Kesaeva's belief in Russian artists, Tsukanov's contribution to the preservation and enhancement of Russian culture, and Kirill's determination to eternalize contemporary art for future generations are, to some extent, attempts to anchor their individual selves in the past as well as in the future. These individuals influence what is legitimate culture in Russian society, and their activities are considered a marker of their moral and spiritual superiority. In the long run, people of this kind might play a larger role in the process than the one or two tycoons, whose influence may end up being much more ephemeral. A side effect of this is that, in fully immersing themselves in the arts in order to escape boredom and fatigue, some men have delegated their business matters to their wives. It is a curious feminization of business through the backdoor, which has potential repercussions for bourgeois gender relations.

6

A Man's World

WHILE GLOBALLY THE position of women has advanced in many parts of the world, today's super-rich still live in the *Mad Men* era, claims former *Financial Times* journalist Chrystia Freeland. The richer you get, the more patriarchal family life becomes.[1]

The role women play in creating a social and cultural context for upper-class life has not been lost on sociologists, particularly those from the United States. C. Wright Mills and E. Digby Baltzell in the 1950s and later G. William Domhoff were fascinated by the informal rituals at play between the genders.[2] Then, in the 1980s, sociologist Susan Ostrander published a thorough empirical study of US upper-class women, in which she scrutinized their role as guardians of their families' social lives.[3] Upper-class women, she found, overwhelmingly concerned themselves with their children's education and upbringing, including the suitability of their friends and future partners. They took charge of representative roles when it came to hosting guests and maintaining the family image, for example, by patronizing the arts or engaging in charity work. The women Ostrander interviewed in the 1970s would readily accept that they needed to be subservient and submissive to their husbands to keep things afloat.[4]

The sociologist Tomke Böhnisch confirms that it makes sense for bourgeois women to adhere to traditional gender norms and not rock the boat too much. The social status of bourgeois women comes and goes in accordance with their marital status, she argues. In her study, she found that the wives of top German executives enjoyed all of the perks that an elevated social position allows, but once divorced, they lost their status and place in society.[5] The upper ranks in many societies still frown upon divorce, and this protects women from being disposed of too easily. Being in charge of child rearing and domestic affairs gives them a well-defined role in the home, and their informal labor secures the symbolic power and material privilege of their class.

Gender Relations in Russia

Gender relations in Russia are frustratingly complex. A certain complexity is probably inevitable given Russia's rollercoaster history with regard to gender equality. Shortly after the 1917 Revolution women gained many rights that were years ahead of those enjoyed by their Western counterparts, especially with regard to abortion and divorce. From the Second World War onward the Soviet military produced a range of heroines, from fighter pilots and snipers to the first female cosmonauts. The scale of female involvement in the Soviet labor market was unprecedented, and so was the child-raising infrastructure. Deeply impressed with the large numbers of female engineers and medical doctors that the Soviet Union produced and employed, many Western feminists, most famously Angela Davis, envied Soviet women for the equality they appeared to enjoy.

Yet those feminists were generally unaware of the reality of women's lives in the Soviet Union. From the Stalin era onward the notion that equality meant the blurring of gender difference was denounced as "primitive."[6] Abortion was recriminalized for nearly two decades from 1936. In the 1960s powerful pro-family propaganda campaigns, designed to increase the birth rate, persuaded many women that motherhood should have absolute priority in their lives.

After 1991 the same, if not even more, rigid ideas about gender norms were promoted, but in a environment where alternative views could now be freely expressed. The extensive social support infrastructure that allowed women with children to stay in work was soon consigned to history. No sizeable feminist movement in Russia existed to challenge the new reality.[7] "Feminism is wrong," declares one of the heroines in Peter Pomerantsev's *Nothing Is True and Everything Is Possible*. "Why should a woman kill herself at a job? That's a man's role. It's up to us to perfect ourselves as women."[8] One of my interviewees, Lyudmila, thirty-three, the wife of a wealthy businessman who owns a private jet company, has an answer for Pomerantsev's heroine: "Because some men leave their wives. And what should these women do then?"

Yet there is a twist in Russia's gender relations. Within the boundaries of their patriarchal world, women manage to dominate in some spheres of private and professional life. This paradox was cuttingly portrayed by Andrey Zvyagintsev in his Oscar-nominated movie *Leviathan* (2014), where all institutions, from the court to the family, are headed by men but overseen by women. Part of this twist is that women in the film are not only ascribed typical female attributes such as reliability and responsibility but are also depicted as stronger and steadier. In general the film portrays Russian men as infantile, if not weak.

It is a portrayal that has its basis in fact. Vera, who runs a property development firm in Moscow's city center, compares herself to her brother: "While I love my work, he loves to live," she said. "He is forty. He lives in the here and now." She was very open about her desire to find a husband and start a family. When I pressed her, she expressed some concern about it; she was now thirty, and time may be running out. "Women think about tomorrow, about their parents and their future family—men don't," she sighed.

This is a view many agree with. Karina, forty-seven, from Rublyovka, considers girls to be more adaptive than boys: "Boys need extra help to develop their skills and discover their potential." This shaped the educational choices she made for her son and two daughters. While the highly confident boy was sent to a private school in England and would later go to a West Coast university, Karina never considered a Western university education for her daughters. They went to the Higher School of Economics and Moscow State University. Karina explained to me that it is more important that things work out in her daughters' family lives, rather than in the workplace. Consequently, although her daughters received decent university educations, only her son was granted the privilege of UK schooling and a US university degree.

Patriarchal gender norms pervade Russian society from the bottom to the top. The image of motherhood experienced yet another boost when Putin launched a campaign to increase the birth rate.[9] When I asked for their views on this, my interviewees all told me that they saw motherhood as essential for every woman. A particularly extreme opinion was voiced by the elderly businessman Leonid, in his eighties: "To give birth, that's the most important thing a woman has to do in life," he said. A woman is "not a fully fledged human being," he continued, if she has not managed to start a family by the age of thirty.

In a family, you see, it must be absolutely clear who the first person is and who comes second, who the major is and who the assistant. There can't be two majors. Consequently, when the talk comes to giving girls the same rights as boys, first of all, the question comes up as to why girls need these rights at all? It is a woman's duty to take care of the family.

I started to feel increasingly uneasy, but Leonid persisted with his monologue. "Once the family exists, a woman can start thinking about her own plans, but first she must make sacrifices for the family," he pronounced.

Girls need to be consciously disciplined and kept down; they need to have their wings severely clipped; they mustn't have a chance to divert. When girls get the same upbringing as boys, that is, when girls develop into proper personalities, that's when they have problems in their family lives.

Leonid conceded that some women are exceptionally successful, "but those women don't have a fully fledged family," he insisted. He picked out one example: "I know one woman, I won't say her name." He paused for a moment, but then continued: "A very young woman, maybe the number one in the country, very talented, she's part of the presidential entourage. But she has no family!" Leonid now paused another time for effect and then said very slowly, stressing every syllable: "That's not right!"

A week after my interview with Leonid I met the famous writer and businessman Lev, who at just under forty is almost half Leonid's age. He told me that motherhood was important for women for pragmatic reasons. "It's normal for a woman to do business or to go into politics, but only if she has first realized herself as a mother." Lev explained further:

If she has not yet realized herself as a mother, but works full-time or does full-time politics or something else, she is deprived of that energetic spirit and that level of self-realization that you find with women who have already succeeded as mothers. To realize herself in this sense is fundamental. The earlier it takes place in a woman's life, the more stable it will be.

This mindset is predicated on the logic of highly traditional gendered upbringing. Girls, being domestically orientated, need disciplining, but do not need extra educational support because they are more adaptive and because motherhood is seen as their main duty. Boys, who are more independent but also more impulsive by nature, need their more infantile biology schooled out of them. What follows, as explained to me by the founder of an educational agency that places Russian children in UK schools and universities, is that boys need the best education. Furthermore, as future breadwinners, they should make pragmatic educational choices, studying business, economics, or law. When girls start university, he continued, there is a feeling among parents that they need to be looked after, which leads many to insist that their daughters carry on living at home during their university years (as in the case of Karina). He frequently meets parents who want their daughters to go to university primarily to find a husband; university was one of the most successful marriage markets in Soviet times. However, some parents dismiss this idea as outdated and believe that their daughters no longer use university as a marriage market; nor do they get married as young as they used to. In any case, the different expectations toward boys and girls, paradoxically, allow girls much greater freedom in their choices about what to study. Many go to art school.

Bourgeois Masculinity

The political elite in Russia was—and still is today—even more male dominated than in many Western countries. In addition, gender roles and perceptions in Russia have prevented women from getting to the top of the business world. Since the early 1990s, from the former party functionaries to the underground world of the black market economy, business has been engineered by and for men. Success stories in the family are almost always male, while mothers, however highly educated, have generally played supporting roles.[10] Men have also dominated informal networking, access to which is often closed to women, such as bonding over heavy drinking, hunting in remote areas in Siberia, or visiting the sauna (for which hotels all over the country routinely prebook prostitutes to entertain male-only groups of travelers).

The hedonistic lifestyles of this generation of elites produced an army of young female gold-diggers. Film producer Peter Pomerantsev followed one of them, a twenty-two-year-old woman from a mining town in Donbas, into the gloomy world of Moscow's high-end nightclubs, where hundreds of *tyolki* (bimbos, or, literally, heifers), as the men call them, fight for the attention of a few mega-rich. The men sit in the darkened VIP lounges while the girls dance below on the dance floor, flirting with shadows they hope will invite them up. At twenty-two, Pomerantsev's heroine is already getting a little old for a successful career as a mistress. Prepared to settle for a millionaire fresh from the provinces (a "dunce"), or "one of those dull expats," she eventually gets lucky. This is at least partly thanks to her cunning. She is invited into a VIP lounge where girls perform oral sex all night, hoping to be discovered. She refuses, believing it will make her stand out. It does, and soon after she is invited to take a trip on a private jet.[11]

Virility is central to the most famous example of *proper* masculinity in Putin's Russia, namely the image of Putin himself. He has the right patriotic machismo, the right blend of charm, soberness, and crudeness.[12] Russians adore men who combine a certain roughness with killer charm, such as the poet Vladimir Mayakovsky in the 1910s and 1920s and the singer-songwriter Vladimir Vysotsky half a century later. Both men were womanizers, and had deep, raspy voices with which they would recite their love poems and love songs.

Masculinity does not exist as an isolated concept, but only in relation to femininity.[13] Vasily, forty-two, a broad-shouldered army officer–turned-businessman with a big, clean-shaven head and a neck as wide as his cheekbones, told me that the Western education system is effeminate. He sends his son to a military academy in St. Petersburg: "For now, that's the best education model for boys," he said. "There they are taught to become proper men and not merely to do some accounting. There the male part of the elite is formed. The children are always kept busy and the value system is right."

While others echo Vasily's thoughts in public, hardly any of the elite go as far as to send their sons to the military. Unlike in the United Kingdom, Russia no longer has a tradition of military service among its elite, as it had in tsarist times. It is far more common for even middle-class parents to buy their sons out of national service or, alternatively, keep them in education until the age of twenty-seven, when conscription expires. This might seem odd given how hard the Kremlin pushes a patriotic rhetoric. Russia's elite is, however, hardly alone in not contributing to this rhetoric's implementation: One just needs to look at the numerous US politicians who approved of the wars in Vietnam or Iraq but avoided participating or having their sons participate.

In Russia, *good* fathers provide but are also concerned about maintaining a warm and loving relationship with their children. Television

anchor Dmitry Kiselyov, a father of five, married for the sixth time, emphasized this. In contrast to Soviet times, he said, in today's Russia, being
multiply divorced and remarried is not an issue, "but it is absolutely unacceptable to abandon your children." Western observers are often surprised
at the easy way Russian men interact with their children. The American
wife of the manager of a luxury hotel in Moscow, who quickly became part
of Moscow's high society, expressed to me her dislike, if not disgust, of
many rich Russian men ("They are terribly coarse and rough," she said),
but one thing about them commands her respect: "Almost all of them are
totally amazing when they are with their children."

While he looks up to his father as his role model, Filip, twenty-eight,
resents the fact that he was not there while he was growing up: "Of course,
I suffered a psychological trauma," he complained. His father left the family just at the time when Filip was starting school: "It's precisely during
those critical school years that you need your father by your side. What
I got from him was mainly financial."

Some fathers acknowledge their lack of engagement with their children back in the 1990s. The businessman Roman missed out on taking
part in the upbringing of the children he had with his first wife. He puts
this neglect down to his youth and his business activities, which took up
all of his time when those children were growing up: "It's as if everything
passed by without me." Roman is now determined to be more engaged
with the children from his second marriage: "It's been a very different
experience for me with these children compared to the older ones. I relate
to them in a totally different way. It's different emotions."

Roman does not think that he is alone in this. "People have become
more experienced, more mature, and more patient." He has never considered leaving his business and moving abroad for his children's education,
as some of his friends and acquaintances have done. "These men become
abnormal," he said. "They don't work, they take their child to school, wait
till the child returns home in the evening. At such a young age, like fifty
or so, a man can't retire."

One topic that came up in several interviews was boredom.
Paradoxically, achieving success can be a trigger for feeling unfulfilled.
Not yet fifty, *Forbes*-listed entrepreneur Gennady told me, while smoking his seventh cigarette, that he wants to retire: "I'm fed up with all
this. I've done it for so long," he said, glaring down at the Hudson from
The Standard's roof terrace. "Did you know, I was one of the first businessmen in Russia, or the Soviet Union, as it still was then? I've already

tried everything. I've already received all the decorations one can receive. Everybody you can think of has written about me. I don't like this anymore; I stopped liking it long ago." Gennady said that he wanted to do something else with his life, something more exciting. However, he seemed at a loss to decide what that could be: "There are many people who like ticking the boxes on their list. I lost this desire long ago. I'm not interested in ticking the boxes. I'm interested in something else, but it is very difficult to say what it is."

Gennady is not the only Russian entrepreneur who is tired of doing business. There seems to be a more general feeling among upper-class Russians that the chase for money is losing its appeal and people are searching for something to put meaning back into their lives. Vyacheslav, fifty-five, is now an entrepreneur, but said he misses his former career in the diplomatic service: "Whenever I read statements by famous people who say that their work is their hobby and they love doing it, I ask myself: How on earth did they manage that?" I noticed some sadness in his voice and, a little embarrassed, glanced at a photo on his desk that showed the businessman in a camouflage jacket and with a Kalashnikov posing with a solemn smile over a massive dead elk.

Following my glance, Vyacheslav said: "That was the last time I went hunting in Chukotka." Chukotka is Russia's most northeastern region, from the cliffs of which, on a clear day, one can see Alaska across the Bering Strait. "It is a stunning part of the world. Very untouched. You get to many places only by helicopter. Well, I love hunting," he continued with a spark in his eyes. "It's in my blood. My ancestors back in the fifteenth century were already hunters." Vyacheslav's face darkened, making him look ten years older: "I know, thanks to my business activities I can allow myself such costly hobbies, but I can't say that I like being a businessman."

It is easy to imagine Vyacheslav in the diplomatic service. He sounds like a diplomat—pausing for a moment before answering questions; speaking slowly, but clearly; delivering measured, thoughtful answers. He said he regretted giving up his own personal goals for the sake of his family. When I pressed him, he admitted his own ambition played a part in the change of his career. "Once I set as my goal being part of the top 1 percent of managers in the country, I had no choice but to leave the foreign office and do business," he explained. For Vyacheslav and his family, a foreign service salary would have been far too low. Now, he said, he wants his children to make up for his lost dreams. He is adamant that they choose what they want to do in life in a way that he has not been able to, most likely outside of business.

Once efficient management structures are in place, many companies can function sufficiently well without their founders. This is both gratifying and alarming, since this can often come with the realization that they themselves have become dispensable. "What I dread is that I won't be needed anymore," said Yefim, who, by his late forties, has amassed a personal fortune of more than a billion US dollars. "I'm scared of this more than anything else." When we met at his Knightsbridge apartment in London, Yefim fussed over making tea and talked in a long-winded, almost rambling way. He told me that he had withdrawn from the day-to-day running of his company a couple of years previously. However, he remains an "honorary person," a "company soul," or "figurehead"—all of which terms he used about himself—but without "any real responsibility." This depresses him sometimes, and he is longing for something more concrete. The most dreadful scenario for him is to wake up and discover that actually nobody is counting on him anymore, he said. "That's a horrifying prospect."

One of my interviewees who does find his work interesting is Konstantin Ernst, whose career as the head of Channel One allows him to engage in the arts and indulge his passion for film, as well as carrying out special projects such as producing the opening ceremony of the Sochi Winter Olympics. He said that in his youth he had dreamed of becoming an actor but instead followed in the footsteps of his father, a famous geneticist, and became a biologist, doing research on in vitro fertilization. His excitement did not last long. "I was terribly bored," he sighed. "I could see my whole life ahead of me. First I would become a professor, then the director of a research institute." But Ernst wanted to leave a mark on history. "Over the last twenty-five years I have personally taken part in all the important events happening in this country," he said. "History is like literature. Those who write about it the most beautifully will leave an enduring legacy for future generations."

Ernst represents a more intelligentsia-style of masculinity. His stamina goes along well with the enthusiasm of those patrons who balk at the notion that they might become disillusioned with the arts. Some are even energetically starting new projects, such as setting up museums and collecting. They do not seem to experience the same tiredness and boredom as the men described earlier. It is as though artistic passion helps keep bourgeois men happy and contented.

Gay Bourgeois Masculinities

I had not done my homework before I went to interview Gleb back in May 2008. Had I Googled the advertising boss, the Internet would have told me—in no uncertain terms—that this man, with his slightly messy blond hair and lean, sporty physique, was not only the archetypal dark-suited businessman portrayed on his company's website, but one of the most flamboyant members of Moscow's eccentric gay arts communities. On the morning we met, Gleb assumed I knew exactly who he was. He leaned back in his chair and talked at length and in a relaxed way about homosexuality in Russia. A "new tolerance" had captured the country's upper class, he said.

> Russia will never be a politically correct country. The young generation just takes it as a part of the new world, especially those who were schooled in the West or lived there for a number of years. And especially those in the luxury class [top assets and income], they don't care a hoot about who you believe in, what sexual orientation you have, what gender you are, how old you are.

No matter how homophobic Russia is, he said, nobody in big business is interested whether he, the head of the most important company in his field, is gay or not. Indeed, he insisted that being gay in Moscow had become somewhat fashionable, defying all the deeply ingrained (and soon to be refreshed) homophobic attitudes among Russians: "The gay community in Moscow is the litmus test for every place that wants to be *en vogue*." This includes places frequented both by liberals and others sympathizing with oppositional views and people loyal to the Kremlin, he added.

Moving among Moscow's *beau monde* and world of show business, Gleb encounters a reality very different from that of the average gay man in Russia. This is not something entirely new: Historically, celebrities in the arts and the entertainment industry have been to some extent exempt from homophobia. This was the case, for example, for the composer Pyotr Tchaikovsky; the founder of the Ballet Russe, Sergei Diaghilev; and the grand filmmaker Sergei Eisenstein. Today it holds true at least to some extent in the music industry. For those inside the industry, it is easy to forget that this is a bubble, not the "real" world. The fact remains that to enjoy an unfettered and relaxed gay existence in Russia one needs to move in the right circles. Outside of this, homosexuality remains taboo and homophobia is generally and notoriously aggressive.

While Gleb credited the influence of Western gay culture with bringing about a change in attitudes among privileged young Russians, he rejected much of the gay rights movement. Even though his coming out was well publicized, he did not want to become a role model for others: "That's the last thing I wanted," he said.

In order to show their support, my business partners did a very silly thing. We've got a table with different country flags on it, and in the middle of these flags they put a rainbow flag. I asked them to remove it instantly. Sorry, that's absolutely silly. My secretary is a Zenit [football] supporter; let's put up a flag for him as well? Sometimes the defense of gay rights is simply absurd.

In May 2014 the European Union included Dmitry Kiselyov on its sanctions list for his controversial television coverage of the Malaysia Airlines plane crash in eastern Ukraine, which lost 298 people their lives. A year earlier Putin appointed this energetic man as the head of Rossiya Segodnya. This is Russia's biggest international news agency and an important government mouthpiece, incorporating the former RIA Novosti news service and the international radio service Voice of Russia. Kiselyov is famous for his trenchant and irate performances in his weekly Sunday TV news bulletin, among them his ferocious anti-Western attitudes and homophobic statements, the latter including the demand that gays should be barred from donating sperm or blood and their hearts should be buried or burned rather than used for organ donation.[14]

At the beginning of our first interview, Kiselyov told me he only had half an hour. Nearly three hours and two black teas later I was still there, sitting on an old sofa in his Soviet-style office. We had gone through pictures of his house in Crimea, discussed all manner of subjects, and got along swimmingly—until I asked about his hatred for homosexuals. The conversation turned sour: "The English," he said, assuming I was English myself, "are so fond of their privacy and say that it comes before everything else, yet they organize gay parades."

Where is the privacy? Then be private and do these things at your place or in a nightclub, but you don't need to impose it on me. Let's organize a parade of the sexual majority. Why only the minority? It's not democratic to impose your will noisily and aggressively on all of us. They are telling me how I should behave and how I should relate to them. That's not normal! It's not cultivated because it runs counter to our cultural traditions. They must not interfere with how I raise my children. In my opinion homosexuality is against nature. At any rate, it's not productive.

Regarding gay pride, the homosexual Gleb and the homophobe Kiselyov might well be in agreement, with both being antagonistic toward it. Gleb's reluctance to identify with anything like a collective gay culture is deeply anchored in Russian culture and history, among both homophobes and homosexuals.[15] Both Gleb and Kiselyov regard the LGBT movement as a destructive import from the West.

Perhaps their agreement is not all that surprising. Like Kiselyov, Gleb is deeply patriotic, Russian-Orthodox, and, most importantly, upper-class. Here class outranks sexual identity. Just as the elite tolerance of bourgeois homosexual men is predicated on their class status, and not their sexuality, so do elite homosexual men identify with the elite rather than with other gay men. There is thus a striking parallel between women and gay men within the elite: Rather than using their position to combat discrimination, they juxtapose themselves as individuals to social groups outside the elite—fellow women and the gay community, respectively.

The mainstream view in Russia is that young children need their mothers, for their motherly instinct and because there are elements of parenting that cannot be learned.[16] Fathers cannot step in; however, female nannies can. If gay Gleb had children, he would employ a female nanny. In the early stages of the child's development, the nanny would need to be from the correct ethnic group. "Only a Slavic woman can really provide the tenderness a toddler needs," he said. "When the child grows up, one can think about a nanny who speaks a foreign language. This is an imperial Russian tradition. A German, French, or English nanny; I don't know yet where from." Pragmatism for Gleb is just as important as imperial tradition. Concluding his thoughts about a future with children, he said: "We'll decide according to the economic and political necessities of the actual moment where the nannies will come from and what languages my children will learn."

While the gay men among my interviewees have the confidence, power, and agency to organize their lives as they wish (including fulfilling their patriarchal role), this is not true for the gay women. Lesbians have traditionally suffered less in Russian society, so long as they did not overtly express their sexuality beyond what could pass as tight female friendship. This is the tried and tested mode of survival for lesbians in Russia.[17] Darya and Alexandra, both in their twenties, are gay and both have partners. They keep their sexuality—which they are reluctant to define as gay, straight, or bisexual—very low-key. While Darya's mother is very liberal and accepting, Alexandra's mother dismisses her daughter's lesbianism as a result of her not yet having encountered a really capable male lover. (The mother's glamorous friends support her in this assessment. Together they have hired a succession of handsome young men to seduce Alexandra and show her the pleasures of heterosexual love. Their actions, they admitted, have so far been in vain.)

Bourgeois Women

Russia does not differ much from other countries when it comes to the number of women at the very top of society. Russia's *Forbes 200* from 2016 listed only three women. The government led by Prime Minister Dmitry Medvedev had three women out of thirty-two senior government members in 2016. After the September 2016 parliamentary elections, the female proportion in the Russian state duma rose to a little more than 15 percent. Most of these female politicians hold very conservative views.

Women should pursue "their own thing," I was told by Gregory, the son of an oligarch. "They should feel like fully fledged members of society," he said. The thirty-one-year-old father-to-be believes that "women should be independent, at least at one stage in their lives. Among the Russian upper classes, hardly any women stay at home. They hire their staff and do their own thing, either work or other activities." Gregory assured me that his mother, a trained French-Russian translator, has "her own thing going." She sings classical music and performs at concerts. His aunt, a businesswoman, looks after family business projects: "She is the sort of woman who's had a serious career."

Yelena, Anastasia, and Natalya, ages between fifty and around sixty-five, have all set up their own successful businesses. Yelena has a clear idea about what the concept "double burden" means: "When a man comes home, an exhausted wife will look after him and bring him his slippers and everything. When a woman comes home exhausted from a long day at work, she still, at home, remains a woman and is responsible for the family."

Everything about Yelena is glamorous: her grass-green blouse, her blood-red lipstick, her long eyelashes, and her long silver cigarette holder. She is a regular face among the celebrity jet set. Her husband, a scientist, keeps to himself. She told me that her husband enjoys the fact that she shows him great respect, especially for his intellect, even though she thinks that "women have a much easier game than men." She could see that I was puzzled by her logic, so she explained, after stubbing out her cigarette in the ashtray and rearranging her blouse: "First, women reason like housewives, in terms of expenses and income, how to feed the family the next day. Second, when men have to drink a lot, women can just smile. Such things help them navigate their way through life."

Some of the powerful women I spoke to have, at least in part, reversed traditional gender roles in their private lives. Anastasia has always worked in male-dominated business fields and has also always been the primary breadwinner for her family. Husbands have come and gone. Now in her fifties, she is married to Misha, her former fitness trainer, who is fourteen years her junior. Misha started working for Anastasia when he was twenty-three and she was thirty-seven. The slim brunette with a short haircut conceded that she had misgivings about the relationship, given the difference in their social status. All the same, she decided to commit to it because her exclusive social world—between the male-dominated businesses and the fences of her luxury suburb—did not offer many opportunities to meet new men. Anastasia was soon pregnant with Misha's daughter, who is now eight years old. He looks after the girl.

For more than a decade they led a happy family life, with her working while he stayed at home, supported by a little army of domestic personnel. But then, Misha, who was thirty-seven at the time, had an affair with a twenty-six-year old. According to Anastasia, he impressed the young woman with his Rolex watch and Lexus (which had been paid for by Anastasia, of course). Anastasia was outraged and ready to kick him out, but not onto the street. She had found him a flat in central Moscow, the rent for which she would pay. In addition he would get $3,000 per month for his maintenance. Misha tried this for a while, but then crawled back to Anastasia. After fourteen years of untrammeled luxury, getting by on $3,000 per month was not an option.

Yelena and Anastasia are very feminine and glamorous in their appearance. This is not unusual. Businesswomen in Russia often have an air of girlish femininity, while at the same time they are very tough in their business style.[18] I have met a number of Western observers who are amazed when they see high-powered Russian women using their physical attractiveness in the workplace, flirting, giggling like teenage girls, and basking in male attention rather than striving to be treated as equals. What works to their advantage is that women who present themselves as very feminine are often underestimated. "Of course, I know how to use my looks," said Anastasia. "It has always been important in business."

I met Natalya, thirty-eight, for lunch in a restaurant close to her office. She was wearing a tight black trouser suit and a loose rose-colored shirt. As with so many Russian women, she started by checking me out from top to toe, which made me pull down my skirt in embarrassment. Then she ordered a salad and a sparkling mineral water. She told me that she combines "female" grace with uncompromising "male" rigidity and harshness. The media have described her as elegant, but dangerous. Natalya chooses predominantly female staff. Only women sit on her management board. This is because she sees "a much greater sense of responsibility in women." She has faced criticism for this: "You choose your staff in such a way that men cannot survive," people have told her. In person, Natalya comes across as charming and soft, and people have often undervalued her as an entrepreneur. Not everybody in Natalya's circle recognizes that she has a successful role in running the company. Some think she is simply a typical "protégée wife" whose project is financed by her wealthy husband.

This sort of put-down is the product of stereotypes about rich men's wives running businesses that their husbands pay for. The initial storyline in the 1990s for this sort of female business activity was that men often supported their wives' business endeavors to keep them busy.[19] Such businesses were mainly concerned with female beauty: salons, fitness studios, and jewelry boutiques.

Some of my male interviewees openly dismissed their wives' activities as nothing more than frivolity. "My wife is not working," said the billionaire Victor. "She's actually never worked," he added. "Now she's building some flats or something. . . . I think she's suffered from time to time from the fact that she's never done anything proper." Andrey, twenty-four, the son of a businessman, also talked dismissively about his father's new wife: "Does she work? Well, apparently yes, but she doesn't earn anything. It's to keep her occupied," he said. "My father opened a company for her—cosmetics. She owns the company. All the money she makes just about covers the rent." Andrey does not believe that his father's new wife has either the aspiration or ability to succeed in business: "But what does it matter? She gets enough money from my dad anyway."

The Surgut businessman Ivan, sixty, seemed to be in perfect harmony with his wife's activities. He bought her a hotel "so that she wasn't bored," he said with a cheeky smile. Our feast had already lasted for three hours.

I had long lost count of how many shots of vodka he had put away (generously allowing me to sip wine instead). "My plan was that she'd be managing it. She'd be the boss—and I'd have my peace. As it turns out, she's now working more than I do." He followed this with long, deep laughter. "She's a strong and responsible person, and well regarded in town. She is fine with it, so everybody is happy."

Other husbands are less accommodating. I met the forty-eight-year-old Boris in Cafe Akademiya on Kamergersky Lane, a stone's throw from the state duma. The slightly overweight but sprightly businessman was dressed in a smart dark-blue suit. He squeezed our interview into a day packed with lobbying, meeting me just before he had dinner with a politician he hoped would be persuaded to support his business interests. Boris's wife is a psychologist who is fully engrossed in her work, often travels to conferences abroad, and works late into the night if necessary—basically, just the same as he does. Nevertheless, he is not happy when she does it because, in his opinion, it causes her to neglect the family. This struck me as strange because Boris did not grow up in a household with a traditional labor division. His mother was a medical doctor and his father an engineer, and he stressed that he had always respected their work ethos. Moreover, Boris's children were already fourteen and twenty and, at that time, probably did not need to have their mother around the whole time.

A little perplexed, I asked whether he was against women pursuing careers in general. "I'm a sexist," he replied. I was astonished. Did he just say "sexist" in the way that I understand the term? My blank look must have made it clear how baffled I was. "A sexist is not someone who loves sex," he clarified, apparently seriously. I was getting increasingly confused about where this conversation was going but I nodded. He continued:

If God wanted men and women to be the same, he'd have created them the same, but as he didn't, he obviously had a thing about it. So we have different rights and obligations, whether we like it or not. I have to make sure that my family is secure, earn money, protect them, etc. Women have different obligations and earning money is not one of them.

I continued to nod, for no clear reason. I found myself thinking how very curious it was that someone who thinks men should be successful outside the home while their wives are chained to the kitchen sink appropriates the term "sexist" for himself, with the same negative meaning the feminist critique implies. It also struck me as odd that he brought God into the conversation, though just five minutes previously he had said that he was not at all religious. Yet as we saw in chapter 4, self-declared atheists are likely to refer both to their genes and to God to explain their success, so it should not have surprised me that God would also be brought into discussions on gender.

BUSINESS AND POLITICS in Russia remain almost exclusively a man's world and a masculine world. Yet nothing beyond this simple statement is straightforward. Russian women are often considered to be the more responsible and stronger sex, albeit within the narrowly confined margins of persistent patriarchal norms, and those can reproduce truly outdated ideas about gender. Russian upper-class women might even reinforce these ideas rather than fight against them, because—in the context of patriarchal norms—the conservation of gender stereotypes can work in their favor. Gay upper-class identities are equally contradictory: As we have seen, Gleb presented his gay masculinity as unproblematic, despite omnipresent homophobia. This indicates that bourgeois identity is strong—indeed, strong enough to override sexual identity. All the same, the nature of elite masculinity and femininity is also changing. The rise of philanthropy in particular has opened up a world of new lifestyle choices. Male art collectors have taken up philanthropy as an outlet to escape feelings of boredom and fatigue, while bourgeois wives have moved on from running beauty salons to engaging in creative activities or taking over complementary tasks such as charity projects.

7

The Inheritors' Coming of Age

THE POST-SOVIET BOURGEOISIE is sharply differentiated between the generations: accumulators in the older, and inheritors in the younger. While the older generation has become rich without the benefit of inheriting any wealth themselves, the latter has acquired its wealth thanks to its fortuitous birth. The inheritors hence face a particular challenge to find new forms of entitlement to wealth.

The children of rich Russians are not the only ones confronted with this challenge. As the sociologist Mike Savage stresses, the inheritance of accumulated wealth is now the most important component in determining social class.[1] The sociologist Rachel Sherman found that wealthy parents in New York City are very keen to raise morally "good people." "Good" implies consuming within measure and with prudent desires, appreciating the value of work and labor, and being aware of the advantages one's social position brings. Overall, the goal is to teach them how to occupy their social positions appropriately and legitimately without giving them up, and how to be worthy of privilege in a moral sense.[2]

Denis versus the Golden Youth

The issue of inheritance was not salient in the 1990s in Russia. At that time the rich worried more about the immediate risk of their rivals wrestling their wealth from them. In the early 2000s a glamour culture ruled their lifestyles. In these contexts, many parents passed on their ostentatious lifestyles to their offspring. The result was the phenomenon of the "golden youth" (zolotaya molodyozh), that is, fun-seeking, spoiled, and flighty teenagers and young adults.

Denis was a child when his father rose through the ranks of the global *Forbes* rich list. One would think that such quick money and influence would be likely to trigger conspicuous behavior. This was not the case in Denis's family: "Because my father became very successful very quickly, he never had to prove anything to anybody." Denis, a gangly, socially awkward young man in his late twenties, dressed in jeans and sweatshirt, explained this to me in a Prêt à Manger coffee shop two blocks from Wall Street. I asked him where he had lived in Moscow when he was growing up. He seemed slightly embarrassed and said that they lived in Rublyovka, Moscow's glamorous luxury suburb. "For my family, to live in Rublyovka was not a question of prestige but a question of security," Denis said defensively. "There was nothing we could do about that. When I was little, it was simply incredibly dangerous in Russia."

Denis fiercely rejects any form of ostentation ("I've got anti-symbols which I follow"). He is particularly concerned not to look like one of the "golden youth": "They're totally dull, those from the elite, particularly if they grew up in Russia," he said with annoyance. The Yale and Harvard graduate, who used to work as a banker on Wall Street and now invests in IT start-ups, continued: "They're interested in things that I'm not interested in at all. Cars and clothes [*shmotki*]." Denis finds their ignorance, snobbishness, and indifference to anybody else in the world particularly annoying: "They don't know New York at all, except for the most expensive restaurants and nightclubs in Manhattan. They are not the slightest bit interested in what's going on around them."

Denis's strong antipathy to the "golden youth" is rooted in a certain familiarity with the social environment he was describing: "Parts of my world in Moscow were like this, and I'm quite glad that I left all that behind me." However, he was at pains to point out that his childhood was not entirely ensconced within this new-money milieu either. His parents, who came from the Soviet intelligentsia, did not send Denis to a private school: "I went to a normal state school in the center of Moscow. Quite a well-known school, but it was not only for rich kids. In my school, showing off money was frowned upon," he explained.

Children who arrogantly boast of their father's wealth may do so quite innocently on the simple grounds that they assume that it is the norm. Sherman collected stories from wealthy New York parents who tried to avoid precisely that. Through constraining their children's consumption of material goods and experiences, the parents hoped also to constrain their children's sense of entitlement. A parallel strategy Sherman found was parents exposing their offspring to children from other social classes. By doing this, the parents aimed to show their children what "normal" life looks like, so that they would learn to appreciate their privilege, as well as acquire social integrity and a sense of obligation to those who have less.[3]

Denis's father applied a similar parental strategy. He sent Denis from an early age to long summer camps for children from rough Siberian oil towns. His educational goals were different from those of Sherman's NYC parents. Denis learned to be a leader: "The main activity there was to set up a model state with a model economy, a president, a parliament, companies, factories, and everything," he recalled. "One summer I was a businessman, another time a parliamentarian, many things." The father's aim was to teach his son to assert himself among children from very different social backgrounds.

While these summer camps taught Denis leadership skills, his sense of superiority stems from elsewhere. Significantly, he expressed this feeling of superiority not only toward the lower classes (those whom he met at those camps) but in particular to wealthy peers. "I've been lucky," he said, slightly nervously, while pushing his shoulder-length hair from his face for the umpteenth time. "I never had to prove anything to anybody, or to show off, because it was clear to everybody anyway who I was."

Indeed, everybody was very aware of the fact that Denis's father made his fortune in the blink of an eye and landed up among the world's very richest. However, Denis grounds his superiority not in his father's wealth, but in the cultural–intellectual elitism of his Moscow intelligentsia family, which boasted famous scientists and celebrated such values and modesty as prescribed by Soviet *kulturnost*: "We've always had the attitude in our family that we don't need to follow the mainstream. We never indulged in all these things [excessive consumerism]. Maybe it's our character, maybe it's our culture and manners."

As much as this seems a self-deception, in many ways it makes sense. A robust family story of an intelligentsia background provides a point of orientation in good times and bad. Much in line with the ethos of the new modesty, Denis's parents were successful in nurturing in him a Soviet-era self-conception that is focused on intellectual independence. The role of money here is simply a supportive one, consolidating free intelligentsia status.

There is, however, a minor chink in his narrative, as in those of other children of the super-rich. I have been surprised time and again that there are few stories of teenage rebellion. Denis confirmed my observation: "In

Russia this is much less prevalent than in the West, this total craziness."
With an innocent look, he told me that he did not rebel as a teenager, nor
later in life, and he stressed that his younger sister did not go through this
either. Denis paused for a moment: "Hold on, I remember one thing." He
acknowledged that he had formerly indulged in a degree of consumerism: "When I was fifteen, fashion was more important to me," he said.
But his parents did not actually mind his passion for fashion, he added.
"And then there was a period when I was really into snowboarding. But,
actually, my parents supported that, too."

Denis's remarks made me realize that we were miles away from each
other in our understanding of teenage rebellion, where perhaps negat-
ing one's parents' views and lifestyles might feature, including becoming
politicized. One reason Denis thinks that he and his sister did not rebel
was that their childhood years were "simply ideal." He wants the same for
his children.

Schooling

Many affluent Russians send their children to Western schools and universities. In the 1990s this was not least to ensure their children's physical
security. In the 2000s it became a question of preferences. According to
a study carried out by the Skolkovo Center for Management, 60 percent
receive at least part, if not all, of their higher education abroad.[4]

Andrey, twenty-four, went to a school in Switzerland from the age
of twelve, after going to a state school in Moscow. He did this while his
father was building up his company, the second biggest in its field in
Russia in terms of production volume. "Why did my father send me to
Switzerland?" he mused. Alluding, perhaps, to a lack of personal reflec-
tion in his parents' decision-making, Andrey acknowledged that they did
what was "fashionable" at that time and "what everyone did."

Media manager Dmitry Kiselyov sent his eldest son to Bloxham School
in Oxfordshire for the last two years of his education, something he soon
came to regret. The school Kiselyov chose was small, not cheap—indeed, he
stressed, the second or third most expensive school in England at that time.
His son did not enjoy his time in the United Kingdom, suffering under
the school's strict discipline. "It was as if he had served in the army. He
was very happy to come back. 'Now I'm back in a free country,'" Kiselyov
remembered his son was saying when he came back home to Russia.

Kiselyov did not want his son to go to university in Britain, for two main reasons. First, he considers the British university curriculum to be too narrowly focused on professional training, rather than providing sufficient general knowledge.

> For example, my ex-wife, who graduated from Cambridge [University], didn't know who started the Second World War. They didn't learn history, but instead specialized too early. You don't get any idea how the world is constructed.

Second, Kiselyov did not want his son to be socialized into a different value system. "I don't want to lose my son. I don't want him to change his mentality," he said. One pressing concern for Kiselyov was the issue of homosexuality, which he hotly debated with me (see chapter 6).

Others also consider Western schooling to be a mistake. The telecommunication entrepreneur Yury Pripachkin, a father of three, is full of regrets at having sent his eldest daughter to school in Switzerland and Spain: "Except for the language skills, this is pointless because the education system in the West is based on a cynical upbringing. Yes, they learn manners but their heads are filled with chaos." Pripachkin's daughter did not finish school in Europe. From the eighth grade she went to school in Russia. "She still managed to enjoy the remnants of the old [Soviet-inspired] education system."

Pripachkin sent his younger boys to a military corps school in Russia. The former military commander is happy with his choice, even though he laments that little has survived from the Soviet education system and that his "children are deprived of the kind of upbringing we had" in the Soviet Union: "There are no values anymore at school; the principles that we used to have are gone. . . . Instead today we have what they call competitiveness. This is a big mistake. This gives birth to a generation that has no values at all."

The decision of Andrey Korkunov, the businessman who had set up a chocolate brand, to send his children to school in Moscow triggered much criticism from his friends and acquaintances: "Oh, they all wanted to dissuade me. They were constantly talking about the huge advantages of Western schooling. But there are two sides to the coin," he suggested. He did not want his children to become alienated from him and his family, "merely for the sake of a better education. A child with a completely different education than your own, with different views and a different culture, will eventually develop into a stranger."

Disillusionment with Western schools has given rise to the question as to whether Russian schools are an alternative and, if so, whether to send children to posh private schools or state schools. Korkunov sent his children to a Russian state school with a focus on languages, rather than one of the fancy new private schools that mushroomed in Moscow in the 1990s and early 2000s. Many rich parents understood quite quickly how much their children would benefit from being surrounded by children from intelligentsia families, instead of being isolated among their own.

If parents are unhappy with the values and cultural resources that schools instill in their offspring, it becomes all the more important for them to take responsibility for passing on the knowledge, skills, and morals that they want their children to have. Vitaly, a wealthy investor in his sixties who made his money in natural resources, has established, in effect, a school for one pupil, his youngest son, Mark. He counted the number of staff working exclusively for the nine-year-old: "It's twenty in total. It's a whole school. Teachers, pedagogues, sport teachers, governesses, and many more."

The aim of employing this little army is to boost the boy's abilities, especially in sports. Vitaly did not hide his competitiveness: "Mark plays tennis and golf very well and he's good at swimming. At what age did you stand on skis for the first time?" he asked, turning to me with a quizzical glance. "Also at three? Okay, well," Vitaly appeared to be disappointed to learn Mark was not the only one. "He learned to ski at that age as well." He is also intellectually strong, Vitaly said with a smug smile. "He reads a lot. He likes Jules Verne." Mark would soon be sent to school in Switzerland.

Despite all the praise for Russian schools and upbringing, billionaires' children usually get educated abroad. Ziyavudin Magomedov's children, for example, go to Harrow (old boys include Winston Churchill and Jawaharlal Nehru) and Ludgrove (the prep school that Princes William and Harry attended). They will go on to study somewhere on the US East Coast, where the billionaire is convinced that education is most dynamic. Veronika Zonabend and Ruben Vardanyan's oldest son studied at Westminster School in London, while the oldest daughter graduated from Robert Bosch United World College in Germany. Vadim Moshkovich's oldest son studies at Stanford, and his oldest daughter is at boarding school in England. Like many of his peers, Moshkovich considers

American higher education to be the best. His son is "in heaven" at Stanford. "He gets by on less then $500 a month," Moshkovich added with some pride. Nevertheless, also like many of his peers, Moshkovich wants his children to return to Russia: "If I'm successful, all my children will come back. Russia is their home. One's home is the place one wants to return to, the place one loves."

Parenting and the Legacy of the Soviet Intelligentsia

The shift toward a new modesty is especially relevant to parents who are critical of the golden youth's extremes of hedonism and consumerism. Natalya, the wife of a billionaire and businesswoman in her own right, told me what a challenge it had been to bring up her children, one daughter and two sons. "We know a huge number of the 'golden youth:' They are destroyed by money and opportunities from the very beginning." When they were little, Natalya feared that her children's privilege could cause them to become morally corrupt: "I tried hard to limit the influence of our wealth on my children. We had to think about it all the time and control the process very strictly."[5]

As Natalya went on, it almost sounded as if, in comparison to middle-class parents, rich parents are at a disadvantage because of the extra challenges their privileged environment creates. She sees it as a mother's obligation not to spoil her children, but to offer them "a healthy challenge." The example she eventually gave is a simple one: Her children knew that she and her husband would always finance and support them, "but they mustn't ever quit university or get kicked out. That would be the end. This was set in stone." This does not sound at all harsh, given that the Russian university system does not usually fail students who show a minimum amount of effort. Natalya's children did well. She sees their success as based on hard work: "My older son is less talented than the younger one, and also less than my daughter. He understood perfectly well that his future depended on working hard and only on that. This played a big role in his life."

People use very different means to instill some "normality" and modesty in their children. Kirill, a banker and art collector in his late forties, hails from a simple social background. He is concerned that his daughters might become spoiled. "Our children use the Metro. We made a point of teaching them how to use it. They need to be aware that life can also be very different," he said. Kirill's family trips into the world of ordinary people provide not only life training, but personality training: "Alongside this, we want them to realize that fashion is not the most important thing in life, but to develop different interests, tastes, and values."

In criticizing a crude, money-orientated personal outlook, some Russian bourgeois parents revive Soviet-era values. The billionaire Roman Avdeev surprised me by appealing to Soviet mores. He wants to instill in his twenty-three children (nineteen of whom were adopted) three main things: first, a spirit of communality; second, some Russianness; and third, those values "we shared within the former Soviet space." After praising his parents' and grandparents' values (see chapter 3), he explained that he would like to see similar nonelitist values develop in his older children. His perception of these values is fairly straightforward: "That success is closely linked to money as it has been in our country for the last few decades is fundamentally wrong. Success is when someone realizes themselves."

The billionaire Alexander Mamut, who bought the UK book retailer Waterstones in 2011, would probably agree with Avdeev. Mamut wrote in a column for *Forbes* that he sees his task as a father to help his children discover their own path and achieve their own success. Success does not need to be narrowed down to business and money, he argued, not even to achieve similar things as their parents. It is just as good to write a great novel, invent something useful, or direct a film, he wrote, consciously or unconsciously setting the bar rather high.[6]

Promoting an image of himself as a scion of an intelligentsia family, Mamut wants for his children a world of values similar to the ones he experienced himself in his childhood and youth. His column for *Forbes* reads like an excerpt from a Soviet textbook. When he was a little boy, he wrote, he got up at eight o'clock in the morning. His father, an academic lawyer, was already working at his desk. On Sundays the parents went to either a museum or the conservatory. Then friends came to visit. They would sing songs and play the piano. All the basic values were in place: a life with one woman, a strong work discipline, holidays with educational aims, and a library at home with a special shelf for poetry (his father had a huge library). They would read serious literature in their spare time.

Such Soviet-era cultural values do not include aspiring to material wealth. On the contrary, the Soviet intelligentsia wanted to think of themselves as enjoying freedom and independence from material urges. This idea is partly refreshed today. The most straightforward expression is in the desire to have their offspring excel in education. Marina, thirty-eight, the wife of a wealthy businessman, praised the talent of her husband's daughter, who is from his first marriage. She was about to finish her first year at the Mechanical Mathematics Faculty at Moscow State University. Marina's stepdaughter's degree was financed by the state. "For me that's just incredible. She's so talented and diligent! That she got into university on her own merit!" To make it into university "on your own merit" means not having needed the help of bribe-paying or intervening parents. Marina saw a bright future for her husband's daughter, most likely as a scientist.

The Inheritors' Coming of Age

In terms of the future of their companies, only a third of the respondents in a study carried out by Skolkovo considered the possibility of transferring their business to one of their children. Fifty-five percent had doubts that their present-day big business would ever turn into a family dynasty.[7] Russian media often draw attention to the lack of a spirit of entrepreneurship among the children of Russia's rich. They are said to feel entitled and self-righteous and follow the path of least resistance—which often means nepotism—and end up working either for their parents' companies, the companies of business partners, or those of associates or old friends.[8] Among my young interviewees, however, this was not always true. Although he was, admittedly, an exception, twenty-four-year-old Andrey did tell me that he had a problem with having simply been born into wealth:

> I don't always feel comfortable. After all, I am using someone else's money. From one perspective you can say that simply because I'm my father's son I've got the right to go on some luxurious holiday. Yet I didn't earn the money for it and actually I don't deserve this money for any other reason than that I'm my father's son. . . . It's actually quite out of order.

Hardly anybody else was as self-questioning as Andrey, but many adhere to the general idea that it is important to be hard working to be the deserving children of rich parents. Yulia understands this completely. With her killer heels, long wavy chestnut hair, high cheekbones, and tall, slim figure, she was another female interviewee who looked like she had just stepped off the catwalk. She presented herself as being particularly entrepreneurial.

I was very glad when Yulia and I finally sat down on the upper terrace of the Whitney Museum of American Art (my neck was hurting from having to look up at her the whole time). I was also glad when she finally switched from talking about art (she likes contemporary art, but not that much) to talking about her life. For a woman who is still only in her mid-twenties, her CV is impressive. She has carried out projects in many fields: tech, finance, the state sector, media, fashion, and the arts. A couple of days prior to our meeting she received a postgraduate diploma from an East Coast university. Now she was about to return to Moscow to join the management of a large state-aligned company.

Yulia's father is a billionaire with excellent connections to the Kremlin, which is very useful given his broad investment portfolio. Although her management position is a great leap forward for someone her age, Yulia wants to follow in her father's footsteps and set up her own business. Her self-assessment is concerned with merit, experience, and vision, rather than privilege:

> The spirit in my family, together with my personal views, has always driven me to do something by myself. This is important because the more responsibility you take on, the faster things develop. It's important to leave your comfort zone and speed up your development.

Yet thanks to her family, Yulia never had to work in finance or as an analyst or consultant, as many of her peers from university have done. She is very glad to have avoided this as it would only have slowed her down unnecessarily. In general, Yulia has benefitted vastly from the social networks of her well-connected father. She is aware of this when reminiscing about how many interesting things she picked up when her parents had guests over for dinner. However, when it comes to her own career, those aspects disappear from her self-assessment, which is that she has achieved success because of her "inner" strength, her discipline, and her drive.

Olga, a redhead in sandals, emerald trousers, and a wine-red tunic, is less ambitious: "I adore my mother. I want to become like her, in a spiritual sense. I want to be as free and independent as she is. And I want to be successful in my career." Here she paused: "But I will never ever achieve as much success as she has. I can't aim to emulate her in this regard." Denis said much the same. For him it is crucial to achieve his own success: "The most important thing is to achieve something yourself." Denis soberly assessed his chances: "I know I'll never reach my father's level. That's not possible today. But still, I want to achieve something myself, not only in terms of work and money, but also in terms of independence."

Indeed, the rapid accumulation of wealth in the manner of the 1990s is almost certainly not repeatable. Moreover, bourgeois parents are themselves tired of the money-making process and seek new meaning in life. In parallel with their turn to philanthropy, many parents express a preference for their children to pursue professions in the cultural world or an intellectual environment, rather than in business. However, this does not remove the tension between passing on material wealth and cultivating cultural capital in one's children. The model rich people adhere to is the one they themselves experienced in their Soviet families and from their Soviet education.

The Negation of Inheritance

Mikhail Fridman, the founder of Alfa-Bank, has publicly declared that his fortune will go to charitable foundations: "The worst thing I could do to my children is to give them an enormous sum of money." He wants them to achieve their own success in their careers. According to a *Forbes* rating from 2016, his four children would otherwise get $3.3 billion each.[9] Alexander Mamut wrote in *Forbes* that his children would receive enough money to get by, but not enough to get harmed by it. The best investment, he said, would be to put money into Russian foundations and trusts that pursue an enlightening, humanistic mission.[10]

Similar thoughts on inheritance came up in a number of interviews. The billionaire Alexander Svetakov wants to leave large amounts of his wealth to charity: "I've got my letter of wishes. Everything is written in there. My children will inherit, but by far not all." Vadim Moshkovich does not plan to pass on any money to his children: "I've told my children that they won't get it, but they don't yet understand what that means." The Zonabend-Vardanyan family will not bequeath their wealth to their children: "They know that they won't get an inheritance. They'll get an education and somewhere to live. The rest is up to them." I asked Veronika Zonabend how they have responded to this. "They live with it," she laughed. "They understand the rules." The businesswoman explained the couple's rationale:

The burden of increased responsibility shouldn't sit on their shoulders. If they want to continue our foundation, for example, it should be entirely of their own volition, plus they should have the ability to run it. We see many examples of bequeathed businesses where the children's skills are not adequate. That was the problem with monarchy. We are not going to repeat it.

The billionaire Roman Avdeev, who looks to Karl Marx for guidance on the topic of philanthropy (chapter 3), stressed the need for a high tax on inheritance. Consistent with his admiration for Marx and his sharp opposition to inheritance, Avdeev will also leave his fortune to charity:

My task is to teach my children what is good and what is bad. They receive a very good education and learn to speak at least two languages. I want my children to speak English. We have a lot of English-speaking staff at home. The children will also receive a flat and a car. As for the rest, they should have a chance to form their own personalities and find their own path in life.

Is this new altruistic selflessness taking precedence over the children's material interests? Survey data do not confirm this as a mass phenomenon. According to the Skolkovo study, 48 percent of the rich want to bequeath to their children all they have, and another 36 percent most of it. Only 13 percent declared that the major part of their wealth would not go to their children.[11] Nevertheless, the voices of the rich parents making their pledges to charity are clearly audible. This is partly the expression of a generation that is the first to have huge wealth assets to pass on to their offspring. It will be the biggest intrafamilial transfer of wealth the world has ever seen if one considers the small number of people involved. The enormity of this project seems daunting even to the actors involved.

Philanthropy, in the form of large endowments and charity pledges, goes hand in hand with the integration of their children into their projects. Moshkovich's children know all about his philanthropy and the values behind it: "They have to listen; they don't have a choice. My wife supports me in everything and we discuss things. We overlap in our values." Irina Sedykh, the billionaire's wife and herself a philanthropist, involves her teenage sons in much of her work and is delighted with the results. They have volunteered at an oncological children's hospital, and recently one of them donated all his summer job money to charity, she said proudly.

Svetakov often takes his children along to all sorts of charity events. His aim is to get them involved in one way or the other, so "that they won't be indifferent to the fate of others." The driving force behind this wish is not only altruism but also self-protection: "In our country nobody is totally safe from ending up in prison. Today you can be young, healthy, and rich and tomorrow old, unfit, and poor." (Things are different for his wife, whose primary interest is her own charity project, a dog orphanage. "She's definitely more interested in her dogs than my school," he laughed in an indulgent but resigned way.)

The interest in charity among the younger generation is occurring at the same time that their parents' generation is aging and becoming more concerned about their approaching death. Parents may view their children's involvement in their charity foundations as a means of surviving beyond the grave. From the long-term perspective of reproducing social class, such an upbringing does more than back up the neoliberal narrative of meritocracy, claiming that anybody can make it if only they have the talent.

AS THIS FIRST generation of rich Russians grows older, it becomes more aware of its mortality. This process is accompanied by intensified thoughts about inheritance and its legitimacy. As the billionaire Alexander Mamut wrote in *Forbes*, "In Russia there is not a single person whose parents could act as a model of how to handle one's inheritance. We are the first generation and there is a special responsibility on our shoulders."[12]

Along with the right schooling, the inculcation of appropriate manners, a certain cultural understanding, and a training in philanthropy might soon become part of what is accepted by the bourgeoisie as a proper upbringing for their children.[13] As Max Weber wrote, if a fortune is not earned, it should at least be deserved—or rather: feel deserved. Philanthropy allows the offspring of the Russian rich, especially daughters, to be professionally engaged in an area that involves little risk and yet enjoys high status.

In general, it is crucial for rich Russians to find a convincing narrative to support the notion that their children are legitimate heirs. This could work if the children themselves were able to express and articulate privilege in such a way as to signal their underlying virtues and worthiness in an environment marked by extreme inequality. The younger generation of Russia's rich might be able to acquire such habits, skills, values, and dispositions—their habitus—as they have never been particularly preoccupied with money-making. Money has always been there, after all.

What might also be to their benefit is their relative insignificance in society, which keeps them out of the spotlight. This, together with their confidence, international schooling, and large financial resources—despite all the talk about their parents disinheriting them to ensure that they have the drive to achieve—provides them with a very comfortable existence and the luxury of choice to pursue interesting and innovative projects. All of this, when taken together, might enable this first generation of inherited wealth to develop new practices, narratives, and ideas that can speak, perhaps favorably, for their class as a whole.

8

Rich Russians and the West

IN 1957 ISAIAH Berlin made the observation that there had "surely never been a society more deeply and exclusively preoccupied with itself, its own nature and destiny" than Russia: "All, without exception and at enormous length, discuss such issues as what it is to be a Russian; the virtues, vices and destiny of the Russian individual and society; but above all the historic role of Russia among the nations."[1] In particular, since the rise of nationalism as a force in the nineteenth century, Russia's view of itself has been intrinsically linked to its attitude toward the West. Attraction to the West and eagerness to emulate Westerners have been coupled with suspicion, repulsion, and dismissiveness, which was expressed most clearly in the nineteenth century by the Slavophiles. This tension has been immensely important for the history of Russian elites, whose discussions through the years have revolved around the question: To what extent is Russia intrinsically unique?[2]

An important narrative in these debates is of Russia as a Eurasian civilization.[3] In 1921 the linguist Nikolay Trubetskoy and the geographer and economist Pyotr Savitsky, who were both now living in the West, put forward, with other Russian émigrés, the idea that Russia was the driving force of the continent of Eurasia, a civilization distinctively different from Europe. In identifying Russia as Asiatic and juxtaposing it with Western Europe, they echoed earlier Slavophile sentiment but went further in that they viewed the cultural predecessor of Eurasia as the Mongol Empire rather than Kievan Rus. In the later Soviet period Lev Gumilyov (the son of the Russian modernist poet Anna Akhmatova) became the most prominent proponent and theoretician of Eurasianism. According to Gumilyov's theories, which he elaborated in the 1960s and 1970s, Russian civilization is not only unique, but spiritually and intellectually superior to that of the West.

From the post-Soviet period to the present day, nationalists, including intellectuals like Alexander Dugin, have constantly refreshed and updated ultraconservative theories of nationalism. These theories have made dramatic inroads into politics and the intellectual mainstream. Currently, the liberal neo-Westernizer view, which considers Russia to be part of the Western world, is in abeyance, and the opposite, neo-Slavophile, Eurasian view of Russia as unique goes largely unchallenged. In this atmosphere, the conservatism of the Russian Orthodox Church holds sway.

Albert, an investor, praised Russia as "the center of the conservative world" because it combines Orthodoxy and Islam, and is in agreement with the pope with regards to conservative values. "We are strongly against LGBT," he explained to me, leaning back in his chair. Albert is not someone who is purely inward looking—indeed, he is quite the opposite. He collaborates with many Western European countries to exhibit his contemporary art collections. Nevertheless, his conclusion is decisive: "We don't need the Western world as it is now. We want to preserve our civilization as it used to be."

Londongrad

The billionaire Valery, a clear liberal, is frustrated at being able to plan at most one day ahead: "Yes, of course, we are used to adapting quickly to new situations. We had one putsch in 1991, another one in 1993, then we had all kinds of crises, and we coped." His life is deeply anchored in Russia, yet he is prepared to leave the country if necessary, at a moment's notice. His assessment of Russia at the present time is not flattering:

It was basically a madhouse we grew up in, Russia in the 1990s. It is still a madhouse. Our horizon doesn't even go beyond the next day, which is also why our economy is not developing. Nobody can make any plans, and as a result, nobody invests in Russia.

This uncertainty results in rich Russians' lack of trust in their state. Even if they are part of its machinery, it is now the norm for them to establish a second life abroad, somewhere they can get to easily. London has long been favored over New York, Paris, or any other European city as the second home for Russia's rich. In contrast to New York, Britain's capital is only a three-and-a-half-hour flight from Moscow, which allows rich breadwinners to leave their families safe and secure in London while they commute to Moscow on business. The United Kingdom has a large network of private schools to which money provides easy access. The country is reluctant to agree to the extradition of Russian residents in the United Kingdom who have run afoul of their own country's laws. London is one of the key centers of global litigation, and its courts are considered independent and uncorrupt. The UK fiscal regime has some important elements of a tax haven in the sense that privacy is sacrosanct. The law enforcement agencies are much less tough than, for example, in the United States. British regulations are in some respects very unbureaucratic and its governance standards permissive.[4] In contrast to France or Germany, it only takes about one day to set up a business in the United Kingdom.

These are all excellent reasons to opt for London. It does not matter much to rich Russians that the easiest way for foreigners with cash to settle in the United Kingdom is via an investor's visa, which is substantially pricier than its equivalent in, for example, the United States. To gain a UK investor visa, an applicant has to invest $2.5 million in government bonds or approved industries. After a period of five years, visa holders can apply for indefinite leave to remain. Those who have invested more than $12 million can apply for leave to remain after only two years. Russians and Chinese have dominated this visa category since the turn of the century.[5] A large amount of undeclared Russian funds have arrived in London—over $1 billion each month in the mid-2010s, most of which has ended up in the housing market, which has had the effect of pushing up prices.[6]

Most Russians with hundreds of millions of US dollars set up their second lives years ago, in the 1990s and early 2000s. Many of the rich arriving in London in the mid-2010s were rather less rich, with wealth amounting to "only" tens of millions of US dollars. But material wealth is not the only thing that determines the pecking order among new and old arrivals in London. Another is the level of culture. Sitting in his bright, modern wood-and-metal house in Kensington, not far from the Russian embassy, the art collector Igor Tsukanov made it clear that he does not have "anything in common with all the people moving over from Russia today."

The former researcher and financier is deeply engaged with the London art world. His oldest son holds a master's degree in law from Berkeley and lives with his young family in Palo Alto. His second son has a degree from Yale University and works in investment banking in London. His daughter is a boarding pupil at a top girls' school, Wycombe Abbey. Only his wife still has one foot in Russia—the office of her consultancy business is there. But more and more of her clients are moving out of Russia and into London, and her business is following them.

Tsukanov, who made his money in finance, deeply identifies with Russian language, literature, music, and art. "We have a large number of writers who are part of world literature and world culture. Russia has produced music on a par with Germany, and no other country has produced so many high-quality musicians," he said, emphasizing that the music tradition, established in the nineteenth century, survived throughout the Soviet era. Although Tsukanov believes that standards in today's Russian music schools have gone down, he thinks that the old quality is being reincarnated by the Russian teachers who moved to Vienna, London, Paris, and New York. The same is true of literature, he said: "Think of Brodsky who lived in America, Turgenev who lived in France . . . It wasn't important where they lived." As for fine art, that is "less high-quality than music, but there are also some world-class protagonists such as Kandinsky and Malevich." Tsukanov, whose collection of post-war Russian art is one of the biggest in the world, is a rare critical voice concerning patriotic sentiments ("Once people talk about patriotism, they start saying strange things"), but Russian culture is very important to him.

Despite not identifying with patriotism, Tsukanov raised concern about the reputation of Russians in the West and the obstacles they face to be fully accepted in the United Kingdom: "There is a perception here in the UK, especially in newspapers, that Russians with big money came over to become members of English society." He briefly hesitated and then added: "If you look at what Abramovich or Usmanov or Blavatnik have done, that may actually be correct. They first became big industrialists, and once their business was fully established, started doing other things." All three of them—Roman Abramovich, Alisher Usmanov, Leonard Blavatnik—have made it on to the *Sunday Times Giving List*. Abramovich's route into UK society has been infamously prosaic. "What does the UK love most of all after the Queen?" asked Tsukanov. I shrugged my shoulders, and he explained: "Football! Abramovich instantly became a famous person because he's spent billions on Chelsea." Usmanov followed suit and bought a significant stake in Arsenal. "Well, everybody has the desire to improve their image a little," said Tsukanov approvingly.

Nikita, a young banker, is more concerned about stereotypes about Russia. His upbringing and education in an international environment—from school in Germany to a private school in Switzerland, a boarding school in the United Kingdom, and eventually a degree from the London School of Economics—made him acutely aware of a scarcely veiled sense of British cultural superiority over Russia: "In England they think of oligarchs, oil, money, and vodka. In Germany it is vodka, *matry-oshkas*, mafia, criminals, and prostitutes. In France it's wealth, champagne, mafia, and vodka." Even though Nikita has never lived in Russia, he identifies with his parents' country very closely and reminded me of Igor Tsukanov in his desire to promote Russia as a country of culture: "I'd like to see people think of science, culture, history, and literature, instead; not bears and vodka. Anyway," Nikita added, "the rich in Russia drink whiskey and cognac, not vodka."

What Keeps Rich Russians in Russia?

If living abroad is so popular, why do rich Russians tend to keep a strong foothold in Russia? Depending on their position in the state apparatus, some simply have to. A 2013 law forced government officials, their spouses, and children under eighteen to divest themselves of foreign stocks and bank accounts. A good number of politicians preferred to abandon their government positions rather than their houses in Europe, among them Roman Abramovich, who stepped down as the chairman of the legislature in Chukotka. However, even he is still a Russian resident, despite his part-time prominence as a Londoner.[7]

According to Germany's most important scholar on elites, Michael Hartmann, this follows a global trend. Analyzing the richest thousand people on the global *Forbes* list of 2015, he concluded that the phenomenon of a transnational, homeless elite is largely a myth. Especially in times of economic crisis, regular networking and interaction with the authorities and business partners in their home country is crucial to keeping everything afloat.[8] Good relations with the authorities have obvious importance in Russia. A law passed in 2015 that obliges Russian citizens who want to keep their offshore assets out of the country for more than 185 days a year had its intended effect: Many rich Russians rearranged their lives and assets.[9] The 2015 *Forbes Russia* list included only seventeen individuals who were not residing in Russia.[10]

There are also good reasons for upper-class Russians lower down the hierarchy to keep their businesses in Russia. Kirill, a banker and art collector in his late forties, spends most of his time in Moscow, even though his family moved to Germany long ago. "What is going on in Moscow is a big opportunity for people with an entrepreneurial spirit," he said. "You won't find that in Europe at all. Here you can build and create something, even in economically difficult times." I found it hard to imagine someone like Kirill enjoying Moscow's bustling, hedonistic, and at times stressful atmosphere. Neat, slick, and earnest Kirill, a committed teetotaler, sipped herbal tea while I wrapped myself in the blankets the waiter brought me to defend myself from the chilly breeze on the Hyatt rooftop terrace.

There are also cultural reasons for Kirill to be in Moscow. Above all, he enjoys his high status in the Moscow art scene. In Germany he has experienced great difficulties when trying to break down cultural boundaries and integrate into German society, despite his perfect command of the language. He explained: "You know I'll never get to the same level in German society that I have here. I will never belong to the kinds of close-knit circles I belong to here." One reason for this is that Germany breaks down into small units—Berlin, Hamburg, Munich. Kirill's family lives in Hamburg, where he has observed a particular elitism. Unless you belong to or have good connections with a specific family, "you've got no chance." He sighed: "You need to represent something historical." Kirill needs the gravitas in society that he commands in Moscow in order not to be bored, he explained. So he has transferred his aspirations for social inclusion in other cultures to his children and grandchildren, who, he hopes, will one day belong to these circles and enjoy the high status he will be unable to gain anywhere outside of Russia. His ambition is for them to "feel at home anywhere on the planet."

Interpersonal East–West Tensions

The Georgian entrepreneur and philanthropist David Iakobachvili, born in 1957, is known to be friendly and charming. I can confirm this from my second encounter with him at the St. Petersburg Economic Forum in 2015, as well as from a phone call I received from him in 2017 in which he agreed to my text about our interview. Our phone talk was a heartwarming conversation with a few laughs thrown in. In the version I had sent to Iakobachvili, I had described him as a Mexican-mustachioed Georgian and he, understandably, could not quite see where the "Mexican" came from. Why not Georgian-mustachioed, he asked me, with laughter in his voice.

Despite these pleasant later encounters, things were rather different during our first meeting in 2009. This took place on an exceptionally hot and humid summer afternoon. Iakobachvili was in a grumpy mood. I asked him what he thought of his Western elitist peers. He told me he had experienced a lot of disappointment, especially when dealing with Western bankers: "Well, there are some Western bankers who are decent," he admitted. Indeed, he does have a number of very good banker friends from Europe and the United States. One of his closest friends, from Sweden, had a collection of self-playing musical instruments that was taken over by the art-loving Iakobachvili and is now the chief exhibit in his museum.[11] Nevertheless, he has had bitter experience in dealings with some Western bankers who are "villains and rogues [zhuliki]," as he called them. "They smile at you as if they were your best friends—and then they deceive you." (Things got a little lighter once we talked about art, some pieces of which reflect a spirit of interpersonal East–West interaction. Iakobachvili showed me a bronze statue that ornaments his office desk: "Look, this is an Austrian one. It was once in Lenin's office. Lenin got it from [the American oil industrialist Armand] Hammer as a present.")

Some of my interviewees displayed considerable emotion when talking about the West. This seems to stem at least partly from the inferiority complex that many of them experienced in the past. Alexander, a businessman and investor in his early sixties, was unusually open and self-aware. He used to feel that there was a big difference between him and Westerners, he told me. In the first post-Soviet decade, Alexander considered his knowledge to be very limited compared to that of the Western people he was dealing with: "I had this feeling of inferiority, well, a complex actually."

This was a mass phenomenon. We all noticed the gaps in our knowledge. We noticed the gaps in our experience, which we couldn't possibly close or even hide. Everybody who had dealings with Westerners, especially with experts, suffered from this complex.

After a deep sigh, Alexander added, in a more confident voice: "That has gone now. This is a great relief because interacting with Westerners has become much more pleasant." He said that in hindsight he understood that this inferiority complex in relation to the West stemmed not from an actual lack of knowledge on the part of himself or his Russian peers, but because of the pretentiousness of some Westerners. He suspects that some of the people he had dealings with understood innately how to play the game and to pretend more knowledge than they actually had, whereas he had to learn from scratch how to do this. "That was a huge problem for me," he said.

His inferiority complex has now been replaced by supreme confidence—again something that he shares with other rich Russians. Alexander believes that the new generation of rich Russians has become equal, if not superior, to the Western elite: "Whether they live in Russia or in the West is purely a question of choice and preference. It's no longer a question of what they know or don't know," he concluded.

In other words, it is not just knowledge that bourgeois Russians have acquired. They have also learned how to play the game—and demonstrate their own pretentiousness. This attitude usually goes hand in hand with an element of defiance. Many Russians have developed a dismissive attitude toward the West's proclaimed values and norms in a number of different spheres, such as democracy, human rights, and the rule of law. They see these as hollow and hypocritical.

Russia's Uniqueness and Superiority over the West

Many of my interviewees harbor romanticized mythologies about Russia's elite—not only about the collective characteristics that make them superior to the West, but also about their relationship with the masses.

When Irina Sedykh explained that some of her philanthropic activities are aimed at compensating for the layoffs at her husband's factory (chapter 5), she mentioned that she considered things to be worse outside of Russia: "As far as I know, American companies are much more cynical in this respect." Sedykh is not inclined to anti-Americanism; on the contrary, she seems very open to the world and very keen on cultural exchange, particularly when it comes to charitable work. However, she genuinely feels for those ordinary Americans who are unprotected when losing their jobs: "Nobody there cares about what will happen to the workers and their families. You mustn't forget, if you make one worker redundant, there are at least two other people who are financially reliant on this one person."

Sedykh's perception of Russian employers' great sense of care goes back to Russia's nineteenth-century literature. While the capitalist West needed institutions to regulate the elite's patronage in relation to the poor, the Slavophiles saw social care in Russian society as something that was developing organically. Gregory's ideas reflect this approach. I met the thirty-one-year-old, the son of an oligarch, on the banks of the Moscow River in a cafe on Red October Island, named after the former chocolate factory. Like Sedykh, Gregory was convinced that the Russian elite "is closer to the people and cares more about them" than is the case with Western elites. Gregory assured me that he knows this because he grew up in the West, first in France, then in the United States. He believes that Russia's rich "don't detach themselves from the people by raising high walls; they treat simple people with a great openness." Yet Gregory's own family reality is rather similar to that which he criticizes in the West. First, their luxury houses in the Moscow suburbs are hidden behind high walls. Second, the last person in his family who had any dealings with the common folk was his grandfather, who started from humble beginnings as a peasant boy from the provinces before he worked his way up in the Ministry of Foreign Trade in the 1950s.

When it comes to superior collective elite traits, the myth is that Russian businessmen are more vibrant, energetic, and open-minded than their Western counterparts. Many see Russia's achievement in developing capitalism within just a couple of decades, when it took the West over two hundred years, as proof of Russia's superiority. The telecommunications entrepreneur Yury Pripachkin, born in 1960, considers the youth of Russia's entrepreneurs as one of its vital strengths. They are, on average, a generation younger than those in the West. In addition, they are self-made, more energetic, and more hands-on. This group, he explained to me, is composed of "people who have done everything by themselves." Alluding to the bailout of banks in the United Kingdom in 2008, Pripachkin challenged the Western argument that the mentality of Russian businessmen is stunted by the Soviet past, whereas that of Western businessmen is not. "Many Western businessmen have a socialist mentality. They think the state must come and help them out of a mess," Pripachkin said. In his opinion, Russia's younger and more innovative generation of self-made businessmen is more readily able to weather the ongoing economic storm.

The businessman Arseny echoed Pripachkin's description of dynamic Russian capitalists when he named the characteristics he regards as specifically Russian: openness and absolute generosity in terms of emotions as well as finances; a passionate curiosity about knowledge; the ability to be spontaneous and to improvise; enjoyment of speed and even uncertainty; the inclination to be audacious, even verging on insolent; and a tendency toward lavish tastes. Arseny could not live in the West, he said: "I would get terribly bored." Despite being (more or less) openly gay in an extraordinarily homophobic Russia, he sees political correctness as a repellent Western trait. He argued that it suppresses a person's intellect, originality, and individuality, whereas in Russia all these "wonderfully terrible peculiarities" have ample room to develop.

I was sitting for almost one and a half hours at a table by the window of Cafe Pushkin, a restaurant in central Moscow with kitsch nineteenth-century interior, waiting for Victoria, the daughter of a wealthy businessman. The waiter eyed me with suspicion when all I ordered until Victoria arrived was a pot of tea. However, as soon as Victoria walked in, along with her mother, Alla, and greeted the waiter as well as me, he was all smiles and courteous behavior toward me.

Victoria and Alla looked like candidates for a TV show on "glamorous Moscow": ash blond, super-chic, and extremely thin. Alla, fifty-going-on-thirty, could easily be mistaken for her daughter's sister. But they were different in their ways of conversing, both seeming to enjoy playing their mother–daughter roles. Both drank green tea and just picked at their salads, but Alla smoked, for which her daughter reprimanded her. Alla had promised her that she would give up by the time Victoria finished her degree at the Chelsea College of Arts, but did not keep her promise. Now, only half a year after graduating, Victoria had already set up her own fashion line together with a friend. She was very happy to return from London to Russia, and seemed to be flourishing. What this energetic young woman loves about Moscow is the freedom she enjoys there: the freedom of opportunity, to be able to start a business at a young age instead of slowly climbing up hierarchical ladders, to break rules instead of being stifled by them. "Freedom, yes, I think we've got much more freedom in everything," she stressed, while her mother nodded in agreement. "And everything is faster here. . . . You don't know what will be happening tomorrow. I'd be bored in the West. London was all right for some time, but I got bored there, too."

Curious to see what their reactions would be, I asked whether this freedom depended on giving bribes. "I never give bribes," Victoria replied sweetly. When I dug deeper, she explained that she left the nitty-gritty detail of her fledgling company to whizz lawyers who acted on her behalf but who did everything by the book. I asked what freedom meant for those who did not have such lawyers. "I can only speak for myself," she replied, in the charming manner I had come across before when Russians tried to

avoid a question. After all, it is not her fault that her father is so successful, she said. The least she could do was make the most of her position by
working very hard.

Given that the world of the elite is tightly knit and everyone knows about
everyone else, I had been picking up snippets about how well Victoria's
business was doing throughout my interviews. People in the know had
explained to me that she had a great partnership with her mother, who
kept an eye on her back-room staff and allowed her to focus on creative
fashion work. Victoria had been able to take advantage of a favorable trend
in the retail sector. Russia's tit-for-tat sanctions had not extended to the
import of clothes, and Victoria's designs are not that much cheaper than
those imported from the West because, like other local designers, she uses
expensive imported fabrics. However, she is able to reap the rewards of a
new consumer preference for Russian-made goods. Being in Moscow has
helped her stay in step with the capricious tastes of her peers. With the
support of celebrity friends who model her new lines and provide glowing
feature interviews in glossy magazines, she is able to set an example to her
friends and their mothers.

Suspicion toward the West

Media manager Dmitry Kiselyov's biography is in many ways representative of post-Soviet political history. In the 1990s, the then gentle, soft-
spoken graduate in Scandinavian studies was, both in his journalism
and his tastes, an exemplary European. He not only embraced everything
Western but promoted it and brought it to the country via *Window to
Europe*, a TV program aired on ORT, Russia's main channel at that time.
He even took an English wife, "a woman from Cambridge." They were
married for six years. Things have changed since then, and he would not
want to repeat that experience:

> Of course, I have foreign friends but I don't especially aim to
> have foreign friends. No question, my close friends are Russians.
> Foreigners are completely different. A friend can mean completely
> different things. If I say "friend," I have one thing in mind; if you
> say it, you might mean something completely different. When my
> former English wife said, "This color is red," and when I said it, we
> meant completely different things. For her "fast" meant one speed
> and for me it meant a completely different speed.

Kiselyov's negative feelings toward the West, which developed throughout the 2000s, proved to be useful when the Kremlin needed someone forceful to promote its image in the 2010s. Kiselyov was more than up to the job. He even reminded the world in March 2014, on the day of the Crimea referendum, that Russia was the only country in the world capable of turning the United States into radioactive dust.[12]

Kiselyov has a large number of like-minded colleagues and competitors in the media business. Aram Gabrelyanov, an ethnic Armenian Russian who grew up in Dagestan, set up Russia's largest tabloid empire (which is now co-owned by Yury Kovalchuk and Gennady Timchenko, two of Putin's closest cronies, who are both on the list of US sanctions). The media magnate has always dreamed of becoming Russia's Rupert Murdoch. His journalists have never written negatively about Putin, "the father of the nation."

Gabrelyanov is convinced that the West aims to destroy Russia and break it up into at least twenty parts in order to exploit and control its rich natural resources. "If it weren't for Putin, Russia wouldn't exist as a state anymore," he said. In his glass-walled office from which he has a good view of his newsroom with its hundreds of journalists, he asked me: "Why did they break up Yugoslavia into ten states? Why? And Iraq, Libya, and so on? Also in Russia, they want us to hate one another in order to make profitable deals with each of the twenty or so devolved, weaker new states," he said. The argument that the West would not benefit from a destabilized Russia did not hold sway with Gabrelyanov. "If Russia didn't have nuclear weapons and a strong army, built by Putin from scratch, they [the Americans] would have long since come over and destroyed us."

Igor Morozov is a man of conviction. Having made money in banking in the 1990s, Morozov later moved into politics. Both in his former work as a duma deputy and in his current position as a member of the Federation Council, Russia's upper house, the former sportsman has focused on international relations, an area in which he acquired expertise while studying for two doctorates, one in law, the other in economics. Morozov and his wife are sophisticated people; worldly, articulate, and educated. She speaks fluent English; he knows English, German, and Persian. Modest in looks and behavior, there is little to indicate that the couple are fairly wealthy, with nearly three thousand hectares of agricultural land in their possession—apart, that is, from the photos on their phones of their horses, a special breed of Arab, which they flew to a Dubai horse show.

At a dinner hosted by yet another Russian patriot, Morozov quietly listened as I told him about what struck me as paranoid scaremongering by the media figures Kiselyov and Gabrelyanov, and which, given that these two men reach out to millions of Russians via their news outlets, can potentially have a dramatic impact.[13] After I had finished, Morozov, himself the author of a lengthy monograph titled *Geopolitical Realities and Security* and holder of a medal For the Return of Crimea, calmly pronounced that I reasoned in a typical European way. I was worried about the effect of an unstable Ukraine because this could have consequences for European countries in terms of migration, economy, and security. Americans, he said, were physically so far away that such considerations did not concern them. In fact, a destabilized Europe would make it easier for the Americans to extend their power and control over the whole continent.

Stalin in Chelsea

During a trip to New York I was invited to attend a PR event of a chic Russian-owned Manhattan antiques shop. Everything was fancy. The subtly tanned host was a young man with a gym-honed physique, complemented by the most perfect manicure. The champagne-sipping ladies elegantly balanced on pencil-thin heels, mingling with effortlessly stylish and arty people.

I chatted with Masha, the owner's wife, a very pleasant woman in her thirties, whose family had moved to Spain in the early 1990s. Despite being perfectly turned out, thanks to good dentistry, professional fashion styling, and a sexy, slender physique, she came across as genuinely natural. She was born into an engineer's family in Novosibirsk. After graduating from an international school, she did an economics degree at a UK business school. She worked for her father's company for a few years before meeting her husband, Vadim, the son of a *Forbes*-listed oil and gas businessman (whose wealth peaked in 2011 at about $2 billion).

Most of Vadim's business is in Latin America and Canada, so the young couple settled in New York City. Vadim has a longstanding passion for antiques, and a year earlier he finally decided to realize his dream of owning a small antiques boutique. Masha liked the idea. She loves meeting new people: the quirky antique art dealers, the international ladies of fashion who constitute her husband's main clients, and the people from the neighborhood, who drop in every so often for a glass or two.

Masha and I got talking about the Moscow Metro and how it is superior to the New York subway. We agreed that this was not least because of the resources that were put into it and the work done by some of the best engineers of the early 1930s. We also agreed that it greatly boosted Stalin's popularity. Stalin was not all good though, Masha added. I nodded, signaling that I agreed that this was indeed the case. However, I quickly understood that Masha's and my views on Stalin were very different. Stalin did not go far enough, she said with a kind of polished, professional smile on her face, which I assumed she learned at her international school. Yes, it had been crucial to eliminate all of those Trotskyists and Leninists who would only have sabotaged the Soviet Union's leap into an industrialized future, she explained. Stalin had never been a Leninist, which accounts for Lenin's suspicion toward him shortly before his death in early 1924. Both Lenin and his wife, Nadezhda Krupskaya, became very wary of Stalin. Lenin had only put up with the young Stalin before the First World War because he successfully staged bank robberies to boost the underground party's fighting fund. So obviously Stalin had to settle accounts with Lenin and his legacy.

Masha went on to explain why it had been necessary for Stalin to eliminate other revolutionaries and their sympathizers, such as the old Bolshevik Nikolai Bukharin, one of Lenin's "fellow travelers." Bukharin had great charisma and was very popular, but he sided with the rich peasants. Industrialization could not have gone ahead while the peasants clung to their old ways of production, so Stalin had to get rid of Bukharin, she said. Masha is convinced that it was also necessary for him to liquidate the Red Army's high command in 1937.

Masha was now quite animated. No matter how Bolshevik Marshal Tukhachevsky and the other senior commanders perceived themselves, they had a tsarist mindset, she said. They would have become a massive problem, hindering more courageous military strategies during the Second World War. If anything, Stalin was not tough enough, she said firmly. He had allowed other massively destructive saboteurs to live, such as the Red Army general Andrey Vlasov, who collaborated with the Nazis after his capture in 1942, and that had been a big mistake.

At this point Masha's husband called his wife over to introduce her to a new customer who was interested in a fine pair of lacquered armchairs. The antique shop staff started collecting the empty Ruinart bottles and champagne glasses. My two favorite pieces of furniture, a 1940s cabinet on sale at $35,000 and an art nouveau coffee table at $40,000, had red stickers on them to indicate that they had already been bought. I went out into the fresh air of a relatively clear New York September night, preoccupied with the conversation we had just had.

As cosmopolitan and sophisticated as Masha is in most respects, her expensive European schooling and university education have failed to turn her into a humanist. Patriotic thinking, including seeing Stalin as the great modernizer and overseer of the Soviet Union's rise to global superpower status, is clearly more persuasive for her. As we saw in the case of Kremlin TV presenter Dmitry Kiselyov in chapter 4, repression of their own family members during Stalin's terror does not necessarily stop Russians from worshiping him and associating him more with the glory of Soviet victory in the Second World War and with the country's economic development than with atrocities and terror.

MANY RICH RUSSIANS criticize what they see as a morally bankrupt West in a way that suggests that Russia is different—a form of Russian exceptionalism. In a nutshell, their logic is that Russia is superior because its elite is better. This narrative implies that they are more caring toward ordinary people, more self-assertive, and more competitive than elites in the West. All the same, despite their extravagant wealth and stratospheric life trajectories, some rich Russians still experience the status anxiety that social climbers feel when they are surrounded by elites who have known privilege and status from the cradle.

Such residual status anxiety can be discerned, for example, in the choices rich Russians make about their Western staff: their consultants, lawyers, advisors, wealth managers, and their children's tutors. The four British men we encountered at the Henley Regatta in the preface of this book have all worked for rich Russians. Three of them in particular—Dave, Matt, and Harry (the fourth, George, is the only one from a solidly establishment background)—are ambitious, aspirational, and upwardly mobile, primarily due to the elite education they have enjoyed. This social climbing often comes with a certain level of status anxiety, which makes them, in one respect, not so different from the rich Russians who have employed them. Russian *parvenu* bosses have learned to spot such characteristics, which might help them find a kindred spirit in these clever, thrusting advisors they choose.

Conclusion

THE STORIES, TASTES, views, and ideas about life that are held by the Russian upper class, and which are recorded in this book, reveal a striking continuity between 2008 and 2017, despite the 2008 economic crisis, Putin's return to the presidency in 2012, the Ukraine crisis, the sanctions, and the collapse of the ruble in December 2014. Many explanations for this can be found in Russia's past. Russia's bourgeoisie emerged as recently as the new millennium, and yet its history has its roots in the twentieth century. Since the early 1990s, historians and social scientists have suggested that a large number of that decade's new elites were not *parvenus* in the sense of being social climbers from ordinary backgrounds, but were descendants of privileged or highly educated families. Members of the Soviet intelligentsia were re-emerging in the post-Soviet business world, initially as brutal predators.

The early 1990s were dominated by a single-minded focus on rapid accumulation of private wealth at any cost. This in turn resulted in the ability to wield immense power. At that time Russia did not have a capitalist class to whom this moneyed set could refer to understand what having an elevated position in society might involve. Neither, at this point, did they care since they were so focused on material accumulation. Those heady years live on in people's memories as breathtaking, bustling, and full of boundless life. For the first time it was truly possible to gain influence, discover new worlds, create something new, experiment, or simply make a lot of money. However, Russia's new rich knew that this would not last. In the long run, a social class was unlikely to be reproducible in this way. Something had to change.

When the new moneyed class came of age, things did change. During the course of the 2000s, amid an economic boom, the wealthy grew in size and complexity. Social life began to go beyond the basic liaisons that had been necessary for survival in the cutthroat world of the 1990s. As this book has argued, money ceased to be the only thing that mattered. This change was facilitated by the fact that the Russian upper class had already made its fortune, so its members no longer had to compete with each other as viciously as they had done before. This was followed by a shift toward less brash and more subtle ways of showing off, an expression of spiritual needs, and a desire to display more cultured traits. Bourgeois norms emerged, and links to the past were forged. Even those people whom the world perceived as robber barons mutated into respectable gentlemen.

This involved forging stronger ties with the intelligentsia. While in the early post-Soviet years it was fashionable for the new upper class to discover aristocratic roots, today a Soviet intelligentsia background provides a better provenance. A significant number of my interviewees ascribe symbolic importance to their social backgrounds, which they use to position themselves in society. References to the Soviet intelligentsia contribute to the sense that an elite identity of the past is being reproduced in the present. Accordingly, it has become good manners to know one's family history and to have a family archive.

The Russian bourgeoisie has also embraced the intelligentsia as a group on whom to model themselves. This has led to a merger between wealth and culture, driving the moneyed class to identify with cultural symbols. The intelligentsia has stood in for the missing capitalist class of the past and has provided the new moneyed class with a model both for a superior sense of identity and for a set of ideas and values that they were not able to articulate. The incorporation of culture has, I have argued, led to a civilizing process, with the result that contemporary highbrow culture in Russia closely overlaps with post-Soviet intelligentsia culture. In the process, by affiliating themselves with projects and activities associated with the intelligentsia, the bourgeoisie are remodeling Russia's post-Soviet intelligentsia in line with their evolving bourgeois taste and fashions.

Becoming Bourgeois

Russia's bourgeoisie has been acquiring the characteristics of a social class through the complex mechanisms of social reproduction, as described by Bourdieu. Having started with just a handful of extremely powerful men, the bourgeoisie now spans at least two generations and includes children and wives. Though the latter are easily replaceable, they have begun to play a greater part in the reproduction of the group than was previously the case—for example, by organizing (though not usually leading) social duties such as charitable activities. The children have also moved on from their former image of the spoiled and decadent "golden youth."

This bourgeoisification process has not been straightforward. Indeed, several social hierarchies now exist in parallel. The contradictions generated in the last decades of rapid social change have resulted in multiple, often ephemeral, lifestyle choices. Many wealthy Russians still primarily identify with and express themselves through conspicuous consumption, ostentation, and pomp. Due to their visibility, these are the groups that are still the most prominent in public consciousness and that have provided the foundation for popular stereotypes. However, from a sociological perspective they are of less interest, since they are not the people who set the tone of the social zeitgeist, push forward new ideas, and create new trends.

The most visible feature of the new "culturedness" is a symbolic expression of status that has become less ostentatious and more private in nature. Understatement and self-imposed restrictions on the display of wealth seem to contradict the hedonism of the 1990s, but also, conversely, represent an organic continuity with those times. Opulence, and the awareness that one indulges in opulence, are necessary if one is to develop the ideas that stand in opposition to them. The dynamics of this process are not actually new to Russia. They can be observed in the actions of protagonists in Russian literary classics, such as the works of Tolstoy.

Reference to a privileged family heritage is not the only way to justify one's standing in society. One can also explain one's privileges by reference to the superior genes inherited from one's ancestors. A few of my interviewees took this further and presented themselves as spiritually sophisticated. Some came close to suggesting that their superiority was God-given. The combination of a superior bloodline and spiritual refinement allowed them to perceive themselves as "chosen ones." Such assertions serve to disguise the fact that their privileges are based on class. Capitalism requires the naturalization of power and inequalities if both are to be widely accepted, not only by the lower classes but also by the elites themselves.

In the twenty-first century the Russian bourgeoisie have felt the need to distance themselves from the brutality of the 1990s. At the same time, they have had to find ways of securing legitimacy for their existence, which has its roots in the very same decade. The bourgeoisie do not directly acknowledge their privilege. For example, they do not advocate redistribution policies that could help them appear as a deserving class in the eyes of the population. Rather, they seek legitimacy above all from their peers and from the presidential administration, leaving the longer-term task of acquiring more widespread legitimacy to the next generation.

This indicates that in contemporary Russia, people have had to embrace and combine new, and often contradictory, ideas stemming from diverse periods and sources. For example, laissez-faire capitalism goes together with a strong state, atheism with religiosity, 1990s social Darwinism with Putin-era paternalism, admiration for a Pinochet-style dictatorship with a mission to promote democracy, lifestyle cosmopolitanism with wartime-style patriotism, and modernism with traditionalism. By studying these contradictory amalgams, I have identified the theme of the bourgeois search for legitimacy, and how the new rich recast their range of narratives to suit their present situation.

Feelings of anxiety, in particular status anxiety, are especially pronounced in times of economic, social, and moral collapse, when structures of control and restraint are absent. This is partly due to a lack of routine and clear rules of acceptance. Feelings of (status) anxiety are noticeable in the interviewees' narratives, which suggests that the process of bourgeoisification is still relatively new. This is not surprising, given that these changes in tastes and morals have occurred in the course of just one generation.

The younger generation is already very different. Those in their early twenties have not experienced the same social collapse that afflicted their parents' generation. The stability of their privileged upbringing, education, and life experiences in general contribute to a coherence and consistency that are emerging within Russia's upper class.

The Ideology of Noble Deeds

As the moneyed class in Russia has acquired bourgeois characteristics, it has become more important for its members to feel that they deserve their status and position in society as well as the benefits they have accrued. This was particularly true after the 2000s, when the oil boom freed them from any financial problems, and again after the 2008 and 2014 economic crises, which increased the pressure on them to acquire social legitimacy. As a consequence, many who were preoccupied with business in the 1990s have now turned to philanthropy, art patronage, and engagement in public roles, particularly in the cultural world. Altruistic social practices have become an important tool for gaining a respectable reputation and for being seen as cultured and distinguished. Recognizing the social duty that goes hand in hand with their position in society is also essential if they wish to participate in bourgeois social life. Philanthropy binds them together through their networks of mutual obligations and the shared recognition of their class-based duties. This facilitates cohesion among the various groups and contributes to the development of class-consciousness.

It is the businessmen-turned-art collectors and art patrons who most obviously embody the new bourgeoisie. They have been trying to acquire a sense of noblesse oblige—the understanding that with wealth and power come social responsibilities—by devoting their time to art without using it for material goals. They have elaborated relatively complex ideas about their lives and their identities, and their commitment to art often contains spiritual elements. This process has been partly enabled by the fact that members of the first post-Soviet moneyed generation, though still young, have grown older, have started to contemplate their own mortality, and have become anxious about the legacy they will leave behind. Noble deeds offer a comfort similar to that of religion; they too promise an afterlife of sorts, since the deeds might confer legitimacy beyond the grave.

Noble deeds might also be linked to their ideologies and values—for example, in the preference people give to helping those they consider to be the deserving poor. Children (particularly those who are gifted) are seen to represent the future. They are favored more highly than the elderly, who are no longer of use to the country, and social misfits such as drug addicts, who do not fit into the social-Darwinist paradigm embraced by many Russians. Yet this preoccupation with the survival of the fittest goes hand in hand with a contradictory preference for helping passive beggars, a core tradition in Russian Orthodoxy. In this context patriotism is particularly powerful, since, as a seemingly eternal value in an ever-changing world, it has become a link between past, present, and future. However, patriotic devotion on the part of the moneyed class clearly ends when it comes to the matter of educating their children, acquiring second homes, and determining where to park their money.

The Young Generation

In the process of coming of age as a new class, Russia's bourgeoisie seems to have discovered its children. Children were largely absent in the 1990s, at least from the lives of my male interviewees who were on their way up the social hierarchy. This does not mean that the *nouveaux riches* of that era did not reproduce, but that the role of family and children in identification processes is far greater today than it was back then. Children and the rituals around them provide their parents with an additional mechanism for reassuring themselves of their social status, and for gaining social distinction. They also present an opportunity for vicarious immortalization.

The younger generation's significance is not limited to meeting their parents' needs, but is also important for the social class as a whole. What children do today matters for the future. Discussions around upbringing generate norms and, as a consequence, contribute to the establishment of identities. This process intensifies the interaction between members of the elite and helps to develop its coherence as a class. The children of the first generation of rich were born into wealth, and therefore money-making has never been their primary concern. This has enabled them to devote their energies to developing new interests that go beyond the limits of business activities. This, in turn, has helped them to establish bourgeois identities.

Young upper-class Russians are fully aware that they will not be able to replicate their parents' success in business, given the unique circumstances of the 1990s and the oil boom in the 2000s. This self-awareness, combined with a large inheritance, might also be one of their strengths. Many of them have developed profiles in spheres other than business. Being less money-focused has encouraged them to internalize new values and attitudes. Increased social exclusivity by means of elite schooling and segregated housing has made their social milieu in some respects more narrow and less adventurous than that of their parents. Yet it would seem, from the interviews I conducted, that the younger generation is happy with this. In general they rebel very little against society, and even less against their parents. Instead, they pursue rather conservative, conformist, and uneccentric life paths.

Russia's *Classe Dominante*

The principal research method applied to the gathering of data for this book was a series of qualitative (biographical narrative) interviews with upper-class Russians. The interview analyses were tested against participant observation, media reports, and expert interviews. The overall conclusion drawn from the data—eighty individual interviews, over a hundred expert interviews, and observations—is that Russia's new upper class has developed stable features similar to those Bourdieu called *la classe dominante*: that is, a social class that, besides economic power, also possesses cultural and social hegemony and the ability to develop transcendent ideas.

Sociological concepts used in research on elites and social class, in particular those of Max Weber, Pierre Bourdieu, and C. Wright Mills, have provided a valuable framework. In contrast to many studies in the field, especially Bourdieusian studies, this book did not measure hard-fact lifestyle components, as manifested particularly in material culture, educational careers, consumption, and pastime activities. Instead, it focused on people's ideas, views, and life concepts as they expressed them in their narratives. I did not initially plan to prioritize these over empirical data on their lifestyles and tastes. In fact, I had not anticipated that the process of bourgeoisification would be that advanced. Surprisingly, the ideas my interviewees expressed about their lives and about Russian society turned out to predominate over descriptions of their lifestyles and tastes in relation to consumerism.

An examination of social milieux indicates that Russia's upper class has developed some level of class-consciousness—or, in Weber's words, *Zusammengehörigkeitsgefühl*, a feeling of belonging together—even though they also show some deeply ingrained distrust and suspicion toward one another. Contradictory, ambivalent, and contested as they might be, members of the new bourgeoisie have their specific and firm views about their role and position at the top of Russian society and in relation to the West. They cherish stability, which, according to Pyotr Aven, is a significant reason why they do not want to rock the boat. Their shared social circles, housing spaces, highbrow cultural activities, and philanthropic commitments constitute the birth of a class they feel they belong to, at least to some extent, regardless of how important their individualism is to them.

This does not mean that my eighty interviewees have completely homogenous views and that the group they belong to constitutes a coherent social agent able to act collectively. On the contrary, many of them are fiercely opposed to each other on many issues. For example, some were active during the anti-Putin protests of 2011 and 2012, while others supported the regime. Some are liberal, some firmly anti-Western, while others hold what are very Soviet-type ideas. All the same, they have many common features, attitudes, and interests, which are generated and regenerated as they interact with one another and, in doing so, influence each other's tastes and views.

Unless the changing political climate brings new, symbolically powerful subcultures to the fore, these new and contradictory patterns of bourgeois identity will become more widespread throughout the upper class and perhaps, in coming years, even among other sections of society. The very fact that these new patterns are so ambiguous and contradictory, combining sophisticated manners and charitable projects with, for example, corrupt business practices, should not surprise us. It is certainly the case that some historically "wolfish" characters, such as the robber barons of the late nineteenth century in the United States, put on sheep's clothing, and never removed it. However, many others retained their ambiguities. We can find examples in classical literature such as Chekhov's *The Cherry Orchard*, in which the social *parvenu*, Lopakhin, seems genuinely to want to help the Ranevsky family, impoverished aristocrats about to lose their estate and their beloved cherry orchard, but then happily sacrifices the orchard himself in order to make money.

In the years to come, we will be able to follow how a social class takes shape due to the accumulation of advantages over time. A whole generation, who gained their first "proper" money in the last three decades and had no tradition they could emulate, will transfer it to their children, and within a relatively short period of time. This will be the biggest transfer of assets within the smallest group of people ever to have occurred. Russia will represent a very obvious example of a country in which the inheritance of accumulated wealth far outweighs any other factors in forming social class. But inheritance is not simply a matter of transferring money to one's children. In this context it is responsible for the creation of a new generation of inheritors who want to be perceived as worthy of receiving that wealth. Powerful everyday ideologies and practices will be essential if the bourgeoisie is to reproduce itself and keep its privileged place in a post-Putin Russia.

Notes

PREFACE AND ACKNOWLEDGMENTS

1. Roland Oliphant, "Russian Court 'Seizes' Britain's Most Expensive Home," *The Telegraph*, May 12, 2016, www.telegraph.co.uk/news/2016/05/12/russian-court-seizes-britains-most-expensive-home/.
2. Kseniia Solov'eva, "Pole Chudes: V Gostiakh u Andreiia Borodina i Evo Zheny v Londone," *Tatler*, March 11, 2015, www.tatler.ru/nashi_lyudi/interview_and_photo_set_21/352520_pole_chudes_v_gostyah_u_andreya_borodina_i_ego_zheni_v_londone.php#p=352531.
3. Shaun Walker, "Russian Oligarch Sergei Polonsky: 'Everyone in Russia Has Gone Mad,'" *The Guardian*, November 11, 2013, www.theguardian.com/world/2013/nov/11/russian-oligarch-sergei-polonsky-arrested; and Anton Chugrinov, "10 Samykh Strannykh Postupov Sergeia Poslonskovo," *Snob*, January 13, 2014, https://snob.ru/selected/entry/70381.
4. Connie Bruck, "The Billionaire's Playlist," *The New Yorker*, January 20, 2014, www.newyorker.com/magazine/2014/01/20/the-billionaires-playlist.

INTRODUCTION

1. All further wealth indicators are taken from *Forbes Russia*, unless otherwise indicated. Billionaires are always dollar billionaires.
2. *Forbes Russia*, "Masshtab Vpechatlenii: Boris Mints Rasskazal Forbes o Svoem Muzee," May 30, 2016, www.forbes.ru/forbeslife/321567-masshtab-vpechatlenii-boris-mints-rasskazal-forbes-o-svoem-muzee.
3. Walter Scheidel, *The Great Leveler: Violence and the History of Inequality from the Stone Age to the Twenty-First Century* (Princeton, NJ: Princeton University Press, 2017), 222.
4. The population shrank by 7 million during the 1990s, with early deaths being more prevalent among poorer and less educated sections of society. Nicholas

Eberstadt, *Russia's Peacetime Demographic Crisis: Dimensions, Causes, Implications* (Seattle, WA: National Bureau of Asian Research, 2010). The sociologist Goran Therborn has claimed that the impact of the privatization programs was comparable to the consequences of the forced collectivization in the 1930s. Goran Therborn, *The Killing Fields of Inequality* (Cambridge: Polity Press, 2013), 8.

5. The World Bank, "Life Expectancy at Birth, Male," accessed June 1, 2015, http://data.worldbank.org/indicator/SP.DYN.LE00.MA.IN?page=4.

6. Chrystia Freeland, *Plutocrats: The Rise of the New Global Super-Rich* (London: Penguin, 2013), 72.

7. A famous example of a novelist who captured the mood of the 1990s is the fiction writer Victor Pelevin, especially his novel *Generation P.* (Moscow: Vagrius, 1999). The novel was subsequently turned into a film by the Russian American arthouse filmmaker Victor Ginzburg. Similarly, in *Dead Man's Bluff*, director Aleksei Balabanov portrays—with Quentin Tarantino–style sardonic humor—two hit men who eventually replace their leather jackets with dark suits and take jobs in the Kremlin bureaucracy. The bestselling novel *Almost Zero* was published under the pseudonym Natan Dubovitsky; the author is widely thought to be Putin's spin doctor Vladislav Surkov. The novel's hero is a former publisher-turned-PR man who makes his money out of copyright piracy and other murky practices, while navigating his way through a highly criminal publishing world. Natan Dubovitsky, "Okolonolia," *Russkii Pioner*, June 29, 2009, http://ruspioner.ru/cool/m/single/2007. Violence and crime were, understandably, rarely the topic of academic research, especially of empirical studies. The Russian sociologist Vadim Volkov was one of the few who took the risk of interviewing members of criminal groups, among them protection companies and law enforcement units, in order to explore the role of organized violence in capital accumulation during the 1990s. Vadim Volkov, *Violent Entrepreneurs: The Use of Force in the Making of Russian Capitalism* (Ithaca, NY: Cornell University Press, 2002). Karen Dawisha carried out meticulous research on the corruption and crime surrounding Putin's rise to power. Her book *Putin's Kleptocracy: Who Owns Russia?* became notorious not least because the prospective publisher got cold feet and turned it down for fear of libel actions. This led to some uneasiness about the extent to which powerful Russians are able to impinge on freedom of speech even beyond the borders of their own country. Subsequently another publisher, Simon & Schuster, acquired the rights to the book and published it: see Karen Dawisha, *Putin's Kleptocracy: Who Owns Russia?* (New York: Simon & Schuster, 2014). For the debate regarding the publisher see *The Economist*, "A Book Too Far," April 3, 2014, www.economist.com/blogs/easternapproaches/2014/04/russia.

8. Ivan Szelényi, Gil Eyal, and Elenor Townsley, *Making Capitalism Without Capitalists: Class Formation and Elite Struggles in Post-Communist Central Europe* (London: Verso, 1998), 166–167.

9. Ferdinand Mount, *The New Few: Or a Very British Oligarchy* (London: Simon & Schuster, 2013), 111; and Anders Åslund, "Comparative Oligarchy: Russia, Ukraine, and the United States," in *Europe After Enlargement*, edited by Anders Åslund and Marek Dąbrowski (Cambridge: Cambridge University Press, 2007), 143–164.

10. Jeffrey A. Winters, *Oligarchy* (Cambridge: Cambridge University Press, 2011), 6–7.

11. The businessman Boris Berezovksy, who went into exile in 2000, died in 2013 in London. His cause, organizing opposition to Putin, has been taken up by the former oil tycoon Mikhail Khodorkovsky. The former long-term mayor of Moscow, Yury Luzhkov, who was ousted in 2010, lives with his billionaire wife Yelena Baturina, in Vienna and London. Little has been heard about the former media tycoon Vladimir Gusinsky, who, after falling into disgrace with Putin, fled to Spain in 2000. The former banker Alexander Smolensky, who was caught up in the 1998 financial crisis, has since kept a similarly low profile. David E. Hoffman, *The Oligarchs: Wealth and Power in the New Russia*, 3rd ed. (New York: PublicAffairs, 2011). Before his death Berezovksy held a whole generation of writers and filmmakers under his spell. A novel based loosely on his biography, *Bol'shaia Paika (The Big Slice)*, was subsequently turned into the movie *Tycoon*, which depicts the rise and fall of an oligarch and ends with his death—a premonition of Berezovsky's own fate a decade later. Yuli Dubov, *Bol'shaia Paika* (Moscow: Vagrius, 2005). The writer Ben Mezrich retold Berezovsky's story after the oligarch's death. Ben Mezrich, *Once Upon a Time in Russia: The Rise of the Oligarchs and the Greatest Wealth in History* (London: William Heinemann, 2015).

12. Chrystia Freeland, *Sale of the Century: The Inside Story of the Second Russian Revolution* (London: Little, Brown, 2000).

13. Fiona Hill and Clifford G. Gaddy, *Mr. Putin: Operative in the Kremlin* (Washington, DC: Brookings Institution Press, 2013), 37.

14. As soon as the state bureaucracy under Putin rose in numbers and visibility, a lively discussion about its influence on Russian politics broke out. Some analysts concluded that the *siloviki* had taken control of the state, whereas others questioned this level of influence. See, for example, Ol'ga Kryshtanovskaia and Stephen White, "The Sovietization of Russian Politics," *Post-Soviet Affairs* 25, no. 4 (2009): 283–309; versus Bettina Renz, "Putin's Militocracy? An Alternative Interpretation of Siloviki in Contemporary Russian Politics," *Europe-Asia Studies* 58, no. 6 (2006): 903–924; and David W. Rivera and Sharon W. Rivera, "Is Russia a Militocracy? Conceptual Issues and Extant Findings Regarding Elite Militarization," *Post-Soviet Affairs* 30, no. 1 (2014): 27–50. The most comprehensive account of the *siloviki* was produced by the investigative journalists Andrei Soldatov and Irina Borogan, *The New Nobility: The Restoration of Russia's Security State and the Enduring Legacy of the KGB* (New York: PublicAffairs, 2010).

15. Daniel Treisman, "Russia's Billionaires," *American Economic Review: Papers &
    Proceedings* 106, no. 5 (2016): 238.

16. The 2006 novel *Soulless* by the then alcohol merchant and now television and
    radio presenter Sergey Minaev tells the story of an affluent late-twenties banker
    who misses just one thing in his fast-car and cocaine-filled life: genuine love.
    This bestseller was later turned into a black-comedy drama. Sergei Minaev,
    Dukhless: Povest' o Nenastoiashchem Cheloveke (Moscow: AST, 2006). Conflict
    between the aging first generation of wealth and their offspring who are now
    coming of age is another topic that has preoccupied filmmakers. In Anna
    Melikyan's 2014 film *Zvezda [Star]*, an oligarch wife becomes friends with her
    husband's rebellious son only when she is facing a terminal illness and discov-
    ers that life does not require luxury. In *Elena*, a 2011 drama directed by Andrey
    Zvyagintsev about another oligarch wife, the title character goes so far as to mur-
    der her husband to get his money in order to secure the future of her son and
    grandson from her first marriage, whom her husband dislikes. The ambiguity, if
    not schizophrenic, nature of Russia's rich was described by the British film pro-
    ducer and writer Peter Pomerantsev in his book *Nothing Is True and Everything Is
    Possible* (New York: PublicAffairs, 2014).

17. Mikhail Zygar', *Vsia Kremlevskaia Rat': Kratkaia Istoriia Sovremennoi Rossii*
    (Moscow: Intellektual'naia Literatura, 2016), 63.

18. The share of the poor in Russia dropped from 35.6 million in 2002 to 15.7 mil-
    lion people in 2013, or from 24.6 percent to 11 percent of the population. In
    contrast to this general trend, however, the situation for the remaining poor
    became much worse between the early 2000s and the mid-2010s. They turned
    into an isolated self-reproducing social group with a distinct socioprofessional
    composition and life chances. The Russian economists Natalia Tikhonova and
    Svetlana Mareeva call this group the "new periphery," which risks reproducing
    absolute poverty across generations. Thus, during a time when the upper class
    took clearer shape and a lifestyle detached from the rest of society, with a rapid
    accumulation of cultural, social, and economic resources, this new periphery
    also grew increasingly separated from the rest of Russian society, with a sharp
    decline in the quality of cultural and human capital. Natalia E. Tikhonova and
    Svetlana V. Mareeva, "Poverty in Contemporary Russian Society: Formation of a
    New Periphery," *Russian Politics* 1, no. 2 (2016): 162.

19. The World Bank, "World Data Bank 2016," accessed on February 14, 2017,
    http://databank.worldbank.org/data/reports.aspx?Code=SI.POV.GINI&id=
    af3ce82b&report_name=Popular_indicators&populartype=series&ispopular=y;
    and Thomas F. Remington, *The Politics of Inequality in Russia* (Cambridge:
    Cambridge University Press, 2011), 1.

20. In Russia in 2013 there was a billionaire for every $11 billion in household
    wealth, as compared to a global ratio of one billionaire for every $170 billion. One
    hundred ten billionaires owned 35 percent of all wealth in Russia. Giles Keating,

Michael O'Sullivan, Anthony Shorrocks, James B. Davies, Rodrogo Lluberas, and Antonios Koutsoukis, *Global Wealth Report 2013*, Credit Suisse Research Institute (Zurich: Credit Suisse AG, 2013), 53. In 2015 the top 10 percent of the population controlled 87 percent of all household wealth in Russia, a ratio significantly higher than in the United States, where the richest 10 percent controlled 76 percent, or in China, where the equivalent figure was 66 percent. Markus Stierli, Anthony Shorrocks, James Davies, Rodrogo Lluberas, and Antonio Koutsoukis, *Global Wealth Report 2015*, Credit Suisse Research Institute (Zurich: Credit Suisse AG, 2015), 53.

21. Anthony Shorrocks, James Davies, and Rodrogo Lluberas, *Global Wealth Report 2014*, Credit Suisse Research Institute (Zurich: Credit Suisse AG, 2014), 31, 53. Wealth inequality is greater than income inequality in almost every country, both because of enormously wealthy individuals on the one hand and one-quarter to one-third of the population on the other that has negative or zero net wealth, even in the advanced countries. Branko Milanovic, *Global Inequality: A New Approach for the Age of Globalization* (Cambridge, MA: The Belknap Press of Harvard University Press, 2016), 39.

22. One problem for Russia was that there was not much to fall back on. Despite the long oil boom in the 2000s, Russia did not manage to overtake Romania, Belarus, and Uruguay on the UNDP Human Development Index: "Human Development Reports 2014," *UNDP*, accessed November 12, 2015, http://hdr .undp.org/en/data. Families with children were the largest group to drift into poverty. The share of families with children under sixteen among the income-based poor jumped from 36.2 percent in 2014 to 62.9 percent in 2015. Tikhonova and Mareeva, "Poverty in Contemporary Russian Society," 162.

23. While this is the official number of billionaires, according to *Forbes*, many estimate that the real figure is two or three times higher. As state officials' wealth tends to be somewhat intangible, as in the case of the former head of the Russian Railways Vladimir Yakunin, *Forbes* is unable to accurately access it, a *Forbes Russia* editor explained to me in 2016. The Super-rich in private business often spread their assets across family members in order to avoid publicity and pressure from the state, criminal structures, and the public.

24. Freeland, *Plutocrats*, 193.

25. See, for example, Treisman, "Russia's Billionaires"; Yuko Adachi, *Building Big Business in Russia: The Impact of Informal Corporate Governance Practices* (London: Routledge, 2010); and Stephen Fortescue, *Russia's Oil Barons and Metal Magnates: Oligarchs and the State in Transition* (Basingstoke: Palgrave Macmillan, 2006).

26. A famous early exception was the sociologist Olga Kryshtanovskaya, who scrutinized Russia's elites very closely in the 2000s. Ol'ga Kryshtanovskaia, *Anatomiia Rossiiskoi Elity* (Moskva: A. V. Solov'eva, 2004). A notable recent exception is a 2015 research project carried out by the Skolkovo Wealth

Transformation Centre, overseen by impact investor and social entrepreneur Ruben Vardanyan. The features they observed among rich Russians are very similar to the findings in this book. Skolkovo Wealth Transformation Centre, *Russia's Wealth Possessors Study* (Moscow: Skolkovo Wealth Transformation Centre, 2015).

27. Birgit Menzel, "Russian Discourse on Glamour," *Kultura, Russian Cultural Review* 6 (December 2008): 4–8; Helena Goscilo and Vlad Strukov, *Celebrity and Glamour in Contemporary Russia: Shocking Chic* (London: Routledge, 2011); and Saara Ratilainen, "Business for Pleasure: Elite Women in the Russian Popular Media," in *Rethinking Class in Russia*, edited by Suvi Salmenniemi (Burlington, VT: Ashgate), 45–66.

28. Stephen White, for example, raises concerns even about the use of the term "class" in relation to Russia, arguing that distinctive developments might require distinctive vocabulary. Stephen White, *Politics and the Ruling Group in Putin's Russia* (New York: Palgrave Macmillan, 2002), xiii.

29. See, for example, Peter Rutland, "The Anatomy of the Russian Elite," in *The Palgrave Handbook on Political Elites*, edited by John Higley (Basingstoke: Palgrave Macmillan, 2018), 273–294; David Lane, *Elites and Identities in Post-Soviet Space* (London: Routledge, 2012); Michael Urban, *Cultures of Power in Post-Communist Russia: An Analysis of Elite Political Discourse* (New York: Cambridge University Press, 2010); Vladimir Shlapentokh, "Wealth Versus Political Power. The Russian Case," *Communist and Post-Communist Studies* 37, no. 29 (2004): 135–160; Vladimir Shlapentokh, "Social Inequality in Post-Communist Russia: The Attitudes of the Political Elite and the Masses (1991–1998)," *Europe-Asia Studies* 51, no. 7 (1999): 1167–1181; and Anton Steen and Vladimir Gel'man, *Elites and Democratic Development in Russia* (London: Routledge, 2003).

30. Thorstein Veblen, *The Theory of the Leisure Class* (New York: Dover Publications, 1994 [1899]).

31. Werner Sombart, *Luxury and Capitalism*, introduction by Philip Siegelman (Ann Arbor: University of Michigan Press, 1967 [1913]).

32. Georg Simmel, *Über soziale Differenzierung: Soziologische und psychologische Untersuchungen*, Duncker & Humbolt, 1890, accessed April 15, 2009, http://socio.ch/sim/differenzierung/index.htm; and Georg Simmel, "Die Mode," in *Philosophische Kultur*, 2nd ed. (Leipzig: Alfred Kröner Verlag, 1919), 25–57.

33. Max Weber, "Economy and Society: An Outline of Interpretive Sociology," translation of 4th German edition of *Wirtschaft und Gesellschaft*, edited by Guenther Roth and Claus Wittich (Berkeley: University of California Press, 1978 [1922]), 305–306, 927–937.

34. C. Wright Mills, *The Power Elite* (Oxford: Oxford University Press, 2000 [1956]), 11, 86.

35. Eric Hobsbawm, *Age of Extremes: The Short Twentieth Century, 1914–1991* (London: Michael Joseph, 1994), 225–400.

36. Pierre Bourdieu, "The Forms of Capital," in *Handbook of Theory and Research for the Sociology of Education*, edited by John G. Richardson (New York: Greenwood Press, 1986), 241–258; and Pierre Bourdieu, *Distinction: A Social Critique of the Judgment of Taste* (London: Routledge & Kegan Paul, 1984).

37. Michèle Lamont, *Money, Morals, and Manners: The Culture of the French and American Upper-Middle Class* (Chicago: University of Chicago Press, 1992). For more on the French bourgeoisie see also Michel Pinçon and Monique Pinçon-Charlot, *Grand Fortunes: Dynasties of Wealth in France* (New York: Algora Publishing, 1998).

38. Khan defines elites as those who enjoy vastly disproportional access to, or control over, resources such as political influence, economic power, status, and prestige. Shamus R. Khan, *Privilege: The Making of an Adolescent Elite at St. Paul's School* (Princeton, NJ: Princeton University Press, 2011); and Shamus R. Khan, "The Sociology of Elites," *Annual Review of Sociology* 38 (2012): 362.

39. Rachel Sherman, "Conflicted Cultivation: Parenting, Privilege, and Moral Worth in Wealthy New York Families," *American Journal of Cultural Sociology* 5, no. 1–2 (2016): 1–33; and Sherman, *Uneasy Street: The Anxieties of Affluence* (Princeton, NJ: Princeton University Press, 2017).

40. Michael Hartmann, *The Sociology of Elites* (New York: Routledge, 2006); and Michael Hartmann, *Die Globale Wirtschaftselite: Eine Legende* (Frankfurt/M.: Campus, 2016).

41. Jean-Pascal Daloz, *The Sociology of Elite Distinction: From Theoretical to Comparative Perspectives* (Basingstoke: Palgrave Macmillan, 2009); and Jean-Pascal Daloz, *Rethinking Social Distinction* (Basingstoke: Palgrave Macmillan, 2013).

42. Thomas Piketty, *Capital in the Twenty-First Century* (Cambridge, MA: The Belknap Press of Harvard University Press, 2014). The French version was published in 2013 and the English translation in 2014. Other important works are Anthony B. Atkinson, *Inequality: What Can Be Done?* (Cambridge, MA: Harvard University Press, 2015); Anthony B. Atkinson and Thomas Piketty, eds., *Top Incomes: A Global Perspective* (Oxford: Oxford University Press, 2010); and Danny Dorling, *Inequality and the 1%* (London: Verso, 2014).

43. Mike Savage, "Piketty's Challenge for Sociology," *British Journal of Sociology* 65, no. 4 (2014): 591–606; Mike Savage, "From the 'Problematic of the Proletariat' to a Class Analysis of 'Wealth Elites,'" *Sociological Review* 63, no. 2 (2015): 233; Mike Savage, *Social Class in the 21st Century* (London: Pelican, 2015); and Mike Savage and Karel Williams, *Remembering Elites* (Oxford: Wiley-Blackwell, 2008).

44. The last point is important with regards to those interviewees included in this study who derive their position not purely on the basis of economic resources, but have enough of these other resources to be able to convert them into other forms of capital if they wish. These include some politicians and media celebrities. Although most of them have for a considerable amount of time engaged in highly lucrative business activities, I originally decided to include them for the other resources they possess, such as powerful social networks and influence

over millions of people. Conversely, this also meant that I excluded many top managers who might have earned a small fortune during the height of the oil boom in the mid-2000s, but did not have much to rely on if they lost their positions after the 2008 economic downturn.

45. My understanding of "bourgeoisie" is very similar to the one put forward by the social historian Sven Beckert. In his book *The Monied Metropolis*, Beckert calls New York City's nineteenth-century economic elite "bourgeoisie." This term encompasses those who shared a specific position in the city's social structure in that they owned and invested capital, employed wage workers (or at least servants), and did not work for wages themselves. Among the bourgeoisie were merchants, industrialists, bankers, rentiers, and real estate speculators. This group accumulated unprecedented economic, social, and political power, and by the Gilded Age had metamorphosed into a social class. Sven Beckert, *The Monied Metropolis: New York City and the Consolidation of the American Bourgeoisie, 1850–1896* (Cambridge: Cambridge University Press, 2001), 7.

46. Karl Marx and Friedrich Engels, *The German Ideology. Part One* (New York: International Publishers, 1970), 64.

47. Bourdieu, *Distinction*.

48. For varying definitions and uses of the term in a cultural context of France see Béatrix Le Wita, *French Bourgeois Culture*, translated by J. A. Underwood (Cambridge: Cambridge University Press, 1994).

49. Leon Trotsky, *The History of the Russian Revolution*, translated by Max Eastman (London: Pluto Press, 1977), 23–37.

50. In the Soviet Union the term "bourgeoisie" came to be used pejoratively in relation to the philistine values of the aspiring middle classes, the "petty/petit bourgeoisie." The literary scholar Vera S. Dunham described the petit-bourgeois middle-class layers of the late Stalin era with the term *meshchanstvo*. Vera S. Dunham, *In Stalin's Time: Middleclass Values in Soviet Fiction* (Cambridge: Cambridge University Press, 1976). In post–Soviet Russia, the Russian "bourgeois" (*burzhui*) was initially used ironically for businessmen with a lifestyle exclusively orientated toward consumerism. In the present day, rich people frequently use the term in reference to themselves and their peers—usually not with a derogatory meaning.

51. Marx himself described a somewhat similar phenomenon in his writings on France at the time of Louis Napoleon after 1848. Karl Marx, *Der achtzehnte Brumaire des Louis Bonaparte*, 3rd ed. (Hamburg: Otto Meißner, 1885), accessed July 2, 2016, http://digital.staatsbibliothek-berlin.de/werkansicht?PPN=PPN633 609536&PHYSID=PHYS_0001&DMDID=.

52. Max Weber, *From Max Weber: Essays in Sociology*, translated and edited by Hans Heinrich Gerth and C. Wright Mills (London: Routledge, 1991), 271.

53. According to a 2014 survey carried out by the Levada Center, 49 percent of Russians think that it has never been possible in post–Soviet Russia to make big money by honest means. Another 10 percent think dishonesty was on the agenda fifteen

to twenty years ago but that today one can go down an honest route, whereas another 15 percent assess the contemporary situation as worthy. Levada–Center, "Rossiiane o Biznese i Biznesmenakh," November 5, 2014, www.levada.ru/ 2014/11/05/rossiyane-o-biznese-i-biznesmenah/,Levada-Center.

54. Georg Simmel, "Exkurs über den Adel," in *Soziologie: Untersuchungen über die Formen der Vergesellschaftung*, edited by Georg Simmel (Frankfurt/M.: Suhrkamp, 1992 [1908]), 820.

55. Apart from half a dozen who moved to the West, most of them live in Moscow; a handful live in other cities, such as St. Petersburg; Siberia's biggest city, Novosibirsk; or Siberian oil towns. Most of them are in business; a small number are in politics. Their business activities include natural resources, finance and banking, new technologies, arms, heavy industry, aviation, consumer product manufacturing, retail, legal services, property development, marketing, and media.

56. Russ Alan Prince and Bruce Rogers, "Marketing Luxury to the Super-Rich," *Forbes*, October 8, 2012, www.forbes.com/sites/russprince/2012/10/08/marketing-luxury-to-the-super-rich/#3cac2d375df5.

57. Milanovic, *Global Inequality*, 43.

58. Anthony Shorrocks et al., *Credit Suisse Wealth Report 2016*, Credit Suisse Research Institute (Zurich: Credit Suisse AG, 2016), 26.

59. Shorrocks, *Global Wealth Report 2014*, 25; and Stierli, *Global Wealth Report 2015*, 43. Prior to the 2008 financial crisis, in 2007, about 200,000 families in Russia (about 0.37 percent of all families) had annual incomes of over $1 million, according to a survey conducted by the state insurance company Rosgosstrakh. Thomas F. Remington, "The Russian Middle Class as Policy Objective," *Post-Soviet Affairs* 27, no. 2 (2011): 98.

60. Daniel Bertaux and Paul Thompson, *Pathways to Social Class: A Qualitative Approach to Social Mobility* (Oxford: Clarendon Press, 1997); and Daniel Bertaux, Paul Thompson, and Anna Rotkirch, *Living Through Soviet Russia* (London: Routledge, 2004).

61. I traveled numerous times to Moscow between the spring and summer of 2008, that is, before the financial crisis, up to 2017. To select my subjects, I went through rich lists, primarily *Forbes-200*, published in *Forbes Russia*, and *Finans*, a finance weekly that existed until 2011. More than a third of the people represented in the sample included in this book are mentioned on these lists. As expected, it was not easy to get the interviews and I used a range of approaches to claw my way in. In many cases I relied on the help of other people—friends, acquaintances, or people I simply approached for this purpose—some of whom organized interviews, put me in touch with other people, invited me to social events, or helped me receive press accreditation. One of the first steps to an interview was to get a potential interviewee's phone number, ideally the private mobile phone number. Although unsolicited phone calls are considered intrusive in Russia as they are almost

anywhere, they are still more accepted there than in other European societies. What worked in my favor was that few people had qualms about handing
over a number to a third party. Once I had a phone number, there was a good
chance that the person would at least talk to me, if not agree to an interview.
Undoubtedly, my own bearing influenced people's replies—(and this was not
necessarily in my favor); first, that I am from the West, second, that I am female.
The large majority of my interviewees were male, and I suspect that a male
researcher would have been more likely to hear revealing stories. Female interviewees did confide personal stories to me, but as there were many fewer of
them, the number of such stories was limited. Moreover, two years into my
research and after three rounds of intense interviewing I finally became aware
that to many Russians an unmarried woman in her late twenties could only have
chosen a research topic such as mine with the aim of trying to benefit from (presumably male) contacts gained. Once I got this point, dismissiveness (usually
from males) and hostility (usually from females) made perfect sense.

62. Investigative research was neither my aim, nor would it have been realistic.
In any case, here, again, being female would have been a disadvantage. One
example is Gerry, a hyperenergetic, ever-jolly, down-to-earth Essex man, who
looks after the needs of rich Russians in the UK, dealing with everything from
suburban real estate to central London real estate and from bespoke or designer
handbags for "girlfriends number 4 and 5, the one for Tuesdays and the one
for Wednesdays." When drinking and partying with his clients, and after everybody has a glass of vodka too many, Gerry sometimes hears their darkest secrets.
Some of them, for example, tell him (not "confess to him"—there was no feeling
of guilt involved, Gerry assured me) of the people they had physically eliminated
when, in the early days, they were doing business back home in Russia. I had
no way of knowing whether my interviewees' world of more discerning, cautious tastes, values, and interests excluded those features that. This was a side of
their identity that they would certainly be more willing to share with Gerry than
with me.

63. Michèle Lamont and Ann Swidler, "Methodological Pluralism and the Possibilities
and Limits of Interviewing," *Qualitative Sociology* 37, no. 2 (2014): 159.

64. Steph Lawler, *Identity: Sociological Perspectives*, 2nd ed. (Cambridge: Polity
Press), 24–33.

65. On the benefits of participant observation see Colin Jerolmack and Shamus Khan,
"Talk Is Cheap: Ethnography and the Attitudinal Fallacy," *Sociological Methods &
Research* 43, no. 2 (2014): 178–209; and Shamus Khan, "Saying Meritocracy and
Doing Privilege," *Sociological Quarterly* 54, no. 1 (2013): 9–19.

66. I never intended to and I did not ask the interviewees about their earnings and
sources of incomes. In some cases their wealth was publicly known; they were
either listed on the Russian *Forbes* rich list, were easily classifiable in other ways,
or I received information from a third person, usually the contact person.

67. Following the interviews I transcribed them, usually in full, and classified them. I then translated the sections of the interviews that I wanted to analyze. I was particularly interested in how people constructed and presented their identities and produced their own selves through narrating their biographies, making statements and judgments, and talking about their values, worldviews, and plans. In the next stage of the analysis, I compared the results from the narrative interviews with the expert interviews as well as with contextual data and journalistic material, mainly from online media, and participant observations.

68. See, for example, Kryshtanovskaia, *Anatomiia Rossiiskoi Elity*, 341–342.

69. In the citations Russian names and titles are spelled according to the Library of Congress system. In the main text, however, I transliterated Russian names according to a simplified form of the BGN/PCGN Romanization system of Russian. This simplified version allows converting "ë" to "yo" (for example, Petr becomes Pyotr), simplifying "-ii," "-iy," and "-yy" endings to "-y" (for example, Arkadii becomes Arkady), and omitting apostrophes for "ъ" and "ь" (for example, Ol'ga becomes Olga). Names ending in "ei" are usually shown as "ey" (for example, Andrey and Sergey), but not in cases where famous people predominantly use "ey" (for example, Sergei Eisenstein). "K" turns in many names to "c" and "ks" to "x" (for example, in Victor and Alexander), apart from, again, cases when people routinized a different spelling (for example, Viktor Vekselberg and Ksenia Sobchak). Some interviewees insisted on a specific spelling (for example, David Yakobashvili, who wished his name to be spelled Iakobachvili).

70. Bourdieu, *Distinction*, 6.

71. Bourdieu saw the ability to evaluate styles and assess others as part of "symbolic capital." Pierre Bourdieu, "Social Space and Symbolic Power," *Sociological Theory* 7, no. 1 (1989): 14–25.

72. The intelligentsia consists of professionals engaged in the cultural and educational sectors and, in the case of the Soviet intelligentsia, also includes academically trained technicians, who have historically played a major role in the country's cultural and political development.

73. Others were very unhelpful in all possible ways. Timofey, an eccentric wealth manager, was not in the slightest bit interested in replying to my questions. The three-hour interview included myriad diversions, such as his complex Asian tea ceremonies, long stories about how he confronted a bear in the Siberian taiga, a demonstration of his knife throwing skills, and a tedious game in which Timofey kept moving closer to me on the couch in his penthouse flat off Kutuzovsky Avenue, and I kept moving away.

CHAPTER 1

1. Ernst's mood was less expansive a year and a half later when, through his public relations representative, he asked that I describe my interview with him only in

general terms and avoid quoting him directly, except when the quotations concerned matters that he had publicly discussed before. Since he has not given an
interview for years, I have omitted many quotations that I wanted to include.

2. Federico Varese, *The Russian Mafia: Private Protection in a New Market Economy*
(Oxford: Oxford University Press, 2001), 55–72. For a journalistic account of the
early post-Soviet period see John Kampfner, *Inside Yeltsin's Russia: Corruption,
Conflict, Capitalism* (London: Cassell, 1994).

3. Ben Mezrich, *Once Upon a Time in Russia: The Rise of the Oligarchs and the
Greatest Wealth in History* (London: William Heinemann, 2015), 60ff; Arkady
Ostrovsky, *The Invention of Russia: The Journey from Gorbachev's Freedom to Putin's
War* (London: Atlantic Books, 2015), 313.

4. Lawrence P. King, "Postcommunist Divergence: A Comparative Analysis of
the Transition to Capitalism in Poland and Russia," *Studies in Comparative
International Development* 37, no. 3 (2002): 14.

5. Freeland, *Sale of the Century*, 24.

6. Petr Aven and Alfred Kokh, *Gaidar's Revolution: The Inside Account of the Economic
Transformation of Russia* (London: I. B. Tauris, 2015), 39–44.

7. Caroline Freund, *Rich People, Poor Countries: The Rise of Emerging-Market Tycoons
and Their Mega Firms* (Washington, DC: Peterson Institute for International
Economics, 2016), 42.

8. Maksim Boycko, Andrei Schleifer, and Robert Vishny, *Privatizing Russia*
(Cambridge, MA: MIT Press, 1995).

9. Freeland, *Sale of the Century*, 112.

10. See, for example, Graeme Gill, *Bourgeoisie, State, and Democracy: Russia, France,
Germany, and the USA* (Oxford: Oxford University Press, 2008), 66–105.

11. By the time of the auctions Pyotr Aven had long left the government.

12. Vladimir Potanin, born in 1961, the son of a senior Soviet foreign-trade official,
spent his childhood in Yemen, New Zealand, and Turkey, among other places,
and then graduated from the prestigious Moscow State Institute of International
Relations (MGIMO). He stood out among the oligarchs for being a proper scion
of the Soviet top elite and, more importantly, for being the only ethnic Russian
among the new oligarchs, most of whom were Jewish.

13. Andrew Barnes, *Owning Russia: The Struggle over Factories, Farms, and Power*
(Ithaca, NY: Cornell University Press, 2006), 110–115; and Joseph R. Blasi, Maya
Kroumova, and Douglas Kruse, *Kremlin Capitalism: The Privatization of the
Russian Economy* (Ithaca, NY: Cornell University Press, 1997), 75.

14. Mikhail Glazunov, *Business in Post-Communist Russia: Privatisation and the Limits
of Transformation* (London: Routledge, 2013), 22.

15. Stephen Fortescue, *Russia's Oil Barons and Metal Magnates: Oligarchs and the
State in Transition* (Basingstoke: Palgrave Macmillan, 2006), 55.

16. David E. Hoffman, *The Oligarchs: Wealth and Power in the New Russia* (New York:
PublicAffairs, 3rd ed., 2011), 312–315.

17. Hoffman, *The Oligarchs*, 351; and Ostrovsky, *The Invention of Russia*, 209–214.

18. Freeland, *Sale of the Century*, 121–126.

19. Ivan Zassoursky, *Media and Power in Post-Soviet Russia* (Armonk, NY: M. E. Sharpe, 2002), 85.

20. Hoffman, *The Oligarchs*, 433–434.

21. Patrick Hamm, Lawrence P. King, and David Stuckler, "Mass-Privatization, State Capacity, and Economic Growth in Post-Communist Countries," *American Sociological Review* 77, no. 2 (2012): 295–324.

22. "Corporate raiding" refers to the abuse of the judicial system to seize control of rival companies. Stanislav Markus, *Property, Predation, and Protection: Piranha Capitalism in Russia and Ukraine* (Cambridge: Cambridge University Press, 2015). The hedge fund owner Bill Browder reflected on his encounter with Russian-type raiding, which led to the death of his lawyer and friend Sergei Magnitsky, in *Red Notice: How I Became Putin's No. 1 Enemy* (London: Bantam Press, 2015).

23. Hoffman, *The Oligarchs*, 447.

24. Simon Pirani, *Change in Putin's Russia: Power, Money and People* (London: Pluto, 2010), 29. Capital flight gained strength again after the onset of the 2008 economic crisis, when, after the Wall Street crash, net outflow was greater than the net inflow in the two preceding years. Pirani, *Change in Putin's Russia*, 97.

25. Masha Gessen, *The Man Without a Face: The Unlikely Rise of Vladimir Putin* (New York: Granta, 2012), 15–22. Michael Zygar cautions about overestimating Berezovsky's role in those years. Mikhail Zygar', *Vsia Kremlevskaia Rat': Kratkaia Istoriia Sovremennoi Rossii* (Moscow: Intellektual'naia Literatura, 2016), 13.

26. The understanding that oligarchs such as Berezovsky were corrupt was substantiated in the portrait of him that appeared in the book *Godfather of the Kremlin*, written by Paul Klebnikov, then editor-in-chief of *Forbes Russia*. Paul Klebnikov, *Godfather of the Kremlin: The Life and Times of Boris Berezovsky* (New York: Harcourt, 2000). Klebnikov was assassinated in 2004. It was widely believed that his publications angered some of the rich and powerful he had so vividly depicted. See, for example, Richard Behar, "Kremlin Hits Back After Forbes Editor Paul Klebnikov's Alleged Killer and Others Denied U.S. Visas," *Forbes*, April 13, 2013, www.forbes.com/sites/richardbehar/2013/04/13/kremlin-hits-back-after-forbes-editor-paul-klebnikovs-alleged-killer-and-others-denied-u-s-visas/#70a9ef5e1b79.

27. Richard Sakwa, *Putin and the Oligarch: The Khodorkovsky-Yukos Affair* (London: I. B. Tauris, 2014), 61–67.

28. Thane Gustafson, *Wheel of Fortune: The Battle for Oil and Power in Russia* (Cambridge, MA: The Belknap Press of Harvard University Press, 2012), 297.

29. Henry Meyer, Ilya Arkhipov, and Jake Rudnitsky, "Putin's Pardon of Tycoon Buoys Russia Before Sochi Games," *Bloomberg*, December 20, 2013, www.bloomberg.com/news/articles/2013-12-20/khodorkovsky-free-after-10-years-in-prison-as-putin-signs-pardon.

30. Pirani, *Change in Putin's Russia*, 195.

31. Fiona Hill and Clifford G. Gaddy, *Mr. Putin: Operative in the Kremlin* (Washington, DC: Brookings Institution Press, 2013), 227. In 2013 Rosneft utilized government support to facilitate its takeover of TNK-BP, the merger of BP and the Russian oil company TNK controlled by Alfa Group, a large oil, industrial, trading, and financial conglomerate.

32. Putin's childhood friend and judo trainer Arkady Rotenberg more than doubled his fortune from $1 billion in 2016 to $2.6 billion in 2017. Another judo-loving friend of Putin, Gennady Timchenko, saw his wealth go up by $4.6 billion in 2016, which placed him in the *Forbes* 2017 list at $16 billion. Putin's friends from the Ozero dacha cooperative near St Petersburg on the shore of Lake Komsomolskoye also did well, including Andrey Fursenko, who was subsequently minister of education; Vladimir Yakunin, later head of Russian Railways; and Yury Kovalchuk, head of Bank Rossiya and owner of major Russian media outlets. All of these people ended up on the US or the EU 2014 sanctions lists, facing visa bans and asset seizure, partly because of their close ties to Putin, which allegedly brought them many benefits. For example, in the case of Rotenberg, there were alleged contracts relating to the Sochi Winter Olympics. For more on Putin and his cronies see Yuri Felshtinsky and Vladimir Pribylovsky, *The Age of Assassins: The Rise and Rise of Vladimir Putin* (London: Gibson Square, 2008), 256; and Karen Dawisha, *Putin's Kleptocracy: Who Owns Russia?* (New York: Simon & Schuster, 2014); as well as journalists' accounts, for example, by Dan Alexander, "Russian Billionaires, Including Several Tied to Putin, Are Up $104 Billion in the Last Year," *Forbes*, March 29, 2017, www.forbes.com/sites/danalexander/2017/03/29/putin-vladimir-donald-trump-russia-billionaires-oligarchs/#43f9b8ad43f9.

33. *Vesti.ru*, "Gref: Itogi Privatizatsii ne Budut Peresmotreny," July 10, 2003, www.vesti.ru/doc.html?id=29550.

34. Hilary Appel and Mitchell A. Orenstein, "Why Did Neoliberalism Triumph and Endure in the Post-Communist World?" *Comparative Politics* (April 2016): 313–331.

35. Pirani, *Change in Putin's Russia*, 94.

36. These years brought oilmen back into the game. Vagit Alekperov, deputy minister of oil and gas between 1990 and 1991 and since 1993 president of Lukoil, Russia's largest private oil company, increased his private wealth to $14.8 billion by 2013. Meanwhile, Roman Abramovich, who later became the owner of Chelsea Football Club and the oil company Sibneft, which he bought together with Berezovsky in the loans-for-shares auctions, led the *Forbes Russia* list from 2005 to 2008 with an average net worth of $13.1 billion. In terms of wealth, Abramovich was supplanted by Oleg Deripaska in 2008, who made his fortune from aluminum (with a peak of $16.8 billion in 2011). Vladimir Lisin (metal and steel; $16.1 in 2017) was the richest Russian in 2010 and 2011, and many others were continuously in the top ten, such as Viktor Vekselberg (aluminum and oil; with a peak of $17.2 billion in 2014), and Alexey Mordashov (steel; with

a peak of $18.5 billion in 2011). With $18.4 billion Leonid Mikhelson was the richest Russian in both 2016 and 2017. He made his money with Novatek, a gas giant. For more see *Forbes Russia* and specifically Elena Berezankskaia, "Zavsegdateli Kluba Milliarderov: 10 Samykh Stabil'no Bogatykh Liudei Rossii," *Forbes Russia*, April 18, 2016.

37. Fortescue, *Russia's Oil Barons and Metal Magnates*.

38. Peter Rutland, "The Anatomy of the Russian Elite," in *The Palgrave Handbook on Political Elites*, edited by John Higley (Basingstoke: Palgrave Macmillan, 2018), 273–294.

39. Markus Stierli et al., *Global Wealth Report 2015*, Credit Suisse Research Institute (Zurich: Credit Suisse AG, 2015), 28. See also Daniel Treisman, "Russia's Billionaires," *American Economic Review: Papers & Proceedings* 106, no. 5 (2016): 236–241, 239.

40. Freeland, *Plutocrats*, 150.

41. An example of such a joint venture was Most, set up in 1989 between the US legal firm Arnold and Porter and Vladimir Gusinsky. Eventually, in the 1990s, Gusinksy bought out his American partners. Fortescue, *Russia's Oil Barons and Metal Magnates*, 26.

42. It may seem strange that an institution like the *Komsomol*, that ostensibly supported Soviet rule, should have played such a role in nurturing new capitalist practices incubating private enterprise. Scholars have explained the paradox. The historian Alexei Yurchak, for example, has argued that the *Komsomol*'s economic, cultural, and ideological activity taught its leaders a pragmatic understanding of work, time, money, skills, and professional relations. It also invested its members with a first-hand insight into the hybrid understandings of the official plans, rules, laws, and institutions of the party-state. Alexei Yurchak, "Entrepreneurial Governmentality in Postsocialist Russia: A Cultural Investigation of Business Practices," in *The New Entrepreneurs of Europe and Asia: Patterns of Business Development in Russia, Eastern Europe, and China*, edited by Victoria E. Bonnell and Thomas B. Gold (Armonk, NY: M. E. Sharpe, 2002), 282.

43. Hoffman, *The Oligarchs*, 100–101.

44. For more on this process see Steven L. Solnick, *Stealing the State: Control and Collapse in Soviet Institutions* (Cambridge, MA: Harvard University Press, 1998), 115–117.

45. Freeland, *Sale of the Century*, 117.

46. Freeland, *Plutocrats*, 150.

47. Hoffman, *The Oligarchs*, 107.

48. Freeland, *Sale of the Century*, 115.

49. Zvi Gitelman, cited in Judith D. Kornblatt, *Doubly Chosen: Jewish Identity, the Soviet Intelligentsia, and the Russian Orthodox Church* (Madison: University of Wisconsin Press, 2004), 48. Many of my interviewees from a Jewish background said that they were atheist, and that their Jewish identity was ethnic rather than

religious. As in the Soviet period, they identify themselves as Russian. Ilya referred to himself as *russky* (a term that implies Russian ethnicity) rather than as *rossiisky* (referring to citizenship of the Russian Federation). He said that he cannot relate to the latter term, which never really took hold in Russia. He claimed that he had never experienced any anti-Semitism himself ("My family name doesn't sound Jewish and I don't have typical traits in my appearance"), but he did recount that his parents did not get into the university they wanted to go to because they are Jewish, and "in addition to that, they had to be ten times better in their studies."

50. Amy Chua, *World on Fire: How Exporting Free Market Democracy Breeds Ethnic Hatred and Global Instability* (London: Heinemann, 2003), 77–94.

51. Freeland, *Sale of the Century*, 105–114.

52. Connie Bruck, "The Billionaire's Playlist," *The New Yorker*, January 20, 2014, www.newyorker.com/magazine/2014/01/20/the-billionaires-playlist.

53. On a theoretical discussion of the importance of social connections see Bonnie H. Erickson, "Culture, Class, and Connections," *American Journal of Sociology* 102, no. 1 (1996): 217–251.

54. Freeland, *Sale of the Century*, 25.

55. Oleg Tin'kov, *Ia Takoi Kak Vse* (Moskva: Al'pina Pablisher, 2010).

56. Irina Gruzinova, Mariia Abakumova, and Elena Zubova, "V Chastnom Poriadke. Mnogo Lits Aleksandra Svetakova," *Forbes*, 2015, www.forbes.ru/sp_data/2015/svetakov/index.html.

57. Another of Tinkov's fellow entrepreneurs is Yevgeny Chichvarkin, now a London exile, who discovered his exceptional salesmanship in street-trading in Moscow. He later founded a mobile phone retailer, Yevroset, together with a childhood friend. His company grew at breakneck speed, becoming the mobile market leader in Russia by the 2000s and turning the former street trader into a billionaire. Chichvarkin's parents were a ministry economist and a pilot—not high up in the Soviet hierarchy, but hardly the Soviet proletariat. Still, he is arguably even more of a social climber than Tinkov. Born in 1974, he was ten years younger than Fridman and Khodorkovsky. He did not benefit from a *Komsomol* network or the patronage of top bureaucrats in the lucrative perestroika insider trading and the rigged privatizations. Moreover, seven years Tinkov's junior, Chichvarkin had to make his initial capital in competition with rivals who, by that time, had already built up significant trade and banking groups. *Znak*, "Evgenii Chichvarkin: 'Ia Vernus' v Rossiiu Cherez Piat' Let, Potomu Chto Togda Sluchitsa . . . ,'" December 2, 2012, www.znak.com/2012-12-02/samyy_ekscentrichnyy_biznesmen_sdelal_cherez_znak_com_neskolko_lyubopytnyh_prognozov.

58. Playing down advantage through family background is a widespread phenomenon in many countries. See, for example, Lisa A. Keister, *Getting Rich: America's New Rich and How They Got That Way* (Cambridge: Cambridge University Press, 2005), 62.

59. Gill Eyal and Eleanor Townsley, "The Social Composition of the Communist Nomenklatura: A Comparison of Russia, Poland, and Hungary," *Theory and Society* 24, no. 5 (1995): 723–775.

60. Ivan Szelényi and Christy Glass, "Winners of the Reforms: The Economic and Political Elite," in *Inequality and Social Structure during the Transition*, edited by Vladimir Mikhalev (Basingstoke: Palgrave Macmillan, 2003), 91. All the same, numerically, few of those holding higher or elite positions in 1988 still did so in 1993, and many fell into the abyss. In particular, many of those who had been part of the intelligentsia experienced a decline, if not an outright fall. Theodore P. Gerber and Michael Hout, "Tightening Up: Declining Class Mobility during Russia's Market Transition," *American Sociological Review* 65, no. 5 (2004): 677–703.

61. Henryk Domanski, *On the Verge of Convergence: Social Stratification in Eastern Europe* (Budapest: Central European University Press, 2000). Ivan Szelényi and Szonja Szelényi, "Circulation or Reproduction of Elites During the Postcommunist Transformation of Eastern Europe," *Theory and Society* 25, no. 5 (1995): 623ff.

62. Eric Hanley, Natasha Yershova, and Richard Anderson, "Russia—Old Wine in a New Bottle? The Circulation and Reproduction of Russian Elites, 1983–1993," *Theory and Society* 24, no. 5 (1995): 663.

CHAPTER 2

1. Thorstein Veblen, *The Theory of the Leisure Class* (New York: Dover Publications, 1994 [1899]), 24.

2. Jennifer Patico, *Consumption and Social Change in a Post-Soviet Middle Class* (Stanford, CA: Stanford General, 2008), 6; Seth Graham, "The Wages of Syncretism: Folkloric New Russians and Post-Soviet Popular Culture," *Russian Review* 62, no. 1 (2003): 37–53; Helena Goscilo, "Introduction: A Label Designed to Libel versus Mimetic Modeling and Parthenogenesis," *Russian Review* 62, no. 1 (2003): 10; Serguei A. Oushakine, "The Quantity of Style. Imaginary Consumption in the New Russia," *Theory, Culture & Society* 17, no. 5 (2000): 97–120; and John Kampfner, *Inside Yeltsin's Russia: Corruption, Conflict, Capitalism* (London: Cassell, 1994).

3. Helena Goscilo and Vladimir Strukov excluded Sobchak from their volume on glamour in contemporary Russia due to her notoriety, which they felt rendered her a too-obvious case. Helena Goscilo and Vlad Strukov, *Celebrity and Glamour in Contemporary Russia: Shocking Chic* (London: Routledge, 2011), 11.

4. Julia Ioffe, "The Master and Mikhail," *The New Yorker*, February 20, 1012, www.newyorker.com/magazine/2012/02/27/the-master-and-mikhail.

5. Veblen, *The Theory of the Leisure Class*, chapter V; Georg Simmel, "Die Mode," in *Philosophische Kultur*, 2nd ed. (Leipzig: Alfred Kröner Verlag, 1919).

6. Karen B. Halnon, "Poor Chic: The Rational Consumption of Poverty," *Current Sociology* 50, no. 4 (2002): 501–516.

7. Pierre Bourdieu, "Social Space and Symbolic Power," *Sociological Theory* 7, no. 1 (1989): 14–25.

8. Peter Oakley, "Ticking Boxes: (Re)Constructing the Wristwatch as a Luxury Object," *Luxury: History, Culture, Consumption* 2, no. 1 (2015): 41–60.

9. Richard A. Peterson and Roger M. Kern, "Changing Highbrow Taste: From Snob to Omnivore," *American Sociological Review* 61, no. 5 (1996): 900–907; and Bethany Bryson, "Anything but Heavy Metal: Symbolic Exclusion and Musical Dislikes," *American Sociological Review* 61, no. 5 (2006): 884–899.

10. Simmel, "Die Mode."

11. Lev Tolstoy, *Childhood, Boyhood, Youth,* translated and with an introduction by Rosemary Edmonds (New York: Penguin, 2006), 326–328. On negative sentiments among the intelligentsia towards the West see, for example, Catriona Kelly, *Refining Russia: Advice Literature, Polite Culture, and Gender from Catherine to Yeltsin* (Oxford: Oxford University Press, 2001), 144–147.

12. Katarina Klingseis, "The Power of Dress in Contemporary Russian Society: On Glamour Discourse and the Everyday Practice of Getting Dressed in Russian Cities," *Laboratorium* 3, no. 1 (2011): 105.

13. The tension between Westernized trends and Russian symbols has in some ways set a precedent for fashion designers today. For example, Ulyana Sergeenko, a former billionaire's wife, who is not shy about her background in a Soviet intelligentsia family of linguists, draws upon Russian fairy-tale and military motifs as well as Soviet cartoons, thus expressing a more confident and distinct national identity. Daliya Galieva, "Gangstery, Bandity i ikh Sputnitsy ot Ul'iany Sergeenko," *Fashion Network,* July 5, 2017, http://ru.fashionnetwork.com/news/Gangstery-bandity-i-ikh-sputnitsy-ot-Ul'yany-Sergyeenko,846362.html#.WWEtT8aB3Vo.

14. Frequently changing their clothes was a feature of the "Russian fashion pack," who came to prominence in the world of Paris haute couture in 2012. In describing this group in an article in the *New York Times,* Eric Wilson quoted the assessment on Style.com that hardly anyone "changes outfits more often or with more look-at-me enthusiasm than this group of designers, bloggers and scenemakers." Here dressing appropriately requires diversity of costumes. Eric Wilson, "The Czarinas Are Back," *New York Times,* June 29, 2012, www.nytimes.com/2012/07/01/fashion/the-russians-claim-the-fashion-spotlight.html.

15. Alan Warde, Wendy Olsen, and Lydia Martens, "Consumption and the Problem of Variety: Cultural Omnivorousness, Social Distinction and Dining Out," *Sociology* 33, no. 1 (1999): 120.

16. Eliot Borenstein, *Overkill: Sex and Violence in Contemporary Russian Popular Culture* (Ithaca, NY: Cornell University Press, 2008), 88.

17. Elena Zdravomyslova and Anna Temkina, "Gendered Citizenship in Soviet and Post-Soviet Societies," in *Nation and Gender in Contemporary Europe*, edited by Vera Tolz and Stephanie Booth (Manchester: Manchester University Press, 2005), 110.

18. Veblen, *The Theory of the Leisure Class*, 27.

19. Jean-Paul Daloz, *The Sociology of Elite Distinction: From Theoretical to Comparative Perspectives* (Basingstoke: Palgrave Macmillan, 2009), 142. See also Ashley Mears, "Girls as Elite Distinction: The Appropriation of Bodily Capital," *Poetics* 53, no. 4 (2015): 22–37.

20. The billionaire banker Oleg Tinkov publicly prides himself on a long-lasting marriage going back to the time before he was rich. *Msk Sobaka*, "Oleg Tin'kov," September 2009, 65–66.

21. Daloz, *The Sociology of Elite Distinction*, 73–77.

22. Laurie Taylor, "Super Rich: The 1% of the 1%," *Thinking Allowed*, BBC Radio 4, January 4, 2017, www.bbc.co.uk/programmes/b086s8yv; and Emma Spence, "Unraveling the Politics of Super-Rich Mobility: A Study of Crew and Guests on Board Luxury Yachts," *Mobilities* 9, no. 3 (2014): 412.

23. *Dozhd'*, "Na Volne Sanktsii. Dozhd' Vyiasnil, Kak Nevyezdnye Biznesmeny i Chinovniki Mogut Vse Ravno Otdykhat' Na Evropeiskikh Kurortakh," August 18, 2014, https://tvrain.ru/teleshow/here_and_now/na_volne_sanktsij_dozhd_vyjasnil_kak_nevyezdnye_biznesmeny_i_chinovniki_mogut_vse_ravno_otdy-hat_na_evropejskih_kurortah-374221.

24. The yacht owners I met were mostly modest-looking men, often almost a little shy, concerned about not appearing to be showoffs. One of them was the billionaire Dmitry Pumpyansky, the main shareholder of the steel piles manufacturer TMK and 73rd on the 2016 Russian *Forbes* rich list. I met him only briefly (and never visited his yacht), but he seemed to be very much the same: serious, timid, with a quiet voice and a little frightened look. Judging by his demeanor he was not the stereotypical breezy rich man who loves throwing lavish yacht parties. In 2016, the billionaire was building a 100-meter-long yacht. Anton Verzhbitskii, "Dunya dlia Pumpianskovo. Milliarder Stroit Stometrovuiu Iakhtu," *Forbes*, July 26, 2016, www.forbes.ru/milliardery/325547-dunya-dlya-pumpyanskogo-milliarder-stroit-stometrovuyu-yakht.

25. Tamara Warren, "Luxury in Motion: The Precarious State of the Supercar," *Luxury* 1, no. 1 (2015): 71–91.

26. Jukka Gronow and Sergei Zhuravlev, "'Soviet Luxuries from Champagne to Private Cars," in *Pleasures in Socialism: Leisure and Luxury in the Eastern Bloc*, edited by David Crowley and Susan E. Reid (Evanston, IL: Northwestern University Press, 2010), 133.

27. The safety of other road users has been considered of little importance when roads are closed for motorcades. Accidents happen frequently. At particularly high risk are residents exiting their driveways onto closed streets, sometimes

ignorant of the closure and the heavy official cars approaching at speed. In 2010, the motorcade of the supreme court president, Vyacheslav Lebedev, sped down an oncoming lane, crashing into the old Zhiguli of a woman with her family en route to their dacha. Lebedev reportedly traveled on regardless, leaving it to his staff to sort out the mess. The police rewrote the facts, blaming the woman for the accident. Had she survived, she could have been brought to trial. Witnesses posted videos on the web, whereupon the lead investigator declared that he had no Internet access. Most accidents caused by rich drivers, of course, are never made public, but are "resolved" with the police at the scene of the incident. Julia Latynina, "Life in Putin's Russia," *Washington Post*, June 22, 2008, www.wash ingtonpost.com/wp-dyn/content/article/2008/06/20/AR2008062002596.html. A similar scenario happened to a fellow common car driver, Oleg Shcherbinsky, who was blamed for having caused a accident in 2005, in which the governor of the Altai region, Mikhail Yevdokimov, who actually caused the car accident, was killed. Shcherbinsky was sentenced to four years in prison, but was freed on appeal in early 2006. Simon Pirani, *Change in Putin's Russia: Power, Money and People* (London: Pluto, 2010), 186. The most scandalous case was when, also in 2005, Alexander Ivanov, the son of Sergei Ivanov (who was then defense minister and later the chief of the presidential administration), killed a sixty-eight-year-old woman on a pedestrian crossing. Despite the fact that Alexander was speeding, no charges were brought against him, and Sergei Ivanov pointed out that his son had suffered physical and emotional trauma. A criminal investigation was launched against the dead woman's son-in-law for allegedly assaulting the minister's son. (Alexander Ivanov later died in a diving accident in 2014.)

28. Alena Ledeneva, *Can Russia Modernise? Sistema, Power Networks and Informal Governance* (Cambridge: Cambridge University Press, 2013), 146; and Andrei Soldatov and Irina Borogan, *The New Nobility: The Restoration of Russia's Security State and the Enduring Legacy of the KGB* (New York: PublicAffairs, 2010), 75.

29. Boris Groys, *The Total Art of Stalinism: Avant-Garde, Aesthetic Dictatorship, and Beyond* (Princeton, NJ: Princeton University Press, 1992), 160–166.

30. Isaiah Berlin, "The Remarkable Decade," *Russian Thinkers*, edited by Henry Hardy and Aileen Kelly (London: Penguin, 2008), 130–154.

31. Neither did the Soviet intelligentsia feature the diversity of its nineteenth-century predecessor. See Kelly, *Refining Russia*, 110. For more on intelligentsia characteristics, their history, and development see Gary M. Hamburg, "Russian Intelligentsias," in *A History of Russian Thought*, edited by William Leatherbarrow and Derek Offord (Cambridge: Cambridge University Press, 2010), 44–69.

32. Masha Gessen, *Dead Again: The Russian Intelligentsia After Communism* (London: Verso, 1997), 102.

33. Gessen, *Dead Again*, 7. In fact, status anxiety has a long history in Russia. Already from the 1890s onward the intelligentsia began to despise ordinary people and prize its own elitist character. Nonaristocratic intellectuals increasingly adopted

the mores of their aristocratic peers to form "Society," especially after the defeat of the 1905 revolution. Laura Engelstein, *Slavophile Empire: Imperial Russia's Illiberal Path* (Ithaca, NY: Cornell University Press, 2009), 81–87.

34. Mark Lipovetsky, "New Russians as a Cultural Myth," *Russian Review* 62, no. 1 (2003): 56. On the phenomenon of intelligentsia members perceiving themselves to live outside "class", see Kelly, *Refining Russia*, 109, 208.

35. The term *kulturnost* was introduced to Western readers by Vera S. Dunham, *In Stalin's Time: Middleclass Values in Soviet Fiction* (Cambridge: Cambridge University Press, 1976), 22. See also Catriona Kelly, "Directed Desires: Kul'turnost' and Consumption," in *Constructing Russian Culture in the Age of Revolution, 1881–1940*, edited by David Shepherd and Catriona Kelly (Oxford: Oxford University Press, 1998), 295; Kelly, *Refining Russia*, 312–389; and Benjamin Tromly, *Making the Soviet Intelligentsia: Universities and Intellectual Life under Stalin and Khrushchev* (Cambridge: Cambridge University Press, 2014).

36. Kelly, "Directed Desires," 302.

37. Kelly, "Directed Desires," 304.

38. Kelly, "Directed Desires," 312.

39. Sheila Fitzpatrick, *On Stalin's Team: The Years of Living Dangerously in Soviet Politics* (Princeton, NJ: Princeton University Press, 2015), 109; and Sheila Fitzpatrick, "Stalin and the World of Culture," Lecture, Pushkin House/London, June 22, 2011. From this period onward the pressure for *kulturnost* became a Soviet variation of the process Norbert Elias describes in *The Civilizing Process*. External constraints (*Fremdzwänge*)—in the Russian case a social pressure to acquire *kulturnost*—train individuals in specific habits which, over time, become routinized and internalized, to the extent that they become self-constraints (*Selbstzwänge*). Norbert Elias, *The Civilizing Process* (Oxford: Blackwell, 1982).

40. Fitzpatrick, *On Stalin's Team*, 187–188; and Fitzpatrick, "Stalin and the World of Culture."

41. Susan A. Ostrander, "Surely You're Not in This Just to Be Helpful: Access, Rapport, and Interviews in Three Studies of Elites," in *Studying Elites Using Qualitative Methods*, edited by Rosanna Hertz and Jonathan B. Imber (London: Sage, 1995), 143.

42. Freeland, *Sale of the Century*, 236.

43. Patricia A. Adler and Peter Adler, "The Reluctant Respondent," in *Handbook of Interview Research: Context & Method*, edited by Jaber F. Gubrium and James A. Holstein (Thousand Oaks, CA: Sage, 2002), 518.

CHAPTER 3

1. Thomas Piketty, *Capital in the Twenty-First Century* (Cambridge, MA: The Belknap Press of Harvard University Press, 2014), 443–447. Many cultures distinguish between what they consider deserving and undeserving rich, which is

in line with what Leslie McCalls found in regards to the general population in the United States. Leslie McCalls, *The Undeserving Rich: American Beliefs about Inequality, Opportunity, and Redistribution* (Cambridge: Cambridge University Press, 2013). On this debate see also Katharina Hecht, "A Relational Analysis of Top Incomes and Wealth. Relative (Dis)advantage, Economic Devaluation and the Service of Capital," LSE International Inequalities Institute, London, Working Paper 11, May 2017. When talking about deserving rich, people often refer to success stories such as that of the Chinese Internet magnate Jack Ma, who with his outsider status is a poster boy for aspiring downtrodden nobodies, and computer geeks from Bill Gates to Steve Jobs, who started their businesses from their homes and cultivated their images as "nerds."

2. Sherman, "Conflicted Cultivation," and Sherman, *Uneasy Street*, 198. See also Rubén Gaztambide-Fernández and Adam Howard, "Social Justice, Deferred Complicity, and the Moral Plight of the Wealthy: A Response to 'With Great Power Comes Great Responsibility': Privileged Students' Conceptions of Justice-Oriented Citizenship," *Democracy & Education* 21, no. 1 (2013): 1.

3. Max Weber, *From Max Weber: Essays in Sociology*, translated and edited by Hans Heinrich Gerth and C. Wright Mills (London: Routledge, 1991), 271.

4. David Beetham, *The Legitimation of Power* (Basingstoke: Macmillan, 1991).

5. Rogers Brubaker, "Rethinking Classical Theory: The Sociological Vision of Pierre Bourdieu," *Theory and Society* 14, no. 6 (1985): 755.

6. Levada-Center, "Rossiiane o Biznese i Biznesmenakh," November 5, 2014, www .levada.ru/2014/11/05/rossiyane-o-biznese-i-biznesmenah/,Levada-Center.

7. Animated Soviet Propaganda, "Capitalist Sharks: Soviet Animation vs. Greed and Ambition," *Films for the Humanities and Sciences* (New York: Films Media Group, 2006).

8. On declining living standards, see Simon Pirani, *Change in Putin's Russia: Power, Money and People* (London: Pluto, 2010), 10.

9. Freeland, *Sale of the Century*, 335.

10. Freeland, *Sale of the Century*, 320.

11. Mikhail Khodorkovsky, "Russia Under Putin and Beyond: The Annual Russia Lecture," *Chatham House*, February 26, 2015, www.chathamhouse.org/event/ russia-under-putin-and-beyond-annual-russia-lecture#sthash.PrEWmdaV.dpuf.

12. *Snob Magazine*, "Sobchak & Sokolova s Petrom Avenom: Ne Stuchat' i Ne Sadit'sa," June 2013, https://snob.ru/magazine/entry/61234.

13. Ian Traynor, "Putin Urged to Apply the Pinochet Stick," *The Guardian*, March 31, 2000, www.theguardian.com/world/2000/mar/31/russia.iantraynor.

14. *Snob*, "Sobchak & Sokolova s Petrom Avenom."

15. This was at an event organized by the Russian Political Club in London on October 19, 2015.

16. See, for example, Anders Uhlin, *Post-Soviet Civil Society: Democratisation in Russia and the Baltic States* (London: Routledge, 2006), 163.

17. Pirani, *Change in Putin's Russia*, 150. The Russian American lawyer Alexander Domrin criticized liberals in Russia and the West for hypocritically deploring the absence of a civil society in the early 2000s, remarking that this very absence was widely welcomed at the time when Gaidar was implementing his shock therapy in 1992 because it suppressed the strong popular resistance to privatization and economic liberalization: Russia's radical free market reformers as well as their foreign advisors "cannot be consistent, sincere, or logical" when demanding the strengthening of civil society in Russia today, because it was precisely the absence or weakness of civil society in the early 1990s that allowed them to "pillage the country under the guise of 'reforms.'" Alexander N. Domrin, "Ten Years Later: Society, 'Civil Society,' and The Russian State," *Russian Review* 62, no. 2 (2003): 31ff.

18. See, for example, Alexei Yurchak, *Everything Was Forever, Until It Was No More* (Princeton, NJ: Princeton University Pres, 2006). Alena Ledeneva calls these multiple moralities and ambivalent norms "double deed." Alena V. Ledeneva, *Can Russia Modernise?* 195.

19. Boris Kagarlitsky, "1960s East and West: The Nature of the Shestidesiatniki and the New Left," *Boundary 2* 36, no. 1 (2009): 95–104.

20. Loren R. Graham, *Science, Philosophy, and Human Behavior in the Soviet Union* (New York: Columbia University Press, 1987), 250.

21. Valerie Sperling, *Sex, Politics, and Putin: Political Legitimacy in Russia* (New York: Oxford University Press, 2015), 70.

22. Michael W. Kraus and Dacher Keltner, "Social Class Rank, Essentialism, and Punitive Judgment," *Journal of Personality and Social Psychology* 105, no. 2 (2013): 247–261; and Michael W. Kraus and Bennet Callaghan, "Noblesse Oblige? Social Status and Economic Inequality Maintenance Among Politicians," *PLOS One* 9, no. 1 (2014). In general social scientists regard essentialist views very critically, but there are some who endorse them: for example, the Harvard economist and Mitt Romney advisor Greg Mankiw, who claims to have identified among the wealthy elites higher IQs, higher levels of willpower, perseverance, entrepreneurial spirit, and most importantly, a greater ability to innovate. N. Gregory Mankiw, "Defending the One Percent," *Journal of Economic Perspectives* 27, no. 3 (2013): 21–34. Many rich themselves share Mankiw's view. Even if they stress their biological superiority not as prominently and directly as Kraus and Keltner found it, it is the major way in which people explain their success. See, for example, Ruben Gaztambide-Fernandez, *The Best of the Best: Becoming Elite at an American Boarding School* (Cambridge, MA: Harvard University Press, 2009); Shamus R. Khan, *Privilege: The Making of an Adolescent Elite at St. Paul's School* (Princeton, NJ: Princeton University Press, 2011); Heather B. Johnson, *The American Dream and the Power of Wealth* (New York: Routledge, 2006); and Phillip Brown, Sally Power, Gerbrand Tholen, and Annabelle Allouch, "Credentials, Talent and Cultural Capital: A Comparative Study of Education Elites in England

and France and Their Study on Elite Graduates," *British Journal of Sociology of Education* 37, no. 2 (2014).

23. Robert H. Frank, *Success and Luck: Good Fortune and the Myth of Meritocracy* (Princeton, NJ: Princeton University Press, 2016).

24. Freeland, *Plutocrats*, 151–152.

25. Frank, *Success and Luck*. Acknowledging luck is a privilege only of the very secure, self-ironic, or exceptionally self-reflective people, such as Warren Buffett, who has stated that his rise to riches was pure chance and that his sisters are actually much smarter than he is but as females, they had fewer opportunities in the era in which he and his siblings grew up. *Forbes*, "The Forbes 400 Summit: Bill Gates, Warren Buffett and the Greatest Roundtable of All Time," *Forbes*, October 8, 2012, www.forbes.com/sites/randalllane/2012/09/18/theforbes-400-summit-bill-gates-warren-buffett-and-the-greatest-roundtable-of-all-time/.

26. Eric Hobsbawm, *Age of Empire: 1875–1914* (New York: Vintage, 1989), 92; Vera Tolz, *Russia* (London: Arnold, 2001); and Liah Greenfeld, *Nationalism: Five Roads to Modernity* (Cambridge, MA: Harvard University Press, 1992).

27. *The Economist*, "Russia's Chief Propagandist," December 10, 2013, www.econo mist.com/blogs/easternapproaches/2013/12/ukraine.

28. On the neoconservative alliance between big business and conservative Christianity in the United States see David Harvey, *A Brief History of Neoliberalism* (Oxford: Oxford University Press, 2005), 50.

29. Levada-Center, "Figura Stalina v Obshchestvennom Mnenii Rossii," March 25, 2016, www.levada.ru/2016/03/25/figura-stalina-v-obshhestvennom-mnenii-rossii/.

30. Chrystia Freeland, "Even Plutocrats Can See Profound Inequality Isn't in Their Interests," *The Guardian*, January 25, 2015, www.theguardian.com/commentisfree/2015/jan/25/even-super-rich-see-plutocracy-flawed; and Freeland, *Plutocrats*, ix–xii.

31. Wealthy individuals themselves tend to confirm these views, as does Bill Gates when he says that half of the *Forbes 400* wealthiest Americans got onto the list thanks to hard work, rather than inheritance. Bill Gates, "Why Inequality Matters," *Gatesnotes*, October 13, 2014, www.gatesnotes.com/Books/Why-Inequality-Matters-Capital-in-21st-Century-Review.

32. I asked Avdeev whether he had any ambition to go into politics. He said he would stay true to his word not to embrace Lenin's ideas, including the one that every cook could run the state. He would be better sticking to the trade in which he is experienced and that he is good at.

CHAPTER 4

1. Catriona Kelly, *Children's World: Growing Up in Russia, 1890–1991* (New Haven, CT: Yale University Press, 2007), 8.

2. For more on late-Soviet factory managers see Andrei Shleifer and Daniel Treisman, *Without a Map: Political Tactics and Economic Reform in Russia* (Cambridge, MA: MIT Press, 2000), 30.

3. The journalist Eduard Dorozhkin denigrates references to aristocratic backgrounds. When I met him, he was chief editor of *Na Rublyovke*, a weekly newspaper targeted at the inhabitants of the luxury suburb Rublyovka. Referring to the 1917 Revolution, the journalist said: "The aristocracy and the Emperor's family were responsible for the destruction of a great country, and everybody knows that. . . . A normally reasoning person would be terribly embarrassed to have aristocratic ancestry."

4. There were several stories of idealism and passionate revolutionary spirit that guided my interviewees' family members before the 1917 Revolution. The grandfather of the businesswoman Veronika Zonabend was born in Poland into a wealthy Jewish family and would have become the heir to the family's textile factory. Instead, in 1919, age nineteen, he was impassioned by the Bolshevik Revolution and "ran away to help build communism." Zonabend, the wife of the entrepreneur Ruben Vardanyan, formerly CEO and controlling shareholder of Troika Dialog investment bank (and owning assets worth $950 million in 2017), said of her grandfather's story: "It was obviously idealism of some sort." There was no shortage of this in her family: Some of her relatives were among the pioneers of the kibbutz movement, while others left for America and engaged in art. Zonabend herself continues this family tradition with her extensive philanthropic activity.

5. Peter Kolchin, *Unfree Labor: American Slavery and Russian Serfdom* (Cambridge, MA: The Belknap Press of Harvard University Press, 1987); and Alessandro Stanziani, *Bondage: Labor and Rights in Eurasia from the Sixteenth to the Early Twentieth Centuries* (New York: Berghahn Books, 2014).

6. Sheila Fitzpatrick, *Tear Off the Masks! Identity and Imposture in Twentieth-Century Russia* (Princeton, NJ: Princeton University Press, 2005), 14–18.

7. On related topics see Orlando Figes, *The Whisperers: Private Life in Stalin's Russia* (London: Penguin, 2008), 33, 35; Mathew Rendle, "The Problems of Becoming Soviet: Former Nobles in Soviet Society," *European History Quarterly* 3, no. 1 (2008): 7–33; Douglas Smith, *Former People: The Last Days of the Russian Aristocracy* (London: Macmillan, 2012); Daniel Bertaux, "Transmission in Extreme Situations: Russian Families Expropriated by the October Revolution," in *Pathways to Social Class: A Qualitative Approach to Social Mobility*, edited by Daniel Bertaux and Paul Thompson (Oxford: Clarendon Press, 1997), 230–258; and Vikoriia Semenova and Ekaterina Foteeva, *Sud'by Liudei: Rossiia XX Vek. Biografii Semei Kak Ob"ekt Sotsiologicheskovo Issledovaniia* (Moskva: Inst. Sotsiologii RAN, 1996).

8. See Viktoriia Semenova and Paul Thompson, "Family Models and Transgenerational Influences. Grandparents, Parents and Children in Moscow and Leningrad from the Soviet to the Market Era," in *Living Through Soviet Russia*, edited by Daniel Bertaux, Paul Thompson, and Anna Rotkirch (London: Routledge, 2004), 131; and Ekaterina Foteeva, "Coping with Revolution. The Experiences of Well-to-Do Russian Families," in *Living Through Soviet Russia*, 68–90.

9. Fitzpatrick, *On Stalin's Team*, 106ff; and Fitzpatrick, "Stalin and the World of Culture."

10. Fitzpatrick, *On Stalin's Team*, 107, 109–110; and Fitzpatrick, "Stalin and the World of Culture." By this time, society more broadly enjoyed a less spartan lifestyle. See also Jukka Gronow, *Caviar with Champagne: Common Luxury and the Ideals of the Good Life in Stalin's Russia* (Oxford: Berg, 2003).

11. On related topics see Laurie Manchester, *Holy Fathers, Secular Sons: Clergy, Intelligentsia and the Modern Self in Revolutionary Russia* (DeKalb: Northern Illinois University Press, 2008).

12. Segalovich gave me some taste of his grandmother's suffering: "When my grandfather was arrested, my grandmother turned into an 'enemy of the people' and all her friends turned their backs on her. When they saw her on the street, they crossed the road to avoid her. I think there was just one family left which demonstratively kept on being friends with us. They were very scared of being arrested as well. So my mother left for the countryside where she was in hiding for a year."

13. Masha Gessen, *Dead Again: The Russian Intelligentsia after Communism* (London: Verso, 1997), 9–10.

14. Norbert Elias, *The Germans: Power Struggles and the Development of Habitus in the Nineteenth and Twentieth Centuries* (Cambridge: Polity Press, 1996), 49.

15. Michael Voslensky, *Nomenklatura: The Soviet Ruling Class* (Garden City, NY: Doubleday, 1984).

16. On the specifics of a sense of public duty among former aristocrats, see, for example, Geoffrey Hosking, *Russia: People and Empire: 1552–1917* (London: HarperCollins, 1997), 349. Even if they were not aristocratic, their idealism was in tune with the mythology of chivalrous self-sacrifice that rebellious members of the tsarist aristocracy cultivated. In more general terms, on the obligation to provide service to the state, see Pierre Bourdieu, *The State Nobility: Elite Schools in the Field of Power* (Cambridge: Polity Press, 1996).

CHAPTER 5

1. Natalia Dinello, "Philanthropy in Russia and the United States. Elites and Philanthropy in Russia," in *International Journal of Politics, Culture and Society* 12, no. 1 (1998): 111. For an explicitly critical sociological analysis of philanthropy see Linsey McGoey, *No Such Thing as a Free Gift: The Gates Foundation and the Price of Philanthropy* (London: Verso, 2015). The topic has become

obligatory in any study on wealth. See, for example, Michael Featherstone, "Super-Rich Lifestyles," in *Elite Mobilities*, edited by Birtchnell and Javier Caletrío (New York: Routledge, 2013), 110–114.

2. Georg Simmel, "Exkurs über den Adel," in *Soziologie: Untersuchungen über die Formen der Vergesellschaftung*, edited by Georg Simmel (Frankfurt/M.: Suhrkamp, 1992 [1908]), 820.

3. Marcel Mauss, *The Gift: The Form and Reason for Exchange in Archaic Societies*, with a foreword by Mary Douglas (London: Routledge Classics, 2002 [1898]).

4. Charities Aid Foundation, *CAF World Giving Index 2016*, https://www.cafonline .org/docs/default-source/about-us-publications/1950a_wgi_2016_report_web_ v2_241016.pdf; and Julia Khodorova, *Russia Giving: Research on Individual Giving in Russia* (Moscow: CAF Russia, 2014).

5. Coutts, *Million Dollar Donors Report 2014*, http://philanthropy.coutts.com/en/ reports/2014/russia/findings.html.

6. "Rashirennoe Zasedanie Pravleniia TPP RF 'O Sotsial'noi Otvetstvennosti Biznesa v Sovremennoi Rossii,'" December 23, 2003, Chamber of Commerce and Industry of the Russian Federation, http://tpprf.ru/ru/news/5877. Alexander Livshin and Richard Weitz, "Civil Society and Philanthropy Under Putin," *International Journal of Not-for-Profit Law* 8, no. 3 (2006): 7–12. See also the results in the study carried out by the Skolkovo Center for Management. Skolkovo Center for Management, *Issledovanie Vladel'tsev Kapitalov Rossii* (Moscow: Center for Management, Wealth and Philanthropy, 2015), 80.

7. Dinello, "Philanthropy in Russia and the United States," 111–114.

8. N. G. O. Pereira, *The Thought and Teachings of N. G. Černyševskij* (The Hague: Mouton, 1975).

9. Dinello, "Philanthropy in Russia and the United States," 111–114.

10. Zonabend and her husband, Ruben Vardanyan, are among the most experienced philanthropists. Among their largest projects is an international boarding school, United World College Dilijan in Armenia. Zonabend looks after it, while her husband is heavily involved in the development of Moscow School of Management Skolkovo, where a research center was created in 2013 for the study of philanthropy, social entrepreneurship, and ways of passing down assets from the first generation of wealthy people in Russia to the next. The couple, together with their friends, also supported the restoration of the Mains building of Dumfries House, an eighteenth-century estate in Scotland. This project, initiated by Prince Charles, includes an educational program for their and other schools in Armenia.

11. Jamey Gambrell, "Philanthropy in Russia: New Money under Pressure," *Carnegie Reporter* 3, no. 1 (2004), www.carnegie.org/reporter/09/philanthropy/ index.html.

12. Francie Ostrower, *Why the Wealthy Give: The Culture of Elite Philanthropy* (Princeton, NJ: Princeton University Press, 1995), 5f., 36. For a follow-up study on the rich in other countries (here the United Kingdom) see Theresa Lloyd, *Why Rich People Give* (London: Association of Charitable Foundations,

2004); and Beth Breeze and Theresa Lloyd, *Richer Lives: Why Rich People Give* (London: Directory of Social Change, 2013).

13. Livshin and Weitz, "Civil Society and Philanthropy Under Putin"; Khodorova, *Russia Giving*, 19; and Skolkovo Center for Management, *Issledovanie Vladel'tsev Kapitalov Rossii*, 78, 81, 83.

14. Graeme B. Robertson, "Managing Society: Protest, Civil Society, and Regime in Putin's Russia," *Slavic Review* 68, no. 3 (2009): 531.

15. See also the results of the study carried out by the Skolkovo Center for Management, *Issledovanie Vladel'tsev Kapitalov Rossii*, 79.

16. Mauss, *The Gift*.

17. Elite women's engagement in civil society via philanthropy replicates what educated noble and aristocratic women did from the early nineteenth century. See Wendy Rosslyn, *Deeds not Words: The Origins of Women's Philanthropy in the Russian Empire* (Birmingham: University of Birmingham, 2007).

18. Mathew Bishop and Michael Green, *Philanthrocapitalism: How the Rich Can Save the World and Why We Should Let Them* (London: Bloomsbury Press, 2008).

19. Coutts, *Million Dollar Donors Report 2014*. Many of the donations that go beyond the borders of Russia are directed to projects that support exiles from the former Soviet space. An exception here is the Boris Mints Institute for Strategic Policy Solutions to Global Challenges, based at Tel Aviv University. The Jewish billionaire's strong links to Israel are not surprising; what is unusual is that the institute deals with environmental questions, food security, health, and poverty in the global South rather than any Russia-related matters.

20. Livshin and Weitz, "Civil Society and Philanthropy Under Putin."

21. Dinello, "Philanthropy in Russia and the United States," 109–133, 111–114; and Khodorova, *Russia Giving*. This description of Western philanthropy is, of course, a simplification, which many would dispute—for example, John Nickson, *Giving Is Good for You: Why Britain Should Be Bothered and Give More* (London: Biteback Publishing, 2013).

22. Khodorova, *Russia Giving*.

23. Geoffrey Hosking, *Trust: A History* (Oxford: Oxford University Press, 2014).

24. Skolkovo Center for Management, *Issledovanie Vladel'tsev Kapitalov Rossii*, 78, 81.

25. Ostrower, *Why the Wealthy Give*, 36–37.

26. Melanie Fasche, "Making Art History, Wealthy Private Collectors and Contemporary Visual Art," in *Geographies of the Super-Rich*, edited by Iain Hay (Cheltenham: Edward Elgar, 2013), 171–185.

27. Irina Mikhailovskaia and Irina Telitsyna, "Chastnyi Salon," *Forbes Russia*, March 3, 2012, www.forbes.ru/5bissue5d/issue/2012-03-0/81669-chastnyi-salon.

28. Liubov Pulikova, "Chto Leonid Mikhel'son Delaet Na Bolotnoi Za €150 Mln," *Forbes Russia*, February 13, 2017, www.forbes.ru/forbeslife/338935-chto-leonid-mihelson-delaet-na-bolotnoy-za-eu150-mln.

29. Suvi Salmenniemi, "The Making of Civil Society in Russia: A Bourdieuan Approach," *International Sociology* 29, no. 1 (2014): 38–55.

30. The relatively weak engagement of women in elite philanthropy in Russia is unusual, as charity work is the ideal area of activity for bourgeois wives. See Diana E. Kendall, *The Power of Good Deeds: Privileged Women and the Social Reproduction of the Upper Class* (Lanham, MD: Rowman & Littlefield, 2002).

CHAPTER 6

1. Freeland, *Plutocrats*, 86.

2. C. Wright Mills, *The Power Elite* (Oxford: Oxford University Press, 2000 [1956]); Edward D. Baltzell, *Philadelphia Gentlemen: The Making of a National Upper Class* (Philadelphia: University of Pennsylvania Press, 1979 [1958]); and G. William Domhoff, *Who Rules America? Power and Politics in the Year 2000*, 3rd ed. (London: Mayfield Publishing, 2000).

3. Susan A. Ostrander, *Women of the Upper Class* (Philadelphia: Temple University Press, 1984).

4. The French comparativist Jean-Pascal Daloz states that, throughout history, it has been elite women who have most rigidly imposed restrictions on themselves and their daughters, while their husbands might well have welcomed more relaxed rules. One example of this is in fashion, where female-enforced rules have tended to be particularly constraining, as with corsetry in Victorian England. Jean-Pascal Daloz, *Rethinking Social Distinction* (Basingstoke: Palgrave Macmillan, 2013), 135–136.

5. Tomke Böhnisch, *Gattinnen: Die Frauen der Elite* (Münster: Westfälisches Dampfboot, 1999).

6. Rebecca Kay, *Men in Contemporary Russia*, 155.

7. Sperling, *Sex, Politics, and Putin*, 4.

8. Peter Pomerantsev, *Nothing Is True and Everything Is Possible* (New York: PublicAffairs, 2014), 16. On similar attitudes see Elena Gapova, "Gender Equality vs. Difference and What Post-Socialism Can Teach Us," *Women's Studies International Forum* 59 (November–December 2016): 9–16.

9. Michele Rivkin-Fish, "Pronatalism, Gender Politics, and the Renewal of Family Support in Russia: Toward a Feminist Anthropology of Maternity Capital," *Slavic Review* 69, no. 3 (2010): 701–724.

10. Elena Rozhdestvenskaia, "Zarabotat' Svoi Lichny Milliard," *Lenta.ru*, October 20, 2015, http://lenta.ru/articles/2015/10/20/million/.

11. Pomerantsev, *Nothing Is True and Everything Is Possible*, 12–18.

12. Valerie Sperling, "Putin's Macho Personality Cult," *Communist and Post-Communist Studies* 49, no. 1 (2016): 13–23.

13. Sperling, *Sex, Politics, and Putin*, 36.

14. *The Economist*, "Russia's Chief Propagandist," December 10, 2013, www.econo mist.com/blogs/easternapproaches/2013/12/ukraine.

15. Dan Healey, "The Disappearance of the Russian Queen, or How the Soviet Closet Was Born," in *Russian Masculinities in History and Culture*, edited by Barbara E. Clements, Rebecca Friedman, and Dan Healey (Basingstoke: Palgrave Macmillan, 2002), 152–171.

16. Kay, *Men in Contemporary Russia*, 156.

17. For more on lesbians in Russia see Francesca Stella, *Lesbian Lives in Soviet and Post-Soviet Russia: Post/Socialism and Gendered Sexualities* (Basingstoke: Palgrave Macmillan, 2015).

18. Sperling, *Sex, Politics, and Putin*, 9.

19. Alexei Yurchak, "Russian Neoliberal: The Entrepreneurial Ethic and the Spirit of True Careerism," *Russian Review* 62, no. 1 (2003): 84ff.

CHAPTER 7

1. Mike Savage, "Piketty's Challenge for Sociology," *British Journal of Sociology* 65, no. 4 (2014): 591–606.

2. Sherman, "Conflicted Cultivation," and Sherman, *Uneasy Street*, 22–25, 197–229.

3. Sherman, "Conflicted Cultivation," and Sherman, *Uneasy Street*, 210–217.

4. Skolkovo Center for Management, *Issledovanie Vladel'tsev Kapitalov Rossii* (Moscow: Center for Management, Wealth and Philanthropy, 2015), 12.

5. Sherman, "Conflicted Cultivation," and Sherman, *Uneasy Street*, 201–206.

6. Alexander Mamut, "Otsy i Deti. Kolonka Aleksandra Mamuta dlia Forbes," *Forbes Russia*, May 20, 2016, www.forbes.ru/mneniya/tsennosti/320643-ottsy-i-deti-kolonka-aleksandra-mamuta-dlya-forbes.

7. Skolkovo Center for Management, *Issledovanie Vladel'tsev Kapitalov Rossii*, 26.

8. Elma Murtazaev, "Pochemu Deti Milliarderov Ne Speshat Nasledovat' Biznes," *Forbes Russia*, May 25, 2015, www.forbes.ru/mneniya-column/konkurentsiya/ 289427-pochemu-deti-milliarderov-ne-speshat-nasledovat-biznes.

9. Ol'ga Proskurina, "Mikhail Fridman Ostavit Detei Bez Sostoianiia," *Forbes Russia*, May 20, 2016, www.forbes.ru/news/320729-mikhail-fridman-ostavit-detei-bez-sostoyaniya.

10. Mamut, "Otsy i Deti."

11. Skolkovo Center for Management, *Issledovanie Vladel'tsev Kapitalov Rossii*, 44.

12. Mamut, "Otsy i Deti."

13. Skolkovo Center for Management, *Issledovanie Vladel'tsev Kapitalov Rossii*, 84–85.

CHAPTER 8

1. Isaiah Berlin, "Soviet Russian Culture," in *The Soviet Mind*, edited by Henry Hardy, foreword by Strobe Talbott (Washington, DC: Brookings Institution Press 2005 [1957]), 130.

2. For more on Russia's relation to the West see Vera Tolz, "The West," in *A History of Russian Thought*, edited by William Leatherbarrow and Derek Offord (Cambridge: Cambridge University Press, 2010), 197–216; Vera Tolz, *Russia* (London: Arnold, 2001), 70–71; Boris Groys, *Die Erfindung Rußlands* (Munich: Hanser Verlag, 1995); and Michael David-Fox, "Conclusion: Transnational History and the East–West Divide," in *Imagining the West in Eastern Europe and the Soviet Union*, edited by György Péteri (Pittsburgh, PA: University of Pittsburgh Press, 2010), 262.

3. See, for example, Charles Clover, *Black Wind, White Snow: The Rise of Russia's New Nationalism* (New Haven, CT: Yale University Press, 2016); and Marlene Laruelle, *In the Name of the Nation: Nationalism and Politics in Contemporary Russia* (Basingstoke: Palgrave Macmillan, 2009).

4. Nicholas Shaxson, *Treasure Islands: Tax Havens and the Men Who Stole the World* (London: Vintage, 2012), 248; and Mark Hollingsworth and Stewart Lansley, *Londongrad: From Russia with Cash: The Inside Story of the Oligarchs* (London: HarperCollins UK, 2009).

5. Spear's Newschannel, "Russian HNWs Flood to London to Escape Putin's Clampdown," June 16, 2015, www.spearswms.com/russian-hnws-flood-to-london-to-escape-putins-clampdown-2/.

6. Jamie McGeever, "UK Draws Billions in Unrecorded Inflows, Much from Russia—Study," *Reuters*, March 10, 2015, http://uk.reuters.com/article/uk-markets-capital-flows-deutsche-idUKKBN0M61FM20150310. Transparency International has raised concerns that the United Kingdom's Tier 1 investors visa schemes are used as a tool to launder corrupt money. Until early 2015, visas were often awarded before applicants had to open a UK bank account. As a result, there was effectively a "blind faith" period in which there were extremely weak checks on who the investors were and where their money came from. In early 2015 the UK government changed the rules, so now applicants have to open a UK bank account before they can apply for a visa, closing the previous "blind faith" loophole. As a result, the number of applicants dropped sharply. Steve Goodrich, "Whatever Happened to the Great British Gold Rush?" *Transparency International*, February 23, 2017, www.transparency.org.uk/whatever-happened-to-the-great-british-gold-rush/.

7. Zhanna Ul'ianova, "Sovet Federatsii Stal Bednee: Iz Soveta Federatsii Ushli Samye Bogatye Senatory," *RBC News*, April 15, 2014, www.rbc.ru/newspaper/2014/04/15/56beeed79a7947299f72d23e.

8. Hartmann, *Die Globale Wirtschaftselite*. According to Hartmann's study, only three Russians on the global *Forbes* list in 2015 had their main residence outside the Russian Federation. Putin's close friend and hockey buddy Gennady Timchenko, a Finnish citizen, whose wealth amounted to $16 billion in 2017, now lives in Switzerland (although he spends half of the year in Moscow). Dmitry Rybolovlev, who made his money producing potash and is now the majority owner and president of AS Monaco soccer club, lives in Monaco. The veteran Russian tycoon Mikhail Fridman, of Ukrainian Jewish descent, who has reinvented himself as an international investor, lives in Britain. However, not even he can say good-bye to his (business) life in Moscow, where he spends 40 percent of his time. Michael Hartmann, "The International Business Elite: Fact or Fiction?" LSE Conference, Changing Elites in Europe, London, November 26–27, 2015. Hartmann's study is endorsed by Cristobal Young, who found that of all billionaires in the world only 16 percent do not live in their country of birth. Of these 16 percent, 30 percent moved as children, 39 percent moved early in their careers, before they got rich, and only 31 percent moved after they already had their great success. Cristobal Young, *The Myth of Millionaire Tax Flight: How Place Still Matters for the Rich* (Stanford, CA: Stanford University Press, 2018), 47–52.

9. There are, of course, ways to navigate the 2015 anti-offshore law. In order to spend as much time as he wishes in Russia and maintain his Russian residence status, the billionaire Alexander Mamut shifted his foreign-based assets into a trust he set up for his three underage children, who are not Russian residents. Timofei Dziadko, Anatolii Temkin, and Igor' Terent'ev, "Milliader Mamut Perepisal Chast' Svoikh Aktivov Na Troikh Detei," *RBC*, February 25, 2015, www .rbc.ru/business/25/02/2015/54edfff59a7947af8e47ee51.

10. Elena Berezanskaia, "Rodina Zovet: Kak Milliardery Otreagirovali na Prizyv k Deofshorizatsii," *Forbes Russia*, April 20, 2015, www.forbes.ru/milliardery/ 286477-rodina-zovet-kak-milliardery-otreagirovali-na-prizyv-k-deofshorizatsii.

11. The museum, called Sobraniye, also exhibits mechanical rarities, among them music boxes, street organs, gramophones, and phonographs, as well as a collection of old Russian and foreign silver, glass, and crystal, and a collection of Russian bronze.

12. Robert Mackey, "Russia Could Still Turn U.S. 'Into Radioactive Dust,' News Anchor in Moscow Reminds Viewers," *New York Times*, March 16, 2014, https:// thelede.blogs.nytimes.com/2014/03/16/russia-could-still-turn-the-u-s-into-radioactive-dust-news-anchor-in-moscow-reminds-viewers/.

13. Patriotic scaremongering became typical for Putin's conservative turn in his third presidency. See, for example, Witold Rodkiewicz and Jadwiga Rogoża, "Potemkin Conservatism: An Ideological Tool of the Kremlin," *Russian Analytical Digest* 171 (July 14, 2015): 2–4; Marlene Laruelle, "Conservatism as the Kremlin's New Toolkit. An Ideology at the Lowest Cost," *Russian Analytical Digest* 138 (November 8, 2013): 2–4; and Anton Shekhovtsov, *Russia and the Western Far Right: Tango Noir* (London: Routledge 2017).

Bibliography

Adachi, Yuko. *Building Big Business in Russia: The Impact of Informal Corporate Governance Practices.* London: Routledge, 2010.

Adler, Patricia A., and Peter Adler. "The Reluctant Respondent." In *Handbook of Interview Research: Context & Method,* edited by Jaber F. Gubrium and James A. Holstein, 515–535. Thousand Oaks, CA: Sage, 2002.

Alexander, Dan. "Russian Billionaires, Including Several Tied to Putin, Are Up $104 Billion in the Last Year." *Forbes,* March 29, 2017. www.forbes.com/sites/danalexander/2017/03/29/putin-vladimir-donald-trump-russia-billionaires-oligarchs/#43f9b8ad43f9.

Appel, Hilary, and Mitchell A. Orenstein. "Why Did Neoliberalism Triumph and Endure in the Post-Communist World?" *Comparative Politics* (April 2016): 314.

Animated Soviet Propaganda. "Capitalist Sharks: Soviet Animation vs. Greed and Ambition." *Films for the Humanities and Sciences.* New York: Films Media Group, 2006.

Åslund, Anders. "Comparative Oligarchy. Russia, Ukraine, and the United States." In *Europe after Enlargement,* edited by Anders Åslund and Marek Dąbrowski, 143–164. Cambridge: Cambridge University Press, 2007.

Atkinson, Anthony B. *Inequality: What Can Be Done?* Cambridge, MA: Harvard University Press, 2015.

Atkinson, Anthony B., and Thomas Piketty, eds. *Top Incomes: A Global Perspective.* Oxford: Oxford University Press, 2010.

Aven, Petr, and Alfred Kokh. *Gaidar's Revolution: The Inside Account of the Economic Transformation of Russia.* London: I. B. Tauris, 2015.

Baltzell, E. Digby *Philadelphia Gentlemen: The Making of a National Upper Class.* Philadelphia: University of Pennsylvania Press, 1979 [1958].

Barnes, Andrew. *Owning Russia: The Struggle over Factories, Farms, and Power.* Ithaca, NY: Cornell University Press, 2006.

Beckert, Sven. *The Monied Metropolis: New York City and the Consolidation of the American Bourgeoisie, 1850–1896.* Cambridge: Cambridge University Press, 2001.

Beetham, David. *The Legitimation of Power*. Basingstoke: Macmillan, 1991.

Behar, Richard. "Kremlin Hits Back After Forbes Editor Paul Klebnikov's Alleged Killer and Others Denied U.S. Visas." *Forbes*, April 13, 2013.

Berezanskaia, Elena. "Rodina Zovet: Kak Milliardery Otreagirovali na Prizyv k Deofshorizatsii." *Forbes Russia*, April 20, 2015. www.forbes.ru/milliardery/286477-rodina-zovet-kak-milliardery-otreagirovali-na-prizyv-k-deofshorizatsii.

Berezankskaia, Elena. "Zavsegdateli Kluba Milliarderov: 10 Samykh Stabil'no Bogatykh Liudei Rossii." *Forbes Russia*, April 18, 2016.

Berlin, Isaiah. "Soviet Russian Culture." In *The Soviet Mind*, edited by Henry Hardy, foreword by Strobe Talbott, 130–165. Washington, DC: Brookings Institution Press, 2005 [1957].

Berlin, Isaiah. "The Remarkable Decade." In *Russian Thinkers*, edited by Henry Hardy and Aileen Kelly, 130–154. London: Penguin, 2008.

Bertaux, Daniel. "Transmission in Extreme Situations: Russian Families Expropriated by the October Revolution." In *Pathways to Social Class: A Qualitative Approach to Social Mobility*, edited by Daniel Bertaux and Paul Thompson, 248–254. Oxford: Clarendon Press, 1997.

Bertaux, Daniel, Paul Thompson, and Anna Rotkirch, eds. *Living Through Soviet Russia*. London: Routledge, 2004.

Bishop, Mathew, and Michael Green. *Philanthrocapitalism: How the Rich Can Save the World and Why We Should Let Them*. London: Bloomsbury Press, 2008.

Blasi, Joseph R., Maya Kroumova, and Dougas Kruse. *Kremlin Capitalism: The Privatization of the Russian Economy*. Ithaca, NY: Cornell University Press, 1997.

Böhnisch, Tomke. *Gattinnen: Die Frauen der Elite*. Münster: Westfälisches Dampfboot, 1999.

Borenstein, Eliot. *Overkill: Sex and Violence in Contemporary Russian Popular Culture*. Ithaca, NY: Cornell University Press, 2008.

Bourdieu, Pierre. *Distinction: A Social Critique of the Judgment of Taste*. London: Routledge & Kegan Paul, 1984.

Bourdieu, Pierre. "The Forms of Capital." In *Handbook of Theory and Research for the Sociology of Education*, edited by John G. Richardson, 241–258. New York: Greenwood Press, 1986.

Bourdieu, Pierre. "Social Space and Symbolic Power." In *Sociological Theory* 7, no. 1 (1989): 14–25.

Bourdieu, Pierre. *The State Nobility: Elite Schools in the Field of Power*. Cambridge: Polity Press, 1996.

Boycko, Maksim, Andrei Schleifer, and Robert Vishny. *Privatizing Russia*. Cambridge, MA: MIT Press, 1995.

Breeze, Beth, and Theresa Lloyd. *Richer Lives: Why Rich People Give*. London: Directory of Social Change, 2013.

Browder, Bill. *Red Notice: How I Became Putin's No. 1 Enemy*. London: Bantam Press, 2015.

Brown, Phillip, Sally Power, Gerbrand Tholen, and Annablle Allouch. "Credentials, Talent, and Cultural Capital: A Comparative Study of Education Elites in England and France and Their Study on Elite Graduates." *British Journal of Sociology of Education* 37, no. 2 (2014).

Brubaker, Rogers. "Rethinking Classical Theory: The Sociological Vision of Pierre Bourdieu." *Theory and Society* 14, no. 6 (1985): 745–775.

Bruck, Connie. "The Billionaire's Playlist." *The New Yorker*, January 20, 2014. www .newyorker.com/magazine/2014/01/20/the-billionaires-playlist.

Bryson, Bethany. "Anything but Heavy Metal: Symbolic Exclusion and Musical Dislikes." *American Sociological Review* 61, no. 5 (1996): 884–899.

Chamber of Commerce and Industry of the Russian Federation. "Rashirennoe Zasedanie Pravleniia TPP RF 'O Sotsial'noi Otvetstvennosti Biznesa v Sovremennoi Rossii.'" December 23, 2003. http://tpprf.ru/ru/news/5877.

Charities Aid Foundation. *CAF World Giving Index 2016*. www.cafonline.org/docs/ default-source/about-us-publications/1950a_wgi_2016_report_web_v2_241016.pdf.

Chua, Amy. *World on Fire: How Exporting Free Market Democracy Breeds Ethnic Hatred and Global Instability*. London: Heinemann, 2003.

Chugrinov, Anton. "10 Samykh Strannykh Postupov Sergeia Poslonskovo." *Snob*, January 13, 2014. https://snob.ru/selected/entry/70381.

Clover, Charles. *Black Wind, White Snow: The Rise of Russia's New Nationalism*. New Haven, CT: Yale University Press, 2016.

Coutts. *Million Dollar Donors Report 2014*. Accessed January 15, 2015. http:// philanthropy.coutts.com/en/reports/2014/russia/findings.html.

Daloz, Jean-Pascal. *The Sociology of Elite Distinction: From Theoretical to Comparative Perspectives*. Basingstoke: Palgrave Macmillan, 2009.

Daloz, Jean-Pascal. *Rethinking Social Distinction*. Basingstoke: Palgrave Macmillan, 2013.

David-Fox, Michael. "Conclusion: Transnational History and the East–West Divide." In *Imagining the West in Eastern Europe and the Soviet Union*, edited by György Péteri, 258–268. Pittsburgh, PA: University of Pittsburgh Press, 2010.

Dawisha, Karen. *Putin's Kleptocracy: Who Owns Russia?* New York: Simon & Schuster, 2014.

Dinello, Natalia. "Philanthropy in Russia and the United States: Elites and Philanthropy in Russia." *International Journal of Politics, Culture and Society* 12, no. 1 (1998): 109–133.

Domanski, Henryk. *On the Verge of Convergence: Social Stratification in Eastern Europe*. Budapest: Central European University Press, 2000.

Domhoff, G. William. *Who Rules America? Power and Politics in the Year 2000*, 3rd ed. London: Mayfield Publishing, 2000.

Domrin, Alexander N. "Ten Years Later: Society, 'Civil Society,' and the Russian State." *Russian Review* 62, no. 2 (2003): 193–211.

Dorling, Danny. *Inequality and the 1%*. London: Verso, 2014.

Dozhd'. "Na Volne Sanktsii. Dozhd' Vyiasnil, Kak Nevyezdnye Biznesmeny i Chinovniki Mogut Vse Ravno Otdykhat' Na Evropeiskikh Kurortakh." August 18, 2014. https://tvrain.ru/teleshow/here_and_now/na_volne_sanktsij_dozhd_vyjasnil_kak_nevyezdnye_biznesmeny_i_chinovniki_mogut_vse_ravno_otdyhat_na_evropejskih_kurortah-374221.

Dubov, Yuli. *Bol'shaia Paika*. Moscow: Vagrius, 2005.

Dubovitsky, Natan. "Okolonolia." *Russkii Pioner*, June 29, 2009. http://ruspioner.ru/cool/m/single/2007.

Dunham, Vera S. *In Stalin's Time: Middleclass Values in Soviet Fiction*. Cambridge: Cambridge University Press, 1976.

Dziadko, Timofei, Anatolii Temkin, and Igor' Terent'ev. "Milliader Mamut Perepisal Chast' Svoikh Aktivov Na Troikh Detei." *RBC*, February 25, 2015. www.rbc.ru/business/25/02/2015/54edfff59a7947af8e47ee51.

Eberstadt, Nicholas. *Russia's Peacetime Demographic Crisis: Dimensions, Causes, Implications*. Seattle, WA: National Bureau of Asian Research, 2010.

Economist, The. "A Book Too Far." April 3, 2014. www.economist.com/blogs/eastern approaches/2014/04/russia.

Economist, The. "Russia's Chief Propagandist." December 10, 2013. www.economist .com/blogs/easternapproaches/2013/12/ukraine.

Elias, Norbert. *The Civilizing Process*. Oxford: Blackwell, 1982.

Elias, Norbert. *The Germans: Power Struggles and the Development of Habitus in the Nineteenth and Twentieth Centuries*. Cambridge: Polity Press, 1996.

Engelstein, Laura. *Slavophile Empire: Imperial Russia's Illiberal Path*. Ithaca, NY: Cornell University Press, 2009.

Erickson, Bonnie H. "Culture, Class, and Connections." *American Journal of Sociology* 102, no. 1 (1996): 217–251.

Eyal, Gill, and Eleanor Townsley. "The Social Composition of the Communist Nomenklatura: A Comparison of Russia, Poland, and Hungary." *Theory and Society* 24, no. 5 (1995): 723–775.

Fasche, Melanie. "Making Art History, Wealthy Private Collectors and Contemporary Visual Art." In *Geographies of the Super-Rich, Cheltenham*, edited by Iain Hay, 171–185. Cheltenham: Edward Elgar, 2013.

Featherstone, Michael. "Super-Rich Lifestyles." In *Elite Mobilities*, edited by Thomas Birtchnell and Javier Caletrío, 99–135. New York: Routledge, 2013.

Felshtinsky, Yuri, and Vladimir Pribylovsky. *The Age of Assassins: The Rise and Rise of Vladimir Putin*. London: Gibson Square, 2008.

Figes, Orlando. *The Whisperers: Private Life in Stalin's Russia*. London: Penguin, 2008.

Fitzpatrick, Sheila. *Tear Off the Masks! Identity and Imposture in Twentieth-Century Russia*. Princeton, NJ: Princeton University Press, 2005.

Fitzpatrick, Sheila. "Stalin and the World of Culture." Lecture, Pushkin House, London, June 22, 2011.

Fitzpatrick, Sheila. *On Stalin's Team: The Years of Living Dangerously in Soviet Politics.* Princeton, NJ: Princeton University Press, 2015.

Forbes. "The Forbes 400 Summit: Bill Gates, Warren Buffett and the Greatest Roundtable of All Time." October 8, 2012. www.forbes.com/sites/randalllane/2012/09/18/theforbes-400-summit-bill-gates-warren-buffett-and-the-greatest-roundtable-of-all-time/.

Forbes Russia. "Masshtab Vpechatlenii: Boris Mints Rasskazal Forbes o Svoem Muzee." May 30, 2016. www.forbes.ru/forbeslife/321567-masshtab-vpechatlenii-boris-mints-rasskazal-forbes-o-svoem-muzee.

Fortescue, Stephen. *Russia's Oil Barons and Metal Magnates: Oligarchs and the State in Transition.* Basingstoke: Palgrave Macmillan, 2006.

Foteeva, Ekaterina. "Coping with Revolution. The Experiences of Well-to-Do Russian Families." In *On Living Through Soviet Russia,* edited by Daniel Bertaux, Paul Thompson, and Anna Rotkirch, 68–90. London: Routledge, 2004.

Frank, Robert H. *Success and Luck: Good Fortune and the Myth of Meritocracy.* Princeton, NJ: Princeton University Press, 2016.

Freeland, Chrystia. *Sale of the Century: The Inside Story of the Second Russian Revolution.* London: Little, Brown, 2000.

Freeland, Chrystia. *Plutocrats: The Rise of the New Global Super-Rich.* London: Penguin, 2013.

Freeland, Chrystia. "Even Plutocrats Can See Profound Inequality Isn't in Their Interests." *The Guardian,* January 25, 2015. www.theguardian.com/commentisfree/2015/jan/25/even-super-rich-see-plutocracy-flawed.

Freund, Caroline. *Rich People, Poor Countries: The Rise of Emerging-Market Tycoons and Their Mega Firms.* Washington, DC: Peterson Institute for International Economics, 2016.

Frye, Timothy. "Original Sin, Good Works, and Property Rights in Russia." *World Politics* 58, no. 4 (2006): 479–504.

Gambrell, Jamey. "Philanthropy in Russia: New Money under Pressure." *Carnegie Reporter* 3, no. 1 (2004). www.carnegie.org/reporter/09/philanthropy/index.html.

Gapova, Elena. "Gender Equality Vs. Difference and What Post-Socialism Can Teach Us." *Women's Studies International Forum* 59 (November–December 2016): 9–16.

Gates, Bill. "Why Inequality Matters." *Gatesnotes,* October 13, 2014. www.gatesnotes.com/Books/Why-Inequality-Matters-Capital-in-21st-Century-Review.

Gaztambide-Fernández, Rubén. *The Best of the Best: Becoming Elite at an American Boarding School.* Cambridge, MA: Harvard University Press, 2009.

Gaztambide-Fernández, Rubén, and Adam Howard. "Social Justice, Deferred Complicity, and the Moral Plight of the Wealthy. A Response to 'With Great

Power Comes Great Responsibility': Privileged Students' Conceptions of Justice-Oriented Citizenship." *Democracy & Education* 21, no. 1 (2013).

Gerber, Theodore P., and Michael Hout. "Tightening Up: Declining Class Mobility during Russia's Market Transition." *American Sociological Review* 65, no. 5 (2004): 677–703.

Gessen, Masha. *Dead Again: The Russian Intelligentsia after Communism.* London: Verso, 1997.

Gessen, Masha. *The Man Without a Face: The Unlikely Rise of Vladimir Putin.* New York: Granta, 2012.

Gill, Graeme. *Bourgeoisie, State and Democracy: Russia, France, Germany and the USA.* Oxford: Oxford University Press, 2008.

Glazunov, Mikhail. *Business in Post-Communist Russia: Privatisation and the Limits of Transformation.* London: Routledge, 2013.

Goodrich, Steve. "Whatever Happened to the Great British Gold Rush?" *Transparency International*, February 23, 2017. www.transparency.org.uk/whatever-happened-to-the-great-british-gold-rush/.

Goscilo, Helena. "Introduction: A Label Designed to Libel versus Mimetic Modeling and Parthenogenesis." *Russian Review* 62, no. 1 (2003): 1–10.

Goscilo, Helena, and Vlad Strukov. *Celebrity and Glamour in Contemporary Russia: Shocking Chic.* London: Routledge, 2011.

Graham, Loren R. *Science, Philosophy, and Human Behavior in the Soviet Union.* New York: Columbia University Press, 1987.

Graham, Seth. "The Wages of Syncretism: Folkloric New Russians and Post-Soviet Popular Culture." *Russian Review* 62, no. 1 (2003): 37–53.

Greenfeld, Liah. *Nationalism: Five Roads to Modernity.* Cambridge, MA: Harvard University Press, 1992.

Gronow, Jukka. *Caviar with Champagne: Common Luxury and the Ideals of the Good Life in Stalin's Russia.* Oxford: Berg, 2003.

Gronow, Jukka, and Sergei Zhuravlev. "Soviet Luxuries from Champagne to Private Cars." In *Pleasures in Socialism: Leisure and Luxury in the Eastern Bloc*, edited by David Crowley and Susan E. Reid, 121–146. Evanston, IL: Northwestern University Press, 2010.

Groys, Boris. *The Total Art of Stalinism: Avant-Garde, Aesthetic Dictatorship, and Beyond.* Princeton, NJ: Princeton University Press, 1992.

Groys, Boris. *Die Erfindung Rußlands.* Munich: Hanser Verlag, 1995.

Gruzinova, Irina, Mariia Abakumova, and Elena Zubova. "V Chastnom Poriadke. Mnogo Lits Aleksandra Svetakova." *Forbes*, 2015. www.forbes.ru/sp_data/2015/svetakov/index.html.

Gustafson, Thane. *Wheel of Fortune: The Battle for Oil and Power in Russia.* Cambridge, MA: The Belknap Press of Harvard University Press, 2012.

Halnon, Karen B. "Poor Chic: The Rational Consumption of Poverty." *Current Sociology* 50, no. 4 (2002): 501–516.

Hamburg, Gary M. "Russian Intelligentsias." In *A History of Russian Thought*, edited by William Leatherbarrow and Derek Offord, 44–69. Cambridge: Cambridge University Press, 2010.

Hamm, Patrick, Lawrence P. King, and David Stuckler. "Mass-Privatization, State Capacity, and Economic Growth in Post-Communist Countries." *American Sociological Review* 77, no. 2 (2012): 295–324.

Hanley, Eric, Natasha Yershova, and Richard Anderson. "Russia—Old Wine in a New Bottle? The Circulation and Reproduction of Russian Elites, 1983–1993." *Theory and Society* 24, no. 5 (1995): 639–668.

Hartmann, Michael. *The Sociology of Elites*. New York: Routledge, 2006.

Hartmann, Michael. *Die Globale Wirtschaftselite: Eine Legende*. Frankfurt/M.: Campus, 2016.

Hartmann, Michael. "The International Business Elite Fact or Fiction?" Paper at the LSE Conference, Changing Elites in Europe, London, November 26–27, 2015.

Harvey, David. *A Brief History of Neoliberalism*. Oxford: Oxford University Press, 2005.

Healey, Dan. "The Disappearance of the Russian Queen, or How the Soviet Closet Was Born." In *Russian Masculinities in History and Culture*, edited by Barbara E. Clements, Rebecca Friedman and Dan Healey, 152–171. Basingstoke: Palgrave Macmillan, 2002.

Hecht, Katharina. "A Relational Analysis of Top Incomes and Wealth. Relative (Dis) advantage, Economic Evaluation and the Service of Capital." LSE International Inequalities Institute, Working Paper 11, May 2017. www.lse.ac.uk/International-Inequalities/Assets/Documents/Working-Papers/Katharina-Hecht-A-Relational-Analysis-of-Top-Incomes-and-Wealth.pdf.

Hill, Fiona, and Clifford G. Gaddy. *Mr. Putin: Operative in the Kremlin*. Washington, DC: Brookings Institution Press, 2013.

Hobsbawm, Eric. *Age of Empire, 1875–1914*. New York: Vintage, 1989.

Hobsbawm, Eric. *Age of Extremes: The Short Twentieth Century, 1914–1991*. London: Michael Joseph, 1994.

Hoffman, David E. *The Oligarchs: Wealth and Power in the New Russia*, 3rd ed. New York: PublicAffairs, 2011.

Hollingsworth, Mark, and Stewart Lansley. *Londongrad: From Russia with Cash: The Inside Story of the Oligarchs*. London: HarperCollins, 2009.

Hosking, Geoffrey. *Russia: People and Empire: 1552–1917*. London: HarperCollins, 1997.

Hosking, Geoffrey. *Trust: A History*. Oxford: Oxford University Press, 2014.

Ioffe, Julia. "The Master and Mikhail." *The New Yorker*, February 20, 2012. www .newyorker.com/magazine/2012/02/27/the-master-and-mikhail.

Jerolmack, Colin, and Shamus Khan. "Talk Is Cheap: Ethnography and the Attitudinal Fallacy." *Sociological Methods & Research* 43, no. 2 (2014): 178–209.

Johnson, Heather B. *The American Dream and the Power of Wealth*. New York: Routledge, 2006.

Kagarlitsky, Boris. "1960s East and West: The Nature of the Shestidesiatniki and the New Left." *Boundary 2* 36, no. 1 (2009): 95–104.

Kampfner, John. *Inside Yeltsin's Russia: Corruption, Conflict, Capitalism.* London: Cassell, 1994.

Kay, Rebecca. *Men in Contemporary Russia: The Fallen Heroes of Post-Soviet Change?* London: Ashgate, 2006.

Keating, Giles, Michael O'Sullivan, Anthony Shorrocks, James B. Davies, Rodrogo Lluberas, and Antonios Koutsoukis. *Global Wealth Report 2013.* Zurich: Credit Suisse AG, 2013.

Keister, Lisa A. *Getting Rich: America's New Rich and How They Got That Way.* Cambridge: Cambridge University Press, 2005.

Kelly, Catriona. *Children's World: Growing Up in Russia, 1890–1991.* New Haven, CT: Yale University Press, 2007.

Kelly, Catriona. *Refining Russia: Advice Literature, Polite Culture, and Gender from Catherine to Yeltsin.* Oxford: Oxford University Press, 2001.

Kelly, Catriona. "Directed Desires: Kul'turnost' and Consumption." In *Constructing Russian Culture in the Age of Revolution, 1881–1940*, edited by David Shepherd and Catriona Kelly, 291–313. New York: Oxford University Press, 1998.

Kendall, Diana E. *The Power of Good Deeds: Privileged Women and the Social Reproduction of the Upper Class.* Lanham, MD: Rowman & Littlefield, 2002.

Khan, Shamus R. *Privilege: The Making of an Adolescent Elite at St. Paul's School.* Princeton, NJ: Princeton University Press, 2011.

Khan, Shamus R. "Saying Meritocracy and Doing Privilege." *Sociological Quarterly* 54, no. 1 (2013): 9–19.

Khan, Shamus R. "The Sociology of Elites." *Annual Review of Sociology* 38 (2012).

Khodorkovsky, Mikhail. "Russia Under Putin and Beyond: The Annual Russia Lecture." *Chatham House*, February 26, 2015. www.chathamhouse.org/event/ russia-under-putin-and-beyond-annual-russia-lecture#sthash.PrEWmdaV.dpuf.

Khodorova, Julia. *Russia Giving: Research on Individual Giving in Russia.* Moscow: Charity Aid Foundation Russia, 2014.

King, Lawrence P. "Postcommunist Divergence: A Comparative Analysis of the Transition to Capitalism in Poland and Russia." *Studies in Comparative International Development* 37, no. 3 (2002): 3–34.

Klebnikov, Paul. *Godfather of the Kremlin: The Life and Times of Boris Berezovsky.* New York: Harcourt, 2000.

Klingseis, Katharina. "The Power of Dress in Contemporary Russian Society: On Glamour Discourse and the Everyday Practice of Getting Dressed in Russian Cities." *Laboratorium* 3, no. 1 (2011): 84–115.

Kolchin, Peter. *Unfree Labor: American Slavery and Russian Serfdom.* Cambridge, MA: The Belknap Press of Harvard University Press, 1987.

Kornblatt, Judith D. *Doubly Chosen: Jewish Identity, the Soviet Intelligentsia, and the Russian Orthodox Church.* Madison: University of Wisconsin Press, 2004.

Kraus, Michael W., and Dacher Keltner. "Social Class Rank, Essentialism, and Punitive Judgment." *Journal of Personality and Social Psychology* 105, no. 2 (2013): 247–261.

Kraus, Michael W., and Bennet Callaghan. "Noblesse Oblige? Social Status and Economic Inequality Maintenance Among Politicians." *PLOS One* 9, no. 1 (2014).

Kryshtanovskaia, Ol'ga. *Anatomiia Rossiiskoi Elity*. Moskva: A.V. Solov'eva, 2004.

Kryshtanovskaia, Ol'ga, and Stephen White. "The Sovietization of Russian Politics." *Post-Soviet Affairs* 25, no. 4 (2009): 283–309.

Lamont, Michèle. *Money, Morals, and Manners: The Culture of the French and American Upper-Middle Class*. Chicago: University of Chicago Press, 1992.

Lamont, Michèle, and Ann Swidler. "Methodological Pluralism and the Possibilities and Limits of Interviewing." *Qualitative Sociology* 37, no. 2 (2014): 153–171.

Lane, David. *Elites and Identities in Post-Soviet Space*. London: Routledge, 2012.

Laruelle, Marlene. *In the Name of the Nation: Nationalism and Politics in Contemporary Russia*. Basingstoke: Palgrave Macmillan, 2012.

Laruelle, Marlene. "Conservatism as the Kremlin's New Toolkit: An Ideology at the Lowest Cost." *Russian Analytical Digest* 138 (November 8, 2013): 2–4.

Latynina, Julia. "Life in Putin's Russia." *Washington Post*, June 22, 2008. www .washingtonpost.com/wp-dyn/content/article/2008/06/20/AR2008062002596.html.

Lawler, Steph. *Identity: Sociological Perspectives*, 2nd ed. Cambridge: Polity Press.

Le Wita, Béatrix. *French Bourgeois Culture*. Translated by J. A. Underwood. Cambridge: Cambridge University Press, 1994.

Leatherbarrow, William, and Derek Offord, eds. *A History of Russian Thought*. Cambridge: Cambridge University Press, 2010.

Ledeneva, Alena V. *Can Russia Modernise? Sistema, Power Networks and Informal Governance*. Cambridge: Cambridge University Press, 2013.

Levada-Center. "Rossiiane o Biznese i Biznesmenakh." November 5, 2014. www .levada.ru/2014/11/05/rossiyane-o-biznese-i-biznesmenah/.

Levada-Center. "Figura Stalina v Obshchestvennom Mnenii Rossii." March 25, 2016. www.levada.ru/2016/03/25/figura-stalina-v-obshhestvennom-mnenii-rossii/.

Lipovetsky, Mark. "New Russians as a Cultural Myth." *Russian Review* 62, no. 1 (2003): 54–71.

Livshin, Alexander, and Richard Weitz. "Civil Society and Philanthropy Under Putin." *International Journal of Not-for-Profit Law* 8, no. 3 (2006): 7–12.

Lloyd, Theresa. *Why Rich People Give*. London: Association of Charitable Foundations, 2004.

Mackey, Robert. "Russia Could Still Turn U.S. 'Into Radioactive Dust,' News Anchor in Moscow Reminds Viewers." *New York Times*, March 16, 2014. https://thelede .blogs.nytimes.com/2014/03/16/russia-could-still-turn-the-u-s-into-radioactive- dust-news-anchor-in-moscow-reminds-viewers/.

Mamut, Alexander. "Otsy i Deti. Kolonka Aleksandra Mamuta dlia Forbes." *Forbes Russia*, May 20, 2016. www.forbes.ru/mneniya/tsennosti/320643-ottsy-i-deti- kolonka-aleksandra-mamuta-dlya-forbes.

Manchester, Laurie. *Holy Fathers, Secular Sons: Clergy, Intelligentsia and the Modern Self in Revolutionary Russia*. DeKalb: Northern Illinois University Press, 2008.

Mankiw, N Gregory. "Defending the One Percent." *Journal of Economic Perspectives* 27, no. 3 (2013): 21–34.

Markus, Stanislav. *Property, Predation, and Protection: Piranha Capitalism in Russia and Ukraine*. Cambridge: Cambridge University Press, 2015.

Marx, Karl, and Friedrich Engels. *The German Ideology. Part One*. New York: International Publishers, 1970.

Marx, Karl. *Der achtzehnte Brumaire des Louis Bonaparte*. 3rd ed. Hamburg: Otto Meißner, 1885. Accessed July 2, 2016. http://digital.staatsbibliothek-berlin.de/wer kansicht?PPN=PPN633609536&PHYSID=PHYS_0001&DMDID=.

Mauss, Marcel. *The Gift: The Form and Reason for Exchange in Archaic Societies*. Foreword by Mary Douglas. London: Routledge Classics, 2002 [1898].

McCalls, Leslie. *The Undeserving Rich: American Beliefs about Inequality, Opportunity, and Redistribution*. Cambridge: Cambridge University Press, 2013.

McGeever, Jamie. "UK Draws Billions in Unrecorded Inflows, Much from Russia—Study." *Reuters*, March 10, 2015. http://uk.reuters.com/article/uk-markets-capital-flows-deutsche-idUKKBN0M61FM20150310.

McGoey, Linsey. *No Such Thing as a Free Gift: The Gates Foundation and the Price of Philanthropy*. London: Verso, 2015.

Mears, Ashley. "Girls as Elite Distinction: The Appropriation of Bodily Capital." *Poetics* 53, no. 4 (2015): 22–37.

Menzel, Birgit. "Russian Discourse on Glamour." *Kultura: Russian Cultural Review* 6 (December 2008): 4–8.

Meyer, Henry, Ilya Arkhipov, and Jake Rudnitsky. "Putin's Pardon of Tycoon Buoys Russia Before Sochi Games." *Bloomberg*, December 20, 2013. www.bloomberg.com/news/articles/2013-12-20/khodorkovsky-free-after-10-years-in-prison-as-putin-signs-pardon.

Mezrich, Ben. *Once Upon a Time in Russia: The Rise of the Oligarchs and the Greatest Wealth in History*. London: William Heinemann, 2015.

Mikhailovskaia, Irina, and Irina Telitsyna. "Chastnyi Salon." *Forbes Russia*, March 3, 2012. www.forbes.ru/5bissue5d/issue/2012-03-0/81669-chastnyi-salon.

Milanovic Branko. *Global Inequality: A New Approach for the Age of Globalization*. Cambridge, MA: The Belknap Press of Harvard University Press, 2016.

Mills, C. Wright. *The Power Elite*. Oxford: Oxford University Press, 2000 [1956].

Minaev, Sergie. *Dukhless: Povest' o Nenastoiashchem Cheloveke*. Moscow: AST, 2006.

Mount, Ferdinand. *The New Few: Or a Very British Oligarchy*. London: Simon & Schuster, 2013.

Msk Sobaka. "Oleg Tin'kov." September 2009.

Murtazaev, Elma. "Pochemu Deti Milliarderov Ne Speshat Nasledovat' Biznes." *Forbes Russia*, May 25, 2015. www.forbes.ru/mneniya-column/konkurentsiya/289427-pochemu-deti-milliarderov-ne-speshat-nasledovat-biznes.

Nickson, John. *Giving Is Good for You: Why Britain Should Be Bothered and Give More.* London: Biteback Publishing, 2013.

Oakley, Peter. "Ticking Boxes: (Re)Constructing the Wristwatch as a Luxury Object." *Luxury: History, Culture, Consumption* 2, no. 1 (2015): 41–60.

Oliphant, Roland. "Russian Court 'Seizes' Britain's Most Expensive Home." *The Telegraph*, May 12, 2016. www.telegraph.co.uk/news/2016/05/12/russian-court-seizes-britains-most-expensive-home/.

Ostrander, Susan A. *Women of the Upper Class.* Philadelphia: Temple University Press, 1984.

Ostrander, Susan A. "Surely You're Not in This Just to Be Helpful: Access, Rapport, and Interviews in Three Studies of Elites." In *Studying Elites Using Qualitative Methods*, edited by Rosanna Hertz and Jonathan B. Imber, 133–150. London: Sage, 1995.

Ostrower, Francie. *Why the Wealthy Give: The Culture of Elite Philanthropy.* Princeton, NJ: Princeton University Press, 1995.

Ostrovsky, Arkady. *The Invention of Russia: The Journey from Gorbachev's Freedom to Putin's War.* London: Atlantic Books, 2015.

Oushakine, Serguei A. "The Quantity of Style: Imaginary Consumption in the New Russia." *Theory, Culture & Society* 17, no. 5 (2000): 97–120.

Patico, Jennifer. *Consumption and Social Change in a Post-Soviet Middle Class.* Stanford, CA: Stanford General, 2008.

Pereira, N. G. O. *The Thought and Teachings of N. G. Černyševskij.* The Hague: Mouton, 1975.

Peterson, Richard A., and Roger M. Kern. "Changing Highbrow Taste: From Snob to Omnivore." *American Sociological Review* 61, no. 5 (1996): 900–907.

Pelevin, Viktor. *Generation P.* Moscow: Vagrius, 1999.

Piketty, Thomas. *Capital in the Twenty-First Century.* Cambridge, MA: The Belknap Press of Harvard University Press, 2014.

Pinçon, Michel, and Monique Pinçon-Charlot. *Grand Fortunes: Dynasties of Wealth in France.* New York: Algora Publishing, 1998.

Pirani, Simon. *Change in Putin's Russia: Power, Money and People.* London: Pluto, 2010.

Pomerantsev, Peter. *Nothing Is True and Everything Is Possible.* New York: PublicAffairs, 2014.

Prince, Russ Alan, and Bruce Rogers. "Marketing Luxury to the Super-Rich." *Forbes*, October 8, 2012. www.forbes.com/sites/russprince/2012/10/08/marketing-luxury-to-the-super-rich/#3cac2d375df5.

Proskurina, Ol'ga. "Mikhail Fridman Ostavit Detei Bez Sostoianiia." *Forbes Russia*, May 20, 2016. www.forbes.ru/news/320729-mikhail-fridman-ostavit-detei-bez-sostoyaniya.

Pulikova, Liubov. "Chto Leonid Mikhel'son Delaet Na Bolotnoi Za €150 Mln." *Forbes Russia*, February 13, 2017. www.forbes.ru/forbeslife/338935-chto-leonid-mihelson-delaet-na-bolotnoy-za-eu150-mln.

Ratilainen, Saara. "Business for Pleasure: Elite Women in the Russian Popular Media." In *Rethinking Class in Russia*, edited by Suvi Salmenniemi, 45–66. Burlington, VT: Ashgate, 2002.

Remington, Thomas F. "The Russian Middle Class as Policy Objective." *Post-Soviet Affairs* 27, no. 2 (2011): 97–120.

Remington, Thomas F. *The Politics of Inequality in Russia.* Cambridge: Cambridge University Press, 2011.

Rendle, Mathew. "The Problems of Becoming Soviet: Former Nobles in Soviet Society." *European History Quarterly* 38, no. 1 (2008): 7–33.

Renz, Bettina. "Putin's Militocracy? An Alternative Interpretation of Siloviki in Contemporary Russian Politics." *Europe-Asia Studies* 58, no. 6 (2006): 903–924.

Rivera, David W., and Sharon W. Rivera. "Is Russia a Militocracy? Conceptual Issues and Extant Findings Regarding Elite Militarization." *Post-Soviet Affairs* 30, no. 1 (2014): 27–50.

Rivkin-Fish, Michele. "Pronatalism, Gender Politics, and the Renewal of Family Support in Russia: Toward a Feminist Anthropology of Maternity Capital." *Slavic Review* 69, no. 3 (2010): 701–724.

Robertson, Graeme B. "Managing Society: Protest, Civil Society, and Regime in Putin's Russia," *Slavic Review* 68, no. 3 (2009): 528–547.

Rodkiewicz, Witold, and Jadwiga Rogoża. "Potemkin Conservatism: An Ideological Tool of the Kremlin." *Russian Analytical Digest* 171 (July 14, 2015): 2–4.

Rosslyn, Wendy. *Deeds Not Words: The Origins of Women's Philanthropy in the Russian Empire.* Birmingham: University of Birmingham Press, 2007.

Rozhdestvenskaia, Elena. "Zarabotat' Svoi Lichny Milliard." *Lenta.ru*, October 20, 2015. http://lenta.ru/articles/2015/10/20/million/.

Rutland, Peter. "The Anatomy of the Russian Elite." In *The Palgrave Handbook on Political Elites*, edited by John Higley, 273–294. Basingstoke: Palgrave Macmillan, 2018.

Sakwa, Richard. *Putin and the Oligarch: The Khodorkovsky–Yukos Affair.* London: I. B. Tauris, 2014.

Salmenniemi, Suvi. *Rethinking Class in Russia.* Burlington, VT: Ashgate, 2012.

Salmenniemi, Suvi. "The Making of Civil Society in Russia: A Bourdieuan Approach." *International Sociology* 29, no. 1 (2014): 38–55.

Savage, Mike. *Social Class in the 21st Century.* London: Pelican, 2015.

Savage, Mike. "Piketty's Challenge for Sociology." *British Journal of Sociology* 65, no. 4 (2014): 591–606.

Savage, Mike. "From the 'Problematic of the Proletariat' to a Class Analysis of 'Wealth Elites.'" *Sociological Review* 63, no. 2 (2015): 223–239.

Savage, Mike, and Karel Williams. *Remembering Elites.* Oxford: Wiley-Blackwell, 2008.

Scheidel, Walter. *The Great Leveler: Violence and the History of Inequality from the Stone Age to the Twenty-First Century.* Princeton, NJ: Princeton University Press, 2017.

Semenova, Vikoriia, and Ekaterina Foteeva. *Sud'by Liudei: Rossiia XX Vek: Biografii Semei kak Ob''ekt Sotsiologicheskovo Issledovaniia.* Moskva: Inst. Sotsiologii RAN, 1996.

Semenova, Viktoriia, and Paul Thompson. "Family Models and Transgenerational Influences. Grandparents, Parents and Children in Moscow and Leningrad from the Soviet to the Market Era." In *Living Through Soviet Russia*, edited by Daniel Bertaux, Paul Thompson, and Anna Rotkirch, 120–145. London: Routledge, 2004.

Shaxson, Nicholas. *Treasure Islands: Tax Havens and the Men Who Stole the World.* London: Vintage, 2012.

Sherman, Rachel. *Uneasy Street. The Anxieties of Affluence.* Princeton, NJ: Princeton University Press, 2017.

Sherman, Rachel. "Conflicted Cultivation: Parenting, Privilege, and Moral Worth in Wealthy New York Families." *American Journal of Cultural Sociology* 5, no. 1–2 (2016): 1–33.

Shlapentokh, Vladimir. "Social Inequality in Post-Communist Russia: The Attitudes of the Political Elite and the Masses (1991–1998)." *Europe-Asia Studies* 51, no. 7 (1999): 1167–1181.

Shlapentokh, Vladimir. "Wealth Versus Political Power: The Russian Case." *Communist and Post-Communist Studies* 37, no. 29 (2004): 135–160.

Shleifer, Andrei, and Daniel Treisman. *Without a Map: Political Tactics and Economic Reform in Russia.* Cambridge, MA: MIT Press, 2000.

Shorrocks, Anthony, James Davies, Rodrogo Lluberas, and Antonios Koutsoukis. *Credit Suisse Wealth Report 2016.* Credit Suisse Research Institute. Zurich: Credit Suisse AG, 2016.

Shorrocks, Anthony, James Davies, and Rodrogo Lluberas. *Global Wealth Report 2014.* Credit Suisse Research Institute. Zurich: Credit Suisse AG, 2014.

Simmel, Georg. *Über soziale Differenzierung: Soziologische und psychologische Untersuchungen.* Duncker & Humbolt, 1890. Accessed April 15, 2009. http://socio.ch/sim/differenzierung/index.htm.

Simmel, Georg. "Die Mode," *Philosophische Kultur.* 2nd ed. Leipzig: Alfred Kröner Verlag, 1919. http:// socio.ch/sim/phil_kultur/kul_3.htm.

Simmel, Georg. "Exkurs über den Adel." In *Soziologie: Untersuchungen über die Formen der Vergesellschaftung*, ed. Georg Simmel. 816–831. Frankfurt/M.: Suhrkamp, 1992 [1908].

Skolkovo Center for Management, Wealth and Philanthropy. *Issledovanie Vladel'tsev Kapitalov Rossii.* 2015.

Skolkovo Wealth Transformation Centre. *Russia's Wealth Possessors Study.* Moscow: Skolkovo Wealth Transformation Centre, 2015.

Smith, Douglas. *Former People: The Last Days of the Russian Aristocracy.* London: Macmillan, 2012.

Snob Magazine. "Sobchak & Sokolova s Petrom Avenom: Ne Stuchat' i Ne Sadit'sa." June 2013. https://snob.ru/magazine/entry/61234.

Soldatov, Andrei, and Irina Borogan. *The New Nobility: The Restoration of Russia's Security State and the Enduring Legacy of the KGB.* New York: PublicAffairs, 2010.

Solnick, Steven L. *Stealing the State: Control and Collapse in Soviet Institutions.* Cambridge, MA: Harvard University Press, 1998.

Solov'eva, Kseniia. "Pole Chudes: V Gostiakh u Andreiia Borodina i Evo Zheny v Londone." *Tatler,* March 11, 2015. www.tatler.ru/nashi_lyudi/interview_and_photo_set_21/352520_pole_chudes_v_gostyah_u_andreya_borodina_i_ego_zheni_v_londone.php#p=352531.

Sombart, Werner. *Luxury and Capitalism.* Introduction by Philip Siegelman. Ann Arbor: University of Michigan Press, 1967 [1913].

Spear's Newschannel. "Russian HNWs Flood to London to Escape Putin's Clampdown." June 16, 2015. www.spearswms.com/russian-hnws-flood-to-london-to-escape-putins-clampdown-2/.

Spence, Emma. "Unraveling the Politics of Super-Rich Mobility: A Study of Crew and Guests on Board Luxury Yachts." *Mobilities* 9, no. 3 (2014): 401–413.

Sperling, Valerie. *Sex, Politics, and Putin: Political Legitimacy in Russia.* New York: Oxford University Press, 2015.

Sperling, Valerie. "Putin's Macho Personality Cult." *Communist and Post-Communist Studies* 49, no. 1 (2016): 13–23.

Stanziani, Alessandro. *Bondage: Labor and Rights in Eurasia from the Sixteenth to the Early Twentieth Centuries.* New York: Berghahn Books, 2014.

Steen, Anton, and Vladimir Gel'man. *Elites and Democratic Development in Russia.* London: Routledge, 2003.

Stella, Francesca. *Lesbian Lives in Soviet and Post-Soviet Russia: Post/Socialism and Gendered Sexualities.* Basingstoke: Palgrave Macmillan, 2015.

Stierli, Markus, Anthony Shorrocks, James Davies, Rodrogo Lluberas, and Antonio Koutsoukis. *Global Wealth Report 2015.* Credit Suisse Research Institute. Zurich: Credit Suisse AG, 2015.

Szelényi, Ivan, and Szonja Szelényi. "Circulation or Reproduction of Elites during the Postcommunist Transformation of Eastern Europe." *Theory and Society* 25, no. 5 (1995): 615–638.

Szelényi, Ivan, Gil Eyal, and Elenor Townsley. *Making Capitalism Without Capitalists: Class Formation and Elite Struggles in Post-Communist Central Europe.* London: Verso, 1998.

Szelényi, Ivan, and Christy Glass. "Winners of the Reforms: The Economic and Political Elite." In *Inequality and Social Structure during the Transition,* edited by Vladimir Mikhalev, 75–98. Basingstoke: Palgrave Macmillan, 2003.

Taylor, Laurie. "Super Rich: The 1% of the 1%." *Thinking Allowed,* BBC Radio 4, January 4, 2017. www.bbc.co.uk/programmes/b086s8yv.

Tikhonova, Natalya E., and Svetlana V. Mareeva. "Poverty in Contemporary Russian Society: Formation of a New Periphery." *Russian Politics* 1, no. 2 (2016): 159–183.

Tin'kov, Oleg. *Ia Takoi Kak Vse.* Moskva: Al'pina Pablisher, 2010.

Therborn, Goran. *The Killing Fields of Inequality.* Cambridge: Polity Press, 2013.

Tolstoy, Lev. *Childhood, Boyhood, Youth.* Translated and with an introduction by Rosemary Edmonds. New York: Penguin, 2006.

Tolz, Vera. *Russia.* London: Arnold, 2001.

Tolz, Vera. "The West." In *A History of Russian Thought,* edited by William Leatherbarrow and Derek Offord, 197–216. Cambridge: Cambridge University Press, 2010.

Traynor, Ian. "Putin Urged to Apply the Pinochet Stick." *The Guardian,* March 31, 2000. www.theguardian.com/world/2000/mar/31/russia.iantraynor.

Treisman, Daniel. "Russia's Billionaires." *American Economic Review: Papers & Proceedings* 106, no. 5 (2016): 236–241.

Tromly, Benjamin. *Making the Soviet Intelligentsia: Universities and Intellectual Life Under Stalin and Khrushchev.* Cambridge: Cambridge University Press, 2014.

Trotsky, Leon. *The History of the Russian Revolution.* Translated from the Russian by Max Eastman. London: Pluto Press, 1977.

Uhlin, Anders. *Post-Soviet Civil Society: Democratisation in Russia and the Baltic States.* London: Routledge, 2006.

Ul'ianova, Zhanna. "Sovet Federatsii Stal Bednee: Iz Soveta Federatsii Ushli Samye Bogatye Senatory." *RBC News,* April 15, 2014. www.rbc.ru/newspaper/2014/04/15/56beeed79a7947299f72d23e.

UNDP Human Development Index. "Human Development Reports 2014." Accessed November 12, 2015. http://hdr.undp.org/en/data.

Urban, Michael. *Cultures of Power in Post-Communist Russia: An Analysis of Elite Political Discourse.* New York: Cambridge University Press, 2010.

Varese, Federico. *The Russian Mafia: Private Protection in a New Market Economy.* Oxford: Oxford University Press, 2001.

Veblen, Thorstein. *The Theory of the Leisure Class.* New York: Dover Publications, 1994 [1899].

Verzhbitskii, Anton. "Dunya Dlia Pumpianskovo. Milliarder Stroit Stometrovuiu Iakhtu." *Forbes,* July 26, 2016. www.forbes.ru/milliardery/325547-dunya-dlya-pumpyanskogo-milliarder-stroit-stometrovuyu-yakhtu.

Vesti.ru. "Gref: Itogi Privatizatsii ne Budut Peresmotreny." July 10, 2003. www.vesti.ru/doc.html?id=29550.

Voslensky, Michael. *Nomenklatura: The Soviet Ruling Class.* Garden City, NY: Doubleday, 1984.

Volkov, Vladimir. *Violent Entrepreneurs: The Use of Force in the Making of Russian Capitalism.* Ithaca, NY: Cornell University Press, 2002.

Walker, Shaun. "Russian Oligarch Sergei Polonsky: 'Everyone in Russia Has Gone Mad.'" *The Guardian,* November 11, 2013. www.theguardian.com/world/2013/nov/11/russian-oligarch-sergei-polonsky-arrested.

Warde, Alan, Wendy Olsen, and Lydia Martens. "Consumption and the Problem of Variety: Cultural Omnivorousness, Social Distinction and Dining Out." *Sociology* 33, no. 1 (1999): 105–127.

Warren, Tamara. "Luxury in Motion: The Precarious State of the Supercar." *Luxury* 1, no. 1 (2015): 71–91.

Weber, Max. *Economy and Society: An Outline of Interpretive Sociology.* Translation of 4th German ed. of *Wirtschaft und Gesellschaft*, edited by Guenther Roth and Claus Wittich. Berkeley: University of California, 1978 [1922].

Weber, Max. *From Max Weber: Essays in Sociology.* Translated and edited by Hans Heinrich Gerth and C. Wright Mills. London: Routledge, 1991.

White, Stephen, ed. *Politics and the Ruling Group in Putin's Russia.* New York: Palgrave Macmillan, 2008.

Wilson, Eric. "The Czarinas Are Back." *New York Times*, June 29, 2012. www.nytimes .com/2012/07/01/fashion/the-russians-claim-the-fashion-spotlight.html.

Winters, Jeffrey A. *Oligarchy.* Cambridge: Cambridge University Press, 2011.

World Bank, The. "World Data Bank 2016." Accessed February 14, 2017. http://databank .worldbank.org/data/reports.aspx?Code=SI.POV.GINI&id=af3ce82b&report_ name=Popular_indicators&populartype=series&ispopular=y.

World Bank, The. "Life Expectancy at Birth, Male." Accessed June 1, 2015. http:// data.worldbank.org/indicator/SP.DYN.LE00.MA.IN?page=4.

Young, Cristobal. *The Myth of Millionaire Tax Flight: How Place Still Matters for the Rich.* Stanford, CA: Stanford University Press, 2018.

Yurchak, Alexei. "Entrepreneurial Governmentality in Postsocialist Russia: A Cultural Investigation of Business Practices." In *The New Entrepreneurs of Europe and Asia: Patterns of Business Development in Russia, Eastern Europe, and China*, edited by Victoria E. Bonnell and Thomas B. Gold, 278–324. Armonk, NY: M. E. Sharpe, 2002.

Yurchak, Alexei. "Russian Neoliberal: The Entrepreneurial Ethic and the Spirit of True Careerism." *Russian Review* 62, no. 1 (2003): 72–90.

Yurchak, Alexei. *Everything Was Forever, Until It Was No More.* Princeton, NJ: Princeton University Press, 2006.

Zassoursky, Ivan. *Media and Power in Post-Soviet Russia.* Armonk, NY: M. E. Sharpe, 2002.

Zdravomyslova, Elena, and Anna Temkina. "Gendered Citizenship in Soviet and Post-Soviet Societies." In *Nation and Gender in Contemporary Europe*, edited by Vera Tolz and Stephanie Booth, 95–115. Manchester: Manchester University Press, 2005.

Znak, "Evgenii Chichvarkin: 'Ia Vernus' v Rossiiu Cherez Piat' Let, Potomu Chto Togda Sluchitsa . . .'" December 2, 2012. www.znak.com/2012-12-02/samyy_ ekscentrichnyy_biznesmen_sdelal_cherez_znak_com_neskolko_lyubopytnyh_ prognozov.

Zygar', Mikhail. *Vsia Kremlevskaia Rat': Kratkaia Istoriia Sovremennoi Rossii.* Moscow: Intellektual'naia Literatura, 2016.

Index

Note: Note material is indicated by an "n" after the page number and followed by the note number.